Reformed Presbyterian Church in North America

The Psalter, or, Book of Psalms

A Revision of the Metrical Version of the Bible Psalms....

Reformed Presbyterian Church in North America

The Psalter, or, Book of Psalms
A Revision of the Metrical Version of the Bible Psalms....

ISBN/EAN: 9783337099725

Printed in Europe, USA, Canada, Australia, Japan

Cover: Foto ©Lupo / pixelio.de

More available books at **www.hansebooks.com**

THE PSALTER;

OR

BOOK OF PSALMS.

A REVISION OF THE

METRICAL VERSION

OF THE

BIBLE PSALMS,

WITH

ADDITIONAL VERSIONS.

NEW YORK.

1893.

J. W. PRATT & SON,

PRINTERS AND STATIONERS,

88 & 90 GOLD ST., N. Y.

PREFACE.

In this revision of the old Scotch metrical version of the Psalms the following rules have been applied :

I. To remove imperfections in the metre, as far as possible, by slight verbal changes.

1. Transposing words, or slightly modifying the expression to secure the right accent. See for example Psalms 21 : 11 ; 25 : 2, C. M. and S. M.; 102 : 18, L. M.

2. Supplying a wanting syllable, of which there is a multitude of instances. See for example, Ps. 22 : 27, 28, 30. In a large number of cases, it was thought best to leave the ending èd as a separate syllable, marking the è with a grave accent.

II. To recast the entire stanza, where serious defect could not otherwise be remedied.

1. This has been done in eliminating awkward double rhymes, and other serious defects of metre. See e. g. Ps. 1: 3; 2: 6; 41: 1.

2. In two instances, a single stanza of the old version has been expanded into two stanzas, to supply omissions. See Ps. 51 : 11, 12 ; and 135 : 1, 2.

3. In many cases two stanzas of the old version have been condensed into one, or a

number of consecutive stanzas have been recast, in order to remove unnecessary additions. See e. g. Ps. 78: 67, 68; and 106: 28, 29.

III. To secure greater accuracy in the use of the names of the Divine Being, and of the specific designations of the Law of God.

1. The various terms found in Psalm 119, "law," "statutes," "precepts," "commandments," "testimonies," etc., are in both versions used with scrupulous accuracy. No little difficulty was encountered in securing this desirable end, with the hampering limitations of metrical feet and rhyme.

2. The Divine Name has been inserted in every instance in which it was omitted—fifty in all.

3. The Divine Name has been omitted in all cases in which it had been inserted when not in the original. All the more careful attention has been given to this point as other versions—except the New England Psalter—seem to have disregarded it altogether. Take a single Psalm for illustration : In the old version of Psalm 119, the name "God" is introduced twice, and the name "Lord" nineteen times.

4. The Divine Name is kept in its proper connection. In a few instances only was this change necessary. See Psalm 119: 107, 108.

5. The exact name of the Divine Being is indicated in every instance. As far as possible, the name " Jehovah " is retained. When the introduction of the original word would weaken the line, it has been translated "Lord," and the word is printed in capitals, to indicate to the English reader that it represents the covenant name ; " Lord " in small letters represents uniformly the Hebrew " Adonai " ; and " God " stands for the Hebrew names " El," " Eloai " and " Elohim." The pronouns that represent the Divine Being are printed with an initial capital.

In the preparation of this revision the original Hebrew was used throughout, together with the best commentaries, translations, and metrical versions. Among the helps found specially valuable may be mentioned the revision of the New England or Bay State Psalter, by President Henry Dunstar, of Harvard College, a New Rendering of the Hebrew Psalms in English Verse, by Abraham Cole, M. D., LL.D., and the revisions of the Scotch Psalter, by the United Presbyterian Church of our own country and the Presbyterian Church of Ireland.

Whenever the rules adopted permitted, the rendering which seemed to be the best among these versions was accepted. The committee would not fail to express their indebtedness to the admirable work of Dr. John De Witt, of the Theological Seminary of the American Reformed Church, New Brunswick, N. J., entitled, "The Praise Songs of Israel; a New Rendering of the Book of Psalms." Constant and careful use of this book only served to heighten the appreciation of its fine Hebrew scholarship, and poetic spirit. Invaluable aid was rendered by this volume in the difficult question of the Hebrew tenses.

A part of the work assigned to the committee was the preparation of some additional metres. It was judged best to add only a few new versions, and these mainly with a view to command the best church music, heretofore unavailable in the Reformed Presbyterian Church. Most of the versions adopted were taken from Dr. Horatius Bonar, Dr. Cole's New Rendering of the Hebrew Psalms in English Verse, the Revision of the Presbyterian Church of Ireland, and the Revision of the United Presbyterian Church of our own land; all of them were revised again, so far as it seemed necessary to the committee, according to the third rule mentioned above. New versions, affording the use of standard music not available by the Irish and U. P. revisions, were prepared by the committee, of thirteen Psalms. A new long metre version of Psalm 119 was also

PREFACE. vii

prepared. The expansion of each part into six common metre stanzas had led to the introduction of much that is not in the Hebrew. Not being willing to change the number of verses in some of the parts, and not feeling themselves warranted to recast every part, yet deeply impressed with the importance of more closely harmonizing a metrical version of this most beautiful and instructive Psalm, so often employed in our Service of Praise, with the inspired original, the committee decided to prepare a new version throughout, with but four stanzas to each part. In all this work the aim has been to realize, as far as possible under the rules given, and the inherent difficulties of versification, the idea of a good version as expressed in the report adopted by Synod in appointing this committee: " A Version, to be really good, should contain nothing more nor less than the original, and should be expressed in language at once smooth and elegant."

At the meeting of the Reformed Presbyterian Synod, in Belle Center, O., June, 1889, the following action was taken: *Resolved*, That Synod authorize the use in families and churches of this Revision.

THE COMMITTEE.

THE PSALTER;

OR

BOOK OF PSALMS.

Psalm I. C. M.

1 THAT man hath perfect blessedness
 Who walketh not astray
 In counsel of ungodly men,
 Nor stands in sinners' way,

2   Nor sitteth in the scorner's chair;
 2 But, placing his delight
 Upon the Lord's law, meditates
 On His law day and night.

3 3 He shall be like a planted tree
 The water-course beside,
 Which in its season yields its fruit,
 And green its leaves abide.

4   And all he does shall prosper well.
  4 The wicked are not so;
 But like they are unto the chaff,
 Which wind drives to and fro.

5 5 In judgment, therefore, shall not stand
 Such as ungodly are;
 Nor in th' assembly of the just
 Shall wicked men appear.

6 6 Because the way of godly men
 Is to Jehovah known;
 Whereas the way of wicked men
 Shall quite be overthrown.

Psalm II. C. M.

1 1 WHY rage the nations? and vain things
Why do the peoples mind? [things
2 The kings of earth do set themselves,
And princes are combined

2 Against Jehovah and His Christ;
With one consent they say:
3 Let us asunder break Their bands,
And cast Their cords away.

3 4 He that in heaven sits shall laugh;
The Lord shall scorn them all.
5 Then shall He speak to them in wrath,
In rage He vex them shall.

4 6 Yet I My King appointed have
Upon My holy hill;
On Zion Mount His throne is set,
Established by My will.

5 7 The sure decree I will declare;
Jehovah said to Me,
Thou art Mine only Son; this day
I have begotten Thee.

6 8 Ask of Me, and for heritage
The nations I'll make Thine;
And, for possession, I to Thee
Will give earth's utmost line.

7 9 Thou shalt, as with a weighty rod
Of iron, break them all;
Them, as a potter's vessel, Thou
Shalt dash in pieces small.

8 10 Now, therefore, kings, be wise; be
Ye judges of the earth;   [taught,
11 In holy fear Jehovah serve,
And tremble in your mirth.

9   12 Kiss ye the Son, lest in His ire
      Ye perish in the way,
      If once His wrath begin to burn ;
      Blessed all that on Him stay.

Psalm II. 7s.

1   W HY do heathen nations rage?
      Why vain things do peoples mind?
    2 Kings of earth themselves engage,
      Rulers are in league combined.

2   They against Jehovah speak,
        And against His Christ they say :
    3 Let us join Their bands to break
      Let us cast Their cords away.

3   4 He shall laugh who sits above,
        Scorn them all Jehovah shall ;
    5 In His anger them reprove ;
      In displeasure vex them all.

4   6 Yet, according to My will,
        Have I set My King to reign ;
      Him on Zion's holy hill,
      Mine Anointed, I'll maintain.

5   7 Thus hath said Jehovah High,
      I will publish the decree ;
      Thee I own My Son, for I
      Have this day begotten Thee.

6   8 Ask, for heritage I'll make
      All the heathen nations Thine ;
      Thou shalt in possession take
      Earth to its remotest line.

7   9 Iron rod of Thine shall fall ;
        Break them shall Thy sceptre's sway;
      Dash them into pieces small,
      Like the potter's brittle clay.

8 10 Therefore, kings, be wise, give ear;
　　　Hearken, judges of the earth;
　11 Serve Jehovah with due fear,
　　　Mingle trembling with your mirth.

9 12 Worship ye, oh, kiss the Son,
　　　Lest ye perish in the way,
　When His wrath is but begun.
　　　Blessed are all that on Him stay.

Psalm III.　C. M.

1　JEHOVAH, how my foes increase!
　　　Against me many rise.
　2 Of my soul many say, For him
　　　In God no succor lies.

2　3 Thou, LORD, my shield and glory art,
　　　Th' uplifter of my head.
　4 I cried, and from His holy hill
　　　Jehovah answer made.

3　5 I laid me down and slept; I waked;
　　　The LORD supported me;
　6 I will not fear though thousands ten
　　　Set round against me be.

4　7 Jehovah, rise; save me, my God;
　　　Thou hast struck all my foes
　Upon the cheek; the wicked's teeth
　　　Hast broken by Thy blows.

5　8 Salvation to Jehovah doth
　　　Forever appertain,
　And on Thy people evermore
　　　Thy blessing shall remain.

Psalm IV. C. M.

1 GIVE ear unto me when I call,
God of my righteousness;
Have mercy, hear my prayer; Thou hast
Enlarged me in distress.

2 2 O ye the sons of men, how long
Will ye love vanities?
How long my glory turn to shame,
And will ye follow lies?

3 3 But know, Jehovah for Himself
The godly man doth choose;
Jehovah, when on Him I call,
To hear will not refuse.

4 4 Fear, and sin not; talk with your heart
On bed, and silent be.
5 Bring offerings of righteousness,
And in the LORD trust ye.

5 6 O who will show us any good?
Is that which many say;
But of Thy countenance the light,
LORD, lift on us alway.

6 7 Upon my heart, bestowed by Thee,
More gladness I have found
Than they, even then, when corn and
Did most with them abound. ⌜wine

7 8 I will both lay me down in peace,
And quiet sleep will take;
Because Thou only me to dwell
In safety, LORD, dost make.

Psalm V. C. M.

1 JEHOVAH, to my words give ear,
My meditation weigh.
2 Hear my loud cry, my King, my God,
For I to Thee will pray.

2 3 LORD, Thou shalt early hear my
    I early will direct [voice;
  My prayer to Thee; and, looking up,
    An answer will expect.

3 4 For Thou art not a God that doth
    In wickedness delight;
  No evil shall abide with Thee,
  5   Nor fools stand in Thy sight;

4   Thou all ill-doers dost abhor,
  6   Cutt'st off who utter lies;
  Jehovah loathes the bloody man,
    And those who frauds devise.

5 7 But into Thy house I will come
    In Thine abundant grace,
  And I will worship in Thy fear
    Toward Thy holy place.

6 8 Jehovah, in Thy righteousness
    Lead me, for foes lay wait;
  Thy way, wherein I am to walk,
    Before my face make straight.

7 9 For in their mouth there is no truth;
    Their inward part is ill;
  Their throat's an open sepulchre,
    Their tongue doth flatter still.

8 10 O God, condemn them; let them be
    By their own counsel quelled;
  Them, for their many sins, cast out;
    For they 'gainst Thee rebelled.

9 11 But let all joy that trust in Thee,
    And still make shouting noise;
  For them Thou sav'st; let all that love
    Thy name in Thee rejoice.

10 12 Because, Jehovah, to the just
  Thou wilt Thy blessing yield;
  With favor Thou wilt compass him
  About, as with a shield.

Psalm V. S. M.

1 M Y words, Jehovah, hear,
   Regard my secret sigh;
  2 My King, my God, unto the voice
   Attend of this my cry.

2 3 Jehovah, in the morn
   To Thee my cry shall be;
  At morn I order will my prayer;
   I will look up to Thee.

3 4 For Thou art not a God
   That doth in sin delight;
  Sin cannot dwell with Thee, nor stand
  5 The foolish in Thy sight;

4   Ill-doers all Thou hat'st;
  6 Cutt'st off who utter lies;
  Jehovah loathes the bloody man,
   And those who frauds devise.

5 7 But to Thy house I 'll come
   In Thine abundant grace,
  And I will worship in Thy fear,
   Toward Thy holy place.

6 8 Jehovah, lead me on
   In righteousness, I pray;
  Because of those who watch for me,
   To me make straight Thy way.

7 9 For their mouth speaks no truth,
   Their inward part is ill;
  Their throat 's an open sepulchre,
   Their tongue doth flatter still.

8 10 Judge them, O God, defeat
         By plans which they devise;
       Them for their many sins cast out,
         For they against Thee rise.

9 11 Let all who trust Thee joy,
         In shouts their praise proclaim;
       Thou savest them, let all rejoice,
         Who love Thy holy name.

10 12 Jehovah, to the just
         Thou wilt Thy blessing yield;
       With favor Thou wilt compass him
         About as with a shield.

Psalm VI. C. M.

1 JEHOVAH, in Thine anger great
         Do Thou rebuke me not;
       Nor on me lay Thy chast'ning hand,
         In Thy displeasure hot.

2 2 Because I withered am away,
         Jehovah, pity me;
       Jehovah, heal Thou me, because
         My bones vexed greatly be.

3 3 My soul is greatly vexed, but, LORD,
         How long stay wilt Thou make?
       4 Return, Jehovah, free my soul;
         Save for Thy mercy's sake.

4 5 Because of Thee in death there shall,
         No more remembrance be:
       Of those that in the grave do lie,
         Who shall give thanks to Thee?

5 6 I with my groaning weary am,
         All night, till morn appears,
       Through grief I make my bed to swim,
         My couch to flow with tears.

6 7 By reason of my vexing grief,
  Mine eye consumèd is;
  It waxeth old, because of all
  That are mine enemies.

7 8 But now depart from me, all ye
  That work iniquity;
  Because Jehovah heard my voice,
  When I did mourn and cry.

8 9 Unto my supplication's voice
  Jehovah lent His ear;
  When I unto Jehovah pray,
  He graciously will hear.

9 10 Let all be shamed and troubled sore,
  That en'mies are to me;
  Let them turn back, and suddenly
  Ashamèd let them be.

Psalm VI. L. M.

1 LORD, in Thy wrath rebuke me not,
  Nor in Thy hot rage chasten me.
  2 LORD, pity me, for I am weak;
  Heal, LORD, for my bones vexèd be.

2 3 My soul is also sorely vexed,
  But, LORD, how long stay wilt Thou
  4 Return, Jehovah, free my soul; [make?
  O save me for Thy mercy's sake.

3 5 Because all those that are deceased,
  Of Thee shall no remembrance have;
  And who is he that will to Thee
  Give praises lying in the grave?

4 6 I with my groaning weary am,
  And all the night, till morn appears,
  Through grief I make my bed to swim,
  And water all my couch with tears.

5   7 Mine eye, consumed with grief, grows old,
          Because of all mine enemies.
     8 Hence from me, wicked workers all ;
          Jehovah heard my weeping cries.

6   9 Jehovah heard my cry, my prayer
          Jehovah will hear graciously.
     10 Shamed and sore vexed be all my foes ;
          Ashamed and turned back suddenly.

Psalm VII. C. M.

1   1 IN Thee, Jehovah, O my God,
          I confidence repose ;
       Save and deliver me from all
          My persecuting foes ;

2   2 Lest that the enemy my soul
          Should like a lion tear,
       In pieces rending it, while there
          Is no deliverer.

3   3 Jehovah, O my God, if I
          Indeed committed this,
       If it be so that in my hands
          Iniquity there is ;

4   4 If I rewarded ill to him
          That was at peace with me,
       (Yea, ev'n the man that without cause
          My foe was, I did free ;)

5   5 Then let the foe pursue and take
          My soul, and my life thrust
       Down to the earth and let him lay
          Mine honor in the dust.

6   6 Rise in Thy wrath, Jehovah, rise,
          For my foes raging be ;
       And to the judgment which Thou hast
          Commanded, wake for me.

7   7 Of peoples the assembled host
       Around Thee shall draw nigh ;
       And over them do Thou return
          Unto Thy place on high.

8   3 Jehovah shall the people judge ;
       My Judge, Jehovah, be,
       After my righteousness and mine
          Integrity in me.

9   9 O let the wicked's mischief end ;
       But 'stablish steadfastly
       The righteous, for the righteous God
          The hearts and reins doth try.

10 10 In God, who saves th' upright in heart,
       Is my defence and stay.
    11 A righteous Judge is God, and God
          Is wrathful every day.

11 12 If one do not return again,
       Then He His sword will whet ;
       His bow He hath already bent,
          And hath it ready set ;

12 13 He also hath for him prepared
       The instruments of death ;
       Against the persecutors He
          His shafts ordainèd hath.

13 14 Behold, he with iniquity
       Doth travail, as in birth ;
       He also mischief hath conceived,
          And falsehood hath brought forth.

14 15 He made a pit and digged it deep,
       Another there to take ;
       But he is fallen into the ditch
          Which he himself did make.

15 16 On his own head shall be returned
  The mischief he hath wrought;
The violence that he hath done
  Shall on himself be brought.

16 17 According to His righteousness
  Jehovah praise will I,
And will to His name sing, who is
  Jehovah the Most High.

Psalm VIII. C. M.

1 O LORD, our Lord, in all the earth,
  How excellent Thy name!
Who hast Thy glory far advanced
  Above the starry frame.

2 2 From infants' and from sucklings'
  Thou didest strength ordain [mouths
In answer to Thy foes, hater
  And vengeful to restrain.

3 3 When I look up unto the heavens,
  Which Thine own fingers framed,
Unto the moon and to the stars,
  Which were by Thee ordained;

4 4 Then say I, What is man, that he
  Remembered is by Thee?
Or what the son of man, that Thou
  So kind to him shouldst be?

5 5 For Thou a little lower hast
  Him than the angels made,
With glory and with dignity
  Thou crownèd hast his head.

6 6 Of Thy hands' work Thou mad'st him
  All under 's feet didst lay;   [lord.
7 All sheep and oxen, yea, and beasts
  That in the field do stray.

7   8 Fowls of the air, fish of the sea,
      All that pass through the same.
9   O LORD, our Lord, in all the earth,
      How excellent Thy name !

Psalm VIII. 8, 6, 8, 4.

1   O LORD, our Lord, in all the earth,
      How excellent Thy name !
    Who hast Thy glory set above
      The starry frame.

2 2 From infants' and from sucklings'
      Is strength by Thee ordained, [mouths
    That so th' avenger may be quelled,
      The foe restrained.

3 3 When I behold Thy spacious heavens,
      The work of Thine own hand,
    The moon and stars in order set
      By Thy command ;

4 4 O what is man, that Thou shouldst him
      In kind remembrance bear ?
    Or what the son of man, that Thou
      For him shouldst care ?

5 5 For Thou a little lower hast
      Him than the angels made ;
    With honor and with glory Thou
      Hast crowned his head.

6 6 Lord of Thy works Thou hast him
      All unto him must yield ;   [made ;
  7 All sheep and oxen, yea, and beasts
      Which roam the field.

7 8 Fowls of the air, fish of the sea,
      All that pass through the same.
  9 O LORD, our Lord, in all the earth,
      How great Thy name.

Psalm IX. C. M.

1 1 LORD, Thee I'll praise with all my heart,
     Thy wonders all proclaim.
   2 O Thou Most High, in Thee I'll joy,
     Exult, and praise Thy name.

2 3 When back my foes were turned, they
     And perished at Thy sight;   [fell,
   4 For Thou maintainedst my right and
     On throne satst judging right.   [cause;

3 5 The nations great Thou hast rebuked,
     The wicked overthrown;
     Thou hast put out their names, that
     May never more be known.   [they

4 6 The desolations are complete,
     That fell the foe upon;
     Their cities Thou hast overthrown,
     Their memory is gone.

5 7 Jehovah shall forever reign,
     For judgment sets His throne;
   8 In righteousness to judge the world,
     Justice to give each one.

6 9 Jehovah will a refuge be
     For those that are oppressed;
     A refuge will He be, in times
     Of trouble, to distressed.

7 10 And they that know Thy name, in Thee
     Their confidence will place;
     For Thou hast not forsaken them
     That truly seek Thy face.

8 11 The praises of Jehovah sing,
     That dwells on Zion hill;
     Among the nations everywhere
     His deeds record ye still.

9 12 When He doth search out bloody
He then remembers them;   [crimes,
The humble folk He not forgets
That call upon His name.

10 13 Jehovah, pity me ; the grief
Which I from foes sustain,
Behold, ev'n Thou who from death's
Dost raise me up again ;   [gates

11 14 That I, in Zion's daughters' gates,
May all Thy praise advance ;
And that I always may rejoice
In Thy deliverance.

12 15 The nations are sunk in the pit,
Which they themselves prepared;
And in the net which they have hid,
Their own feet fast are snared.

13 16 Jehovah is by judgment known,
Which He Himself hath wrought ;
The sinners' hands do make the snares
Wherewith themselves are caught.

14 17 The wicked shall be backward turned,
Into death's dark abode ;
And all the nations that forget
The great and mighty God.

15 18 For they that needy are shall not
Forgotten be alway ;
The expectation of the poor
Shall not be lost for aye.

16 19 Arise, LORD, let not man prevail ;
Judge nations in Thy sight.
20 That they may know themselves but
The nations, LORD, affright. [men,

Psalm X. C. M.

1 JEHOVAH, wherefore standest Thou
    Away from us so far?
And wherefore hidest Thou Thyself,
    When times so troublous are?

2 The wicked, in his loftiness,
    Doth persecute the poor;
In these devices they have framed,
    Let them be taken sure.

3 The wicked of his heart's desire
    Doth talk with boasting great;
The covetous renounceth, yea
    He doth Jehovah hate.

4 The wicked, in his lofty pride,
    Doth say: He'll not requite;
For in the counsels of his heart
    There is no God of might.

5 His ways at all times grievous are;
    Thy judgments from his sight
Are far removed; at all his foes
    He puffeth with despite.

6 Within his heart he thus hath said:
    I moved shall never be;
And no adversity at all
    Shall ever come to me.

7 His mouth with cursing, fraud, deceit,
    Is filled abundantly;
And mischief underneath his tongue
    There is, and vanity.

8 He closely sits in villages;
    He slays the innocent;
Against the poor that pass him by
    His cruel eyes are bent.

9 9 He, lion-like, lurks in his den ;
　　 He waits the poor to take ;
　　 And when he draws him in his net,
　　 His prey he doth him make.

10 10 Himself he humbleth very low,
　　 He croucheth down withal,
　　 That so a multitude of poor
　　 May by his strong ones fall.

11 11 He thus hath said within his heart :
　　 God hath it quite forgot ;
　　 He hides His countenance, and He
　　 Forever sees it not.

12 12 O Thou Jehovah, rise ; lift up,
　　 O God, Thy hand on high ;
　　 Put not the meek afflicted ones
　　 Out of Thy memory.

13 13 Why is it that the wicked man
　　 Thus doth our God despise ?
　　 That Thou wilt ever it require,
　　 He in his heart denies.

14 14 Thou hast it seen ; mischief and spite
　　 Thou seest to repay ;
　　 The poor commits himself to Thee ;
　　 Thou art the orphan's stay.

15 15 The arm break of the wicked man,
　　 And of the evil one ;
　　 Do Thou seek out his wickedness
　　 Until Thou findest none.

16 16 Jehovah 's King through ages all,
　　 Even to eternity ;
　　 The heathen nations from His land
　　 Are perished utterly.

17 17 The humble ones' sincere desire,
Jehovah, Thou didst hear;
Thou wilt prepare their heart, and Thou
To hear wilt bend Thine ear;

18 18 To judge the fatherless and those
That are oppressed so sore,
That man, that is but sprung of earth,
May them oppress no more.

Psalm XI. C. M.

1 1 IN Jehovah put my trust;
How is it, then, that ye
Say to my soul, Swift as a bird
Unto your mountain flee?

2 2 For, lo, the wicked bend their bow,
Their shafts on strings they fit,
That those who upright are in heart
They privily may hit.

3 3 If the foundations be destroyed,
What hath the righteous done?
4 Jehovah in His temple is,
In heaven, Jehovah's throne.

4 He sees; His eyelids try men's sons.
5 The just Jehovah proves;
But His soul hates the wicked man.
And him that vi'lence loves.

5 6 Snares, fire and brimstone, furious storms
On sinners He shall rain;
This, as the portion of their cup,
Doth unto them pertain.

6 7 For just Jehovah is, and doth
In righteousness delight;
They shall His countenance behold,
Who are in heart upright.

Psalm XII. C. M.

1 JEHOVAH, give salvation; for
  The godly fades away;
  And from among the sons of men
  The faithful do decay.

2 2 Unto his neighbor every one
  Doth utter vanity;
  They with a double heart do speak,
  And lips of flattery.

3 3 Jehovah shall false lips cut off,
  Tongue that speaks proudly thus:
  4 We 'll with our tongues prevail, our lips
  Are ours; who 's lord o'er us?

4 5 For poor oppressed, and for the sighs
  Of needy, rise will I,
  Jehovah saith, and will him save
  From such as him defy.

5 6 Jehovah's words are words most pure,
  They are like silver tried
  In earthen furnace, seven times
  That hath been purified.

6 7 Jehovah, Thou shalt save and keep
  Them ever from this race.
  8 On each side walk the wicked, when
  Vile men are high in place.

Psalm XII. C. P. M.

1 JEHOVAH, help; the godly cease;
  Among the sons of men decrease
    Those who uprightly live. [speak,
  2 With flatt'ring lips they falsehood
  And with a double heart they seek
    Their neighbors to deceive.

2 3 Jehovah shall false lips destroy,
And tongues that boastful words
That say with one accord : [employ ;
4 Our tongues shall in our cause be
Our lips to us alone belong ;   [strong,
Who over us is lord ?

3 5 For those that are oppressed indeed,
For all the poor that sigh in need,
Lo, now will I arise ;
Thus saith Jehovah in His grace :
And them I will in safety place
From such as them despise.

4 6 Pure the LORD'S words, as silver tried
In furnace seven times purified ;
7 O LORD, Thou from this race
Wilt safety for Thy saints provide.
8 The wicked walk on every side,
When vileness has high place.

Psalm XIII. C. M.

1 How long, Jehovah, me forget ?
Shall it for ever be ?
O how long shall it be that Thou
Wilt hide Thy face from me ?

2 2 How long take counsel in my soul
Still sad in heart shall I ?
How long exalted over me
Shall be mine enemy ?

3 3 Jehovah, O my God, regard,
And answer to me make ;
Mine eyes enlighten, lest the sleep
Of death me overtake.

4 4 Lest that mine enemy should say,
Against him I prevail ;
And those that trouble me rejoice
When I am moved and fail.

5 5 But I have all my confidence
      Upon Thy mercy set;
   My heart within me shall rejoice
      In Thy salvation great.

6 6 Unto Jehovah then will I
      Sing praises cheerfully,
   Because He hath His bounty shown
      To me abundantly.

Psalm XIII. 7s & 6s.

1 1 HOW long, O LORD? Forget me
         Wilt Thou for evermore?
      For ever wilt Thou let me
         Thy hidden face deplore?

2 2 How long, my soul, take counsel
         Thus sad in heart all day?
      How long shall foes exulting
         Subject me to their sway?

3 3 O LORD, my God, consider
         And hear my earnest cries;
      Lest I in death should slumber,
         Enlighten Thou mine eyes.

4 4 Lest foe be heard exclaiming,
         Against him I prevailed;
      And they that vex my spirit
         Rejoice when I have failed.

5 5 But on Thy tender mercy
         I ever have relied;
      With joy in Thy salvation
         My heart shall still confide.

6 6 And I'll with voice of singing
         Jehovah praise alone;
      Because to me His favor
         He hath so largely shown.

Psalm XIV. C. M.

1 THAT there is not a God, the fool
  Doth in his heart conclude;
 They are corrupt, their works are vile,
  Not one of them do'th good

2 2 Jehovah on the sons of men
  From heaven did look abroad,
 To see if any understood,
  And did seek after God.

3 3 They altogether filthy are;
  They all aside are gone;
 And there is none that doeth good,
  Yea, sure there is not one.

4 4 These workers of iniquity,
  Do they not know at all,
 That they my people eat as bread,
  Nor on Jehovah call?

5 5 There feared they much; for God is with
  The whole race of the just.
 6 You shame the counsel of the poor,
  Because the LORD's his trust.

6 7 Let Isr'el's help from Zion come!
  When back the LORD shall bring
 His captives, Jacob shall rejoice,
  And Israel shall sing.

Psalm XIV. S. M.

1 THE fool in heart hath said:
  There's no such thing as God!
 They are corrupt, none doeth good,
  Their vile deeds are abroad.

2 2 From heaven Jehovah looked,
  To see men's sons and try
 If any understanding had,
  Or sought his God on high.

3   3 Together all are vile ;
      All are apostate gone ;
      Among them none is doing good,
      There is not even one.

4   4 Who work iniquity,
      Do they not know at all
      That they my people eat as bread,
      Nor on Jehovah call ?

5   5 There fear them seized, because
      God is with people just.
    6 Ye shame the counsel of the poor,
      Who in Jehovah trust.

6   7 Let help from Zion come !
      Back captive Isr'el bring,
      Jehovah ! Jacob then shall shout,
      And Israel shall sing.

Psalm XV.   C. M.

1   WITHIN Thy tabernacle, LORD,
      Who shall abide with Thee ?
    And in Thy high and holy hill
      Who shall a dweller be ?

2   2 The man that walketh uprightly,
      And worketh righteousness ;
    And as he thinketh in his heart,
      So doth he truth express.

3   3 Who doth not slander with his tongue,
      Nor to his friend do'th hurt ;
    Nor yet against his neighbor doth
      Take up an ill report.

4   4 In whose eyes vile men are despised ;
      But who Jehovah fear,
    He honoreth, and changeth not,
      Though to his hurt he swear.

5   5 His coin puts not to usury,
       Nor take reward will he
     Against the guiltless. Who do'th thus
       Shall never movèd be.

Psalm XV. 7s & 6s.

1   WITHIN Thy tent, Jehovah,
       Who shall with Thee abide?
     And on Thy hill so holy,
       Who ever can reside?

2   2 The man whose walk is upright,
       Whose works all righteous are;
     And as in heart he thinketh,
       So doth he truth declare.

3   3 His tongue speaks not in slander,
       Nor harms a friend's good name,
     No tale of scandal spreadeth
       His neighbor to defame.

4   4 His eyes frown on the sinner;
       But who Jehovah fear,
     He honors; never changeth,
       Though to his hurt he swear.

5   5 He gains not by extortion,
       Nor take a bribe will he,
     'Gainst guiltless ones. Thus doing
       He moved shall never be.

Psalm XVI. C. M.

1   KEEP me, O God; I trust in Thee,
       2 Jehovah, I confess:
     Thou art my Lord; apart from Thee,
       No good do I possess.

2 3 To saints on earth, the excellent
   Where my delight's all placed :
 4 Their sorrows shall be multiplied
   To idol gods that haste.

3   Of their drink-offerings of blood
   I will no off'ring make ;
 Yea. neither I their very names
   Up in my lips will take.

4 5 Of mine inheritance and cup
   The LORD's the portion sure :
 The lot that fallèn is to me
   Thou dost maintain secure.

5 6 Unto me happily the lines
   In pleasant places fell ;
 Yea, the inheritance I have,
   In beauty doth excel.

6 7 I bless Jehovah, Him who doth
   By counsel me conduct ;
 And in the seasons of the night
   My reins do me instruct.

7 8 I always have Jehovah set
   Before my face ; for He
 Doth ever stand at my right hand ;
   I shall not movèd be.

8 9 Because of this my heart is glad,
   And joy shall be expressed
 Even by my glory ; and my flesh
   In confidence shall rest.

9 10 Because my soul in grave to dwell
   Shall not be left by Thee ;
 Nor wilt Thou give Thy Holy One
   Corruption there to see.

10 11 Thou wilt me show the path of life;
   Of joys there is full store
Before Thy face; at Thy right hand
   Are pleasures evermore.

Psalm XVII. C. M.

1 HEAR, LORD, the right, attend my
   Unto my prayer give heed, [cry,
That doth not in hypocrisy
   From feignèd lips proceed.

2 2 And from before Thy presence forth
   My judgment do Thou send;
And unto things that equal are
   O let Thine eyes attend.

3 3 My heart Thou provest, and by night
   Dost visit me and try,
But findest naught; because my mouth
   Shall not sin, purposed I.

4 4 As for men's works, I by the word,
   That from Thy lips doth flow,
Have kept myself out of the paths
   Wherein destroyers go.

5 5 Hold up my goings and me guide
   In those Thy paths divine;
So that my footsteps may not slide
   Out of those ways of Thine.

6 6 I called upon Thee have, O God,
   Because Thou wilt me hear;
That Thou mayst hearken to my
   To me incline Thine ear. [speech,

7 7 Thy wondrous loving-kindness show,
   Thou that by Thy right hand
Sav'st them that trust in Thee, from
   That up against them stand. [those

8 8 As apple of the eye me keep,
    In Thy wings' shade me hide
  9 From wasting deadly foes, who me
    Beset on every side.

9 10 In their own pride they are inclosed,
    Their mouth speaks loftily.
 11 Our steps they compass, and to earth
    Down bowing set their eye.

10 12 He like unto a lion is,
    That's greedy of his prey,
    Or lion young, which, lurking, doth
    In secret places stay.

11 13 Arise, Jehovah, disappoint,
    Cast down mine enemy;
    And from the wicked one, Thy sword,
    Do Thou deliver me.

12 14 From men, Thy hand, Jehovah—men
    That love the world, me save,
    Who only in this present life
    Their part and portion have;

13   Whom with Thy treasures Thou dost
    They many sons receive,   [fill;
    And of their great abundance they
    Unto their children leave.

14 15 But as for me, I Thine own face
    In righteousness will see;
    And with Thy likeness, when I wake,
    I satisfied shall be.

Psalm XVIII. C. M.

1 JEHOVAH, Thee, my strength, I'll love;
  2 My fortress is the LORD;
    My rock, and He that doth to me
    Deliverance afford;

2 My God, my strength, whom I will trust,
   A buckler unto me;
  Of my salvation the strong horn,
   And my high tower is He.

3 Unto Jehovah, who of praise
   Is worthy, I will cry;
  And then shall I preservèd be
   Safe from mine enemy.

4 The cords of death encompassed me,
   Sin's floods made me afraid; [drawn,
 5 Bands of the grave were round me
   Death's snares were on me laid.

6 In grief I on Jehovah called,
   Cry to my God did I;
  He from His temple heard my voice,
   To His ears came my cry.

7 Earth, as affrighted, then did shake,
   Trembling upon it seized;
  The hills' foundations then were moved
   Because He was displeased.

8 Up from His nostrils came a smoke,
   And from His mouth there came
  Devouring fire, and coals by it
   Were turned to burning flame.

9 He also bowèd down the heavens,
   And thence He did descend;
  And thickest clouds of darkness did
   Under His feet attend.

10 And He upon a cherub rode,
   And thereon He did fly;
  Yea, on the swift wings of the wind
   His flight was from on high.

10 11 He darkness made His secret place ;
   About Him, for His tent,
   Dark waters were, and thickest clouds
   Of airy firmament.

11 12 And at the brightness of that light
   Which was before His eye,
   His thick clouds passed away, hail
   And coals of fire did fly.   [stones

12 13 Jehovah also in the heavens
   Did thunder in His ire ;
   And there the Highest gave His voice ;
   Hailstones and coals of fire.

13 14 Yea, He His arrows sent abroad,
   And them He scatterèd ;
   His lightnings also He shot out,
   And them discomfited.

14 15 The waters' channels then were seen,
   The world's foundations vast
   At Thy rebuke discovered were,
   And at Thy nostrils' blast.

15 16 And from above He did send down
   And take me from below ;
   From many waters He me drew,
   Which would me overflow.

16 17 From my strong foe He rescued me,
   And such as did me hate ;
   Because He saw that they for me
   Too strong were, and too great.

17 18 They came upon me in the day
   Of my calamity ;
   But evèn then Jehovah was
   Himself a stay to me.

18 19 He to a place where liberty
    And room was hath me brought;
  Because He took delight in me,
    He my deliv'rance wrought.

19 20 According to my righteousness
    The LORD did recompense;
  He me repaid according to
    My hands' pure innocence.

20 21 Jehovah's ways I kept, nor from
    My God turned wickedly.
  22 His judgments were before me, I
    His laws put not from me.

21 23 Sincere before Him was my heart,
    With Him upright was I;
  And watchfully I kept myself
    From mine iniquity.

22 24 According to my righteousness
    Jehovah did requite,
  After the cleanness of my hands
    Appearing in His sight.

23 25 Thou to the gracious showest grace,
    To just men just Thou art;
  26 Pure to the pure, but froward still
    To men of froward heart.

24 27 For Thou wilt the afflicted save,
    In grief that low do lie;
  But wilt bring down the countenance
    Of them whose looks are high.

25 28 For Thou will light my candle so
    That it shall shine full bright;
  My God Jehovah also will
    My darkness turn to light.

26 29 By Thee through troops of men I break,
And them discomfit all ;
And by my God assisting me
I overleap a wall.

27 30 Yea, God is perfect in His way ;
Jehovah's word is tried ;
He is a buckler to all those
Who do in Him confide.

28 31 Who but the LORD is God ? save God
Who is a rock and stay ?
32 'Tis God that girdeth me with strength
And perfect makes my way.

29 33 He made my feet swift as the hind's ;
On my heights made me stand.
34 My hands He taught to war, mine arms
A bow of brass did bend.

30 35 The shield of Thy salvation Thou
Upon me didst bestow ;
Thy right hand held me up, and great
Thy kindness made me grow.

31 36 And in my way my steps Thou hast
Established under me,
That I go safely, and my feet
Are kept from sliding free.

32 37 Mine enemies I did pursue,
And did them overtake,
Nor did I turn again till I
An end of them did make.

33 38 I wounded them, they could not rise,
They at my feet did fall. [war ;
39 Thou me didst gird with strength for
My foes Thou broughtst down all.

34 40 And Thou hast given me the necks
    Of all mine enemies;
  That I might utterly destroy
    Those who against me rise.

35 41 They cried for help, but there was none
    Who would or could them save;
  Yea, they unto Jehovah cried,
    But He no answer gave.

36 42 Then did I beat them small as dust
    Before the wind that flies;
  And I did cast them out like dirt
    Upon the street that lies.

37 43 Thou mad'st me free from people's
    And nations' head to be;   [strife,
  A people whom I have not known
    Shall service do to me.

38 44 At hearing they shall me obey;
    To me they shall submit;
  45 Strangers for fear shall fade away,
    Who in close places sit.

39 46 Jehovah lives, blessed be my Rock;
    My Saviour-God, praised be;
  47 God doth avenge me, and subdues
    The people under me.

40 48 He saves me from mine enemies;
    Yea, Thou hast lifted me
  Above my foes, and from the man
    Of vi'lence set me free.

41 49 Therefore to Thee will I give thanks
    The nations all among,
  And to Thy name, Jehovah, sing
    Loud praises in a song.

42 50 He great deliv'rance gives His king ;
 He mercy doth extend
 To David, His anointed one,
 And his seed without end.

Psalm XIX. C. M.

1 THE heavens God's glory do declare ;
 The skies His hand-works preach.
 2 Day utters speech to day, and night
 To night doth knowledge teach.

2 3 There is no speech, nor tongue to
 Their voice doth not extend. [which
 4 Their line is gone through all the earth,
 Their words to the world's end.

3 In them He set the sun a tent,
 5 Who, bridegroom-like, forth goes
 From 's chamber, as a strong man doth
 To run his race rejoice.

4 6 From heavèn's end he goeth forth,
 Circling to th' end again ;
 And there is nothing from his heat
 That hidden doth remain.

5 7 The LORD'S law perfect is, and turns
 The soul in sin that lies.
 Jehovah's testimony 's sure,
 It makes the simple wise.

6 8 Jehovah's precepts righteous are ;
 They do rejoice the heart ;
 Jehovah's own commands are pure;
 · They light to eyes impart.

7 9 Unspotted is Jehovah's fear,
 It ever doth endure ;
 Jehovah's judgments all are truth,
 And righteousness most pure.

8 10 They more than gold, yea, much fine
To be desirèd are; [gold,
Than honey, honey from the comb
That droppeth, sweeter far.

9 11 Moreover, they Thy servant warn
How he his life should frame;
A great reward provided is
For them that keep the same.

10 12 Who can his errors understand?
From secret faults me cleanse;
13 Thy servant also keep Thou back
From all presumptuous sins;

11 And do not suffer them to have
Dominion over me;
I shall be righteous then, and from
The great transgression free.

12 14 The words which from my mouth proceed,
The thoughts sent from my heart,
Accept, Jehovah, who my Rock
And my Redeemer art.

Psalm XX. C. M.

1 JEHOVAH hear thee in the day
When trouble He doth send;
And let the name of Jacob's God
Thee from all ill defend.

2 2 O let Him send His help to thee,
Out from His holy place;
Let Him from Zion, His own hill,
Sustain thee by His grace.

3 3 Let Him remember all thy gifts,
Accept thy sacrifice;

4 Grant thee thy heart's wish, and fulfil
Thy thoughts and counsel wise.

4   5 In thy salvation we will joy;
In our God's name we will
Display our banner; all thy prayers
Jehovah doth fulfil.

5   6 I know Jehovah saves His Christ;
He from His holy heaven
Will hear Him, with the saving strength
By His own right hand given.

6   7 In chariots some put confidence,
Some horses trust upon;
But we will trust Jehovah's Name,
Who is our God alone.

7   8 We rise, and upright stand, when they
Are bowèd down and fall.
9 Jehovah, save; and let the King
Us hear when we do call.

Psalm XXI. C. M.

1   JEHOVAH, in Thy strength the king
Shall very joyful be;
And in Thy saving help rejoice
Exceedingly shall he.

2   2 For Thou upon him hast bestowed
All that his heart would have;
And Thou from him hast not withheld
Whate'er his lips did crave.

3   3 For Thou with blessings didst him
Of goodness manifold;   [meet
And Thou hast set upon his head
A crown of purest gold.

4 4 When he desirèd life of Thee,
      Thou life to him didst give ;
   Even such a length of days, that he
      For evermore should live.

5 5 In that salvation wrought by Thee
      His glory is made great ;
   Honor and comely majesty
      Thou hast upon him set.

6 6 Because that Thou for evermore
      Most blessèd hast him made,
   And Thou hast with Thy countenance
      Made him exceeding glad.

7 7 Because the king his confidence
      Doth on Jehovah lay ;   [High
   And through the grace of the Most
      Shall not be moved away.

8 8 Thy hand shall all those men find out
      That en'mies are to Thee ;
   Even Thy right hand shall find out
      Of Thee that haters be.   [those

9 9 Like oven of fire Thou shalt them
      When kindled is Thine ire ;   [make,
   Jehovah's wrath shall swallow them,
      Devour them shall the fire.

10 10 Their fruit from earth Thou shalt de-
      Their seed men from among ; [stroy,
   11 For they beyond their might, 'gainst
      Did mischief plot, and wrong. [Thee

11 12 For Thou shalt make them turn their
      When arrows Thou shalt place [back
   Upon Thy strings, and ready make
      To fly against their face.

12 13 Jehovah, in Thy mighty power
Do Thou exalted be ;
So shall we sing with joyful hearts,
And praise Thy power shall we.

Psalm XXI. 12s & 9s.

1 O JEHOVAH, the king in Thy strength
shall be glad,
And shall in Thy salvation rejoice ;
2 For Thou freely didst give him each
wish his heart had,
And request of his suppliant voice.

2 3 All the blessings he craved Thou didst
graciously give,
With the purest of gold he is crowned.
4 When he asked of Thee life, Thou
hast made him to live,
While the ages shall circle around.

3 5 Through salvation from Thee is his
fame widely spread,
Thou didst glory and honor impart ;
6 Yea, most blessèd for evermore Thou
hast him made,
And Thy presence has gladdened his
heart.

4 7 For the king in the name of Jehovah
Most High
Did unwavering confidence place ;
Through His great loving-kindness
he still will rely
On the Highest, and stand by His
grace.

5 8 Thou wilt stretch forth Thy hand on
      the heads of Thy foes,
    On Thy haters a right hand of power;
   9 Then Thy wrath shall around them
      like furnace flames close ;
    Yea, Jehovah's own wrath shall
      devour.

6 10 From the earth shall their race be
      consumed and destroyed,
    And their offspring forever shall fail;
   11 By the evil they plotted, the schemes
      they employed,
    They shall never against Thee pre-
      vail.

7 12 But their back Thou wilt make them to
      turn in swift flight,
    When Thine arrows are aimed at
      their face.
   13 But be Thou, O Jehovah, exalted in
      might ;
    We will sing of Thy power and grace.

Psalm XXII. C. M.

1 MY God, my God, why hast Thou me
     Forsaken ? why so far
   Art Thou from helping me, and from
     My words that roaring are ?

2 2 All day, my God, to Thee I cry,
     Yet am not heard by Thee ;
   And in the season of the night
     I cannot silent be.

3 3 But Thou art holy, Thou that dost
     Inhabit Isr'el's praise.
   4 Our fathers hoped in Thee; they hoped,
     And Thou didst them release.

4 5 When unto Thee they sent their cry,
     To them deliv'rance came ;
     Because they put their trust in Thee,
     They were not put to shame.

5 6 But as for me, a worm I am,
     And as no man am prized ;
     Reproach of men I am, and by
     The people am despised.

6 7 All that me see laugh me to scorn ;
     Shoot out the lip do they ;
     They nod and shake their heads at me,
     And mocking, thus do say :

7 8 He did Jehovah trust, that He
     Would free him by His might ;
     Let Him deliver him, since he
     Had in Him such delight.

8 9 But Thou art He who gave me birth,
     From Thee I being had ;
     And I upon my mother's breast
     By Thee to hope was made.

9 10 And I was cast upon Thy care,
     Even from my birth till now ;
     And from my childhood's dawn, my
     And my support art Thou.   [God

10 11 Be not far off, for grief is near,
     And none to help is found.
   12 Bulls many compass me, strong bulls
     Of Bashan me surround.

11 13 Their mouths they opened wide on me,
  Upon me gape did they,
 Like to a lion ravening,
  And roaring for his prey.

12 14 Like water I'm poured out, my bones
  All out of joint do part;
 Amidst my bowels, as the wax,
  So melted is my heart.

13 15 My strength 's like a potsherd dried;
  My tongue it cleaveth fast
 Unto my jaws; and to the dust
  Of death Thou brought me hast.

14 16 For dogs have compassed me about;
  The wicked that did meet
 In their assembly me inclosed;
  They pierced my hands and feet.

15 17 I all my bones may tell; my foes
  Upon me look and stare.
 18 Upon my vesture lots they cast,
  And clothes among them share.

16 19 Jehovah, be not far; my strength,
  Haste to give help to me.
 20 From sword my soul, from power of
  My precious life set free.   [dogs

17 21 From the devouring lion's mouth
  My life do Thou defend;
 To save from horns of unicorns
  Thou didst me answer send.

18 22 I will show forth Thy Name unto
  Those that my brethren are;
 Amidst the congregation I
  Thy praises will declare.

19 23 Jehovah praise, who do Him fear ;
  Him glorify, all ye
The seed of Jacob ; fear Him, all
  That Isr'el's children be.

20 24 For He despised not, nor abhorred
  The meek one's misery ;
Nor from him hid His face, but heard
  When he to Him did cry.

21 25 Within the congregation great
  My praise shall be of Thee ;
My vows before them that Him fear
  Shall be performed by me.

22 26 The meek shall eat, and shall be filled;
  They also praise shall give
Unto Jehovah, who Him seek ;
  Your heart shall ever live.

23 27 All ends of earth remember shall
  And turn Jehovah to ;
The kindreds of the nations all
  To Him shall homage do ;

24 28 Because unto Jehovah doth
  The kingdom appertain ;
And over all the nations, He,
  As Governor, doth reign.

25 29 Earth's fat ones eat, and worship shall ;
  All who to dust descend
Shall bow to Him ; none of them can
  His soul from death defend.

26 30 A seed shall service do to Him ;
  And to the Lord it shall
A generation counted be
  Throughout the ages all.

27 31 They shall come, and they shall declare
His truth and righteousness
Unto a people yet unborn,
Because He hath done this.

Psalm XXIII. C. M.

1 1 THE LORD's my Shepherd, I'll not
    2 He makes me down to lie [want,
In pastures green; He leadeth me
The quiet waters by.

2 3 My soul He doth restore again;
And me to walk doth make
Within the paths of righteousness
Even for His own Name's sake.

3 4 Yea, though I walk in death's dark vale,
Yet will I fear no ill;
For Thou art with me, and Thy rod
And staff me comfort still.

4 5 A table Thou hast furnished me
In presence of my foes;
My head Thou dost with oil anoint,
And my cup overflows.

5 6 Goodness and mercy all my life
Shall surely follow me;
And ever in Jehovah's house
My dwelling place shall be.

Psalm XXIII. 11s.

1 1 THE LORD is my Shepherd; no want
    shall come nigh.
  2 In pastures of verdure He makes me to
    lie;
Beside restful waters He leads me in
    peace;
  3 My soul to new life He restores by His
    grace.

2 In right ways He leads me for His own
   Name's sake;
4 So when in the valley of death-shade
   I walk,
   Since Thou wilt be with me, no ill
   shall I fear;
   Thy rod and Thy staff give me com-
   fort and cheer.

3 5 Thou spreadest my table in face of my
   foes;
   My head Thou anointest, my cup
   overflows.
6 Thy goodness and mercy pursue my
   life's ways;
   At home with Jehovah I 'll dwell endless days.

Psalm XXIV. C. M.

1 THE earth unto the LORD belongs
   And all that it contains;
   The world that is inhabited,
   And all that there remains.

2 2 For the foundations thereof He
   Upon the seas did lay,
   And He hath it established firm
   Upon the floods to stay.

3 3 Who is the man that shall ascend
   Into Jehovah's hill?
   Or who within His holy place
   Shall have a dwelling still?

4 4 Whose hands are clean, whose heart is
   And unto vanity   [pure;
   Who hath not lifted up his soul,
   Nor sworn deceitfully.

5 5 This is the man who shall receive
      The blessing from the LORD,
   The God of his salvation shall
      Him righteousness accord.

6 6 Lo! this the generation is
      That after Him inquire,
   O Jacob, who do seek Thy face,
      With their whole heart's desire.

7 7 Ye gates, lift up your heads on high ;
      Ye doors that last for aye,
   Be lifted up, that so the King
      Of glory enter may.

8 8 But who of glory is the King?
      The mighty LORD is this ;
   Even that same LORD, that great in
      And strong in battle is.   [might

9 9 Ye gates, lift up your heads ; ye doors,
      Doors that do last for aye,
   Be lifted up, that so the King
      Of glory enter may.

10 10 But who is He that is the King
      Of glory? who is this?
   The LORD of Hosts, and none but He,
      The King of glory is.

Psalm XXIV. 11s.

1 THE earth and the fulness with which
      it is stored,
   The world and its dwellers belong to
      the LORD;
 2 For He on the seas its foundation hath
      laid,
   And firm on the waters its pillars hath
      stayed.

2 3 What man shall the hill of Jehovah
  ascend?
  And who in the place of His Holiness
  stand?
  4 The man of pure heart, and of hands
  without stain,
  Who swears not to falsehood, nor loves
  what is vain.

3 5 He shall from Jehovah the blessing
  receive,
  The God of salvation shall righteousness give.
  6 For this is the people, yea, this is the
  race
  Of those that in Jacob are seeking
  Thy face.

4 7 Ye gates, lift your heads and an entrance display,
  Ye doors everlasting, wide open the
  way;
  The King of all glory high honors
  await,
  The King of all glory shall enter in
  state.

5 8 Who is King of glory? Jehovah the
  strong,
  Jehovah the mighty in war against
  wrong.
  9 Ye gates, lift your heads and an entrance display,
  Ye doors everlasting, wide open the
  way;

6   The King of all glory high honors
  await,
  The King of all glory shall enter in
  state.

10 What King of all glory is this that ye sing?
Jehovah of hosts, He of glory is King.

Psalm XXV. C. M.

1 1 TO Thee I lift my soul, O LORD.
2 My God, I trust in Thee;
Let me not be ashamed, nor let
My foes exult o'er me.

2 3 Let none of those that wait on Thee
Be put to shame at all;
But those who causelessly transgress,
Let shame upon them fall.

3 4 Thy ways, LORD, show; teach me Thy paths,
5 Lead me in truth, teach me;
For of my safety Thou art God;
All day I wait on Thee.

4 6 Thy mercies, that most tender are,
Jehovah, now recall,
And loving-kindnesses; for they
Have been through ages all.

5 7 Let not the errors of my youth,
Nor sins remembered be;
In mercy for Thy goodness' sake,
O LORD remember me.

6 8 Jehovah good and upright is,
The way He'll sinners show;
9 The meek in judgment He will guide,
And make His path to know.

7 10 The whole paths of Jehovah are
Both truth and mercy sure

To such as keep His covenant
And testimonies pure.

8 11 Jehovah, for Thine own Name's sake
I humbly Thee entreat
To pardon mine iniquity,
For it is very great.

9 12 Who fears Jehovah, him He'll teach
The way that he shall choose.
13 His soul shall dwell at ease ; his seed
The earth, as heirs, shall use.

10 14 The secret of Jehovah is
With such as fear His name ;
And He His holy covenant
Will manifest to them.

11 15 My waiting eyes are constantly
Upon Jehovah set ;
For He it is that shall bring forth
My feet out of the net.

12 16 O turn Thee unto me ; do Thou
To me Thy mercy show ;
For I am lone and desolate,
And am brought very low.

13 17 Enlarged the griefs are of my heart ;
Me from distress relieve.
18 See mine affliction and my pain,
And all my sins forgive.

14 19 Consider Thou mine enemies,
Because they many are,
And it a cruel hatred is,
Which they against me bear.

15 20 Do Thou in safety keep my soul ;
Do Thou deliver me ;

　　　　Let me not be ashamed ; for I
　　　　　　Have put my trust in Thee.

16 21 O let integrity and truth
　　　　　　Keep me, who Thee attend.
　　22 Release, O God, to Israel
　　　　　　From all his troubles send.

Psalm XXV. S. M.

1　TO Thee I lift my soul,
　　　2 O LORD ; I trust in Thee,
　　My God ; let me not be ashamed,
　　　　Nor foes exult o'er me.

2　3 Let none that wait on Thee
　　　　Be put to shame at all ;
　　But those who causelessly transgress,
　　　　Let shame upon them fall.

3　4 Thy ways, Jehovah, show ;
　　　　Thy paths, O teach Thou me.
　　5 And do Thou lead me in Thy truth,
　　　　Therein my Teacher be :

4　　For Thou art God that dost
　　　　To me salvation send ;
　　And I upon Thee all the day,
　　　　Expecting, do attend.

5　6 Thy tender mercies, LORD,
　　　　To mind do Thou recall,
　　And loving-kindnesses, for they
　　　　Have been through ages all.

6　7 My sins and faults of youth,
　　　　Jehovah, do forget ;
　　In tender mercy think on me,
　　　　And for Thy goodness great.

7 8 Jehovah's good and just;
 The way He'll sinners show;
 9 The meek in judgment He will guide
 And make His path to know.

8 10 Jehovah's paths are all
 The truth and mercy sure
 To those that do His cov'nant keep,
 And testimonies pure.

9 11 Now for Thine own Name's sake,
 Jehovah, I entreat,
 O pardon mine iniquity;
 For it is very great.

10 12 What man is he that fears
 The LORD, and doth Him serve?
 Him shall He teach the way that he
 Shall choose and still observe.

11 13 His soul shall dwell at ease;
 And his posterity
 Shall flourish still, and of the earth
 Inheritors shall be.

12 14 Jehovah's secret is
 With them that fear His name,
 And He His holy covenant
 Will manifest to them.

13 15 Mine eyes are constantly
 Upon Jehovah set;
 For He it is that shall bring forth
 My feet out of the net.

14 16 Turn unto me Thy face,
 And to me mercy show;
 Because that I am desolate,
 And am brought very low.

15 17 My heart's griefs are increased;
  Me from distress relieve.
  18 See mine affliction and my pain,
  And all my sins forgive.

16 19 Consider Thou my foes,
  Because they many are,
  And it a cruel hatred is
  Which they against me bear.

17 20 O do Thou keep my soul,
  Do Thou deliver me;
  And let me never be ashamed
  Because I trust in Thee.

18 21 Let truth and right me keep,
  For I on Thee attend.
  22 Release, O God, to Israel
  From all his troubles send.

Psalm XXVI. C. M.

1 JUDGE me, Jehovah, for I walked
  In mine integrity;
  I in the LORD have put my trust,
  Slide therefore shall not I.

2 2 Search me, Jehovah, and me try;
  Prove heart and reins, I pray;
  3 For Thy love is before mine eyes;
  Thy truth's paths are my way.

3 4 With persons vain I have not sat,
  Nor with dissemblers gone.
  5 Th' assembly of ill men I hate,
  To sit with such I shun.

4 6 My hands in innocence I'll wash,
     And them will purify;
     Jehovah, then, Thine altar pure
     Encompass round will I.

5 7 That I, with voice of grateful praise,
     May publish and declare,
     And tell of all Thy mighty works,
     That great and wondrous are.

6 8 The habitation of Thy house,
     Jehovah, I love well;
     Yea, in that place I do delight
     Where doth Thine honor dwell.

7 9 With sinners gather not my soul,
     And such as blood would spill;
  10 Whose hands devices mischievous,
     Whose right hand bribes do fill.

8 11 But as for me, I will walk on
     In mine integrity;
     Do Thou redeem me, and do Thou
     Be merciful to me.

9 12 My foot upon an even place
     Doth stand with steadfastness;
     Within the congregations, I
     Jehovah's Name will bless.

Psalm XXVII. C. M.

1 THE LORD's my light and saving
     health;
     Who shall make me dismayed?
     My life's strength is the LORD; of
       whom
     Then shall I be afraid?

2 2 When as mine enemies and foes,
  Most wicked persons all,
 To eat my flesh against me rose,
  They stumbled and did fall.

3 3 Against me though a host encamp,
  My heart yet fearless is;
 Though war against me rise, I will
  Be confident in this.

4 4 One thing I of the LORD desired,
  And will seek to obtain;
 That all life's days I may within
  Jehovah's house remain.

5 That I the beauty of the LORD
  Behold may and admire,
 And that I in His holy place
  May rev'rently inquire.

6 5 For He in His pavilion shall
  Me hide in evil days;
 In secret of His tent me hide
  And on a rock me raise.

7 6 And now, even at this present time,
  My head shall lifted be
 Above all those that are my foes,
  And round encompass me.

8 I therefore to His holy house
  Will joyous off'rings bring;
 Jehovah I will praise, yea, I
  To Him will praises sing.

9 7 Do Thou, Jehovah, hear my voice
  When I do cry to Thee;
 Upon me also mercy have,
  And do Thou answer me.

10 8 When Thou didst say, Seek ye My face,
   Then unto Thee reply
Thus did my heart : Thy gracious face,
   Jehovah, seek will I.

11 9 Far from me hide not Thou Thy face;
   Put not away from Thee
Thy servant in Thy wrath ; Thou hast
   A helper been to me.

12 O God who my salvation art,
   Leave me not, nor forsake ;
10 Though father, mother, both me leave,
   Jehovah will up take.

13 11 Jehovah, teach me in Thy way,
   To me a Leader be
In a plain path, because of those
   That hatred bear to me.

14 12 Give me not to mine en'mies' will ;
   For witnesses that lie
Against me risen are, and such
   As breathe out cruelty.

15 13 I should have fainted had I not
   Believed that I would see
Jehovah's goodness in the land
   Of them that living be.

16 14 Wait on Jehovah and be strong,
   And He shall strength afford
Unto thy heart ; yea, do thou wait,
   I say, upon the LORD.

Psalm XXVIII. C. M.

1 TO Thee I 'll pray, O LORD, my Rock ;
   O answer Thou my cry ;
Lest by Thy silence I become
   As those in grave that lie.

2 2 The voice hear of my humble prayers,
　　When unto Thee I cry;
　When to Thy holy oracle
　　I lift my hands on high.

3 3 With ill men draw me not away
　　That work iniquity;　　　　[in.
　That speak peace to their friends, while
　　Their hearts doth mischief lie.

4 4 Give them according to their deeds,
　　And evil of their way;
　And, as the work of their own hands
　　Deserve, do Thou repay.

5 5 He shall not build, but them destroy,
　　Who would not understand
　Jehovah's works, nor did regard
　　The doing of His hand.

6 6 Blessed be Jehovah evermore,
　　For graciously He heard
　The voice of my petitions, and
　　My prayers He did regard.

7 7 The LORD's my strength and shield;
　　Upon Him did rely;　　[my heart
　I have been helped, and hence my heart
　　Doth joy exceedingly.

8　　I'll praise Him with my song. Their
　　8　Jehovah is alone;　　　[strength
　He also is the saving strength
　　Of His anointed one.

9 9 O Thine own people do Thou save,
　　Bless Thine inheritance;
　Them also do Thou feed, and them
　　For evermore advance.

Psalm XXIX. C. M.

1 O GIVE Jehovah praise, ye sons
  That of the mighty be,
  Yea, to Jehovah do ascribe
  All strength and majesty.

2 The glory due unto His Name
  Give to Jehovah now;
  In beauty of His holiness
  Before Jehovah bow.

3 Jehovah's voice is on the floods;
  The God of glory great
  Doth thunder; on the waters vast
  Jehovah has His seat.

4 The voice is full of power, which
  Forth from Jehovah high; [sounds
  Jehovah's mighty voice is full
  Of glorious majesty.

5 Jehovah's voice asunder doth
  The shiv'ring cedars tear;
  Jehovah doth the cedars break
  That Lebanon doth bear.

6 He makes them like a calf to skip;
  Even that great Lebanon,
  And, like the young of unicorns,
  The mountain Sirion.

7 Jehovah's voice cleaves flames of fire,
8 Jehovah's voice doth shake
  The wilds; the Kadesh wilderness
  Jehovah makes to quake.

9 Jehovah's voice makes hinds to calve,
  It makes the forest bare;
  And in His temple every one
  His glory doth declare.

9 10 The LORD sat on the flood; sit King
    Jehovah ever shall.
 11 The LORD His folk makes strong;
    with peace
    The LORD doth bless them all.

Psalm XXIX. 12s & 11s.

1 GIVE ye to Jehovah, O sons of the
    mighty,
    Give ye to Jehovah the glory and
    power;
 2 O give to the name of Jehovah due
    glory;
    In holy apparel, Jehovah adore.

2 3 The voice of Jehovah comes down on
    the waters,
    In thunder the God of the glory
    draws nigh;
    Lo, over the waves of the wide-flowing
    waters
    Jehovah as King is enthroned on
    high.

3 4 The voice of Jehovah is mighty, is
    mighty,
    The voice of Jehovah in majesty
    speaks;
 5 The voice of Jehovah the cedars is
    breaking,
    Jehovah the cedars of Lebanon
    breaks.

4 6 Like playful calves leaping, they skip
    when He speaketh;
    Lo, Lebanon leaps at the sound of
    His Name!

Like son of the unicorn Sirion is
   skipping;
7 The voice of Jehovah divideth the
   flame.

5 8 The voice of Jehovah—it shaketh the
      desert,
   The desert of Kadesh, it shaketh
      with fear;
   9 The hind of the field into travail-pangs
      casteth;
   The voice of Jehovah the forest strips
      bare.

6   Each one, in His temple, His glory
        proclaimeth.
   10 JAH sat on the flood; JAH is King
        on His throne.
   11 Jehovah all strength to His people
        imparteth;
   Jehovah with peace ever blesseth
      His own.

Psalm XXX. C. M.

1 JEHOVAH, Thee I'll praise, for Thou
      Hast lifted me on high,
   And over me Thou to rejoice
      Mad'st not mine enemy.

2 2 Jehovah, Thou who art my God,
        I in distress to Thee
   With loud cries lifted up my voice,
      And Thou hast healèd me.

3 3 Jehovah, Thou my soul hast brought
      And rescued from the grave;
   That I to pit should not go down,
      Alive Thou didst me save.

4 4 O ye that are His holy ones,
   Jehovah's praise proclaim,
And unto Him give thanks when ye
   Record His holy Name.

5 5 For but a moment lasts His wrath;
   Life in His favor lies;
Though weeping for a night endures,
   At morn doth joy arise.

6 6 In my prosperity I said
   That nothing shall me move.
 7 Jehovah, Thou my mountain hast
   Established by Thy love.

7   When Thou Thy face didst hide, dis-
     Was I and sore dismayed;   [tressed
 8 Jehovah, unto Thee I cried;
   I to Jehovah prayed.

8 9 What profit is there in my blood
   When I to grave go down?
Shall dust give praises unto Thee?
   Shall it Thy truth make known?

9 10 Hear, LORD, have mercy; help me,
      LORD;
 11   Thou didst from sackcloth free;
My grief to dancing Thou hast turned,
   With gladness girded me;

10 12 That sing Thy praise my glory may,
   And never silent be;
My God, Jehovah, evermore
   I will give thanks to Thee.

Psalm XXX. 7s.

1 THEE, Jehovah, will I praise;
   From the depths Thou didst me raise,
And mine adversaries, glad

    Over me, Thou hast not made.
2 LORD, my God, I cried to Thee,
    And in love Thou healedst me.

2 3 Thou, Jehovah, didst me save!
    And from the devouring grave,
    Sending down from heaven above,
    Broughtest up my soul in love;
    And alive Thou keepest me,
    That the pit I should not see.

3 4 Sing unto Jehovah, sing;
    Thanks His saints unto Him bring;
    Call to mind His holiness!
  5 Truly, of His anger, less
    Than a moment is the bound;
    In His favor life is found.

4   Weeping tarries for a night,
    Gladness comes with morning light.
  6 Said I in prosperity,
    I shall never moved be;
  7 Strength, LORD, to my mountain now
    By Thy favor givest Thou.

5   Thou didst hide Thy face from me;
    I was in perplexity;
  8 Unto Thee, Jehovah, I
    Lifted up my fervent cry;
    To Jehovah, in my need,
    Supplication I have made.

6 9 O what profit can there be
    In this blood of mine to Thee,
    If I to corruption go?
    Shall the dust Thy praises show?
    Shall the silent dust express
    All Thy truth and faithfulness?

7 10 Hear Thou, O Jehovah, hear,
And in mercy draw Thou near;
O Jehovah, in Thy love,
Send me succor from above;
11 Thou my mourning from me hast
Into dancing turned, at last.

8 All my sackcloth loosèdst Thou,
Girdedst me with gladness now;
12 Thus my glory praise shall Thee,
And shall never silent be.
Then, O LORD my God, will I
Thee for ever glorify.

Psalm XXXI. C. M.

1 1 IN Thee, Jehovah, do I trust,
Shamed let me never be;
According to Thy righteousness,
Do Thou deliver me.

2 2 Bow down Thine ear to me, with speed
Send me deliverance;
To save me, my strong rock be Thou.
And my house of defence.

3 3 Because Thou art my rock, and Thee
I for my fortress take;
Do Thou me therefore lead and guide,
Even for Thine own Name's sake.

4 4 And since Thou art my saving strength,
Pull me out of the net,
Which they in subtlety for me
So privily have set.

5 5 Into Thy hand I do commit
My spirit; Thou art He,
O Thou Jehovah, God of truth,
Who hast redeemèd me.

PSALM XXXI.

6 6 All those I have abhorred, that do
Regard false vanities;
But as for me my confidence
Upon Jehovah lies.

7 7 I 'll in Thy mercy greatly joy;
For Thou my miseries
Considered hast; Thou hast my soul
Known in adversities;

8 8 And Thou hast not inclosèd me
Within the en'my's hand;
And by Thee have my feet been made
In open place to stand.

9 9 Jehovah, on me mercy have,
For trouble is on me;
Mine eyes, my body, and my soul
With grief consumèd be.

10 10 Because my life with grief is spent,
My years with sighs and groans;
My strength doth fail; and for my sin
Consumèd are my bones.

11 11 I was a scorn to all my foes,
And to my neighbors near
A great reproach have I become,
And to my friends a fear.

12 12 And when they saw me walk abroad,
They from my presence fled;
I like a broken vessel am,
Forgotten as one dead.

13 13 For slanders I of many heard;
Fear compassed me, while they
Against me did consult, and plot
To take my life away.

14 14 But, O Jehovah, I on Thee
　　My confidence did lay ;
　And I to Thee, Thou art my God,
　　Did confidently say.

15 15 My times are wholly in Thy hand ;
　　Do Thou deliver me
　From their hands, that mine enemies
　　And persecutors be.

16 16 Thy countenance to shine do Thou
　　Upon Thy servant make ;
　To me do Thou salvation give
　　For Thy great mercies' sake.

17 17 Jehovah, let me not be shamed,
　　For on Thee called I have ;
　Let wicked men be shamed, let them
　　Be silent in the grave.

18 18 To silence put the lying lips,
　　That grievous things do say,
　And hard reports in pride and scorn,
　　On righteous men do lay.

19 19 How great 's the goodness Thou for
　　That fear Thee hast in store ; [them
　Wrought out for them that trust in
　　The sons of men before.　　[Thee,

20 20 In secret of Thy presence, Thou
　　Shalt hide them from man's pride ;
　From strife of tongues Thou closely
　　As in a tent them hide.　　[shalt

21 21 All blessing to Jehovah give,
　　For He hath magnified
　His wondrous love to me within
　　A city fortified.

22 22 For from Thine eyes cut off I am,
   I in my haste had said ;
   My voice yet heard'st Thou, when to
   With cries my moans I made. [Thee

23 23 O love Jehovah, all His saints,
   Because Jehovah guards
   The faithful ; and proud doers He
   Abundantly rewards.

24 24 Be of good courage, and He strength
   Unto your heart shall send,
   All ye who on Jehovah do
   With confidence depend.

Psalm XXXII. C. M.

1   O BLESSED the man is unto whom
      Have freely pardoned been
   All the transgressions he hath done,
   And covered is his sin.

2 2 Blessed is the man to whom the LORD
      Imputeth not his sin,
   And in whose spirit is no guile,
   Nor fraud is found therein.

3 3 When as I did refrain my speech,
      And silent was my tongue,
   My bones then waxed old because
   I cried out all day long.

4 4 Because on me, both day and night
      Thy hand did heavy lie
   And quickly was my moisture turned
   To summer's drought thereby.

5 5 My sin I have confessed, my guilt
      Have not concealed from Thee ;
   I said, Jehovah, I have sinned ;
   And Thou forgavest me.

6 6 For this shall every godly one
  His prayer direct to Thee;
 In such a time he shall Thee seek
  As found Thou mayest be.

7 Surely when floods of waters great
  Do swell up to the brim,
 They shall not overwhelm his soul,
  Nor once come near to him.

8 7 Thou art my hiding-place, Thou shalt
  From trouble keep me free;
 Thou, with songs of deliverance,
  About shall compass me.

9 8 I will instruct thee, and thee teach
  The way that thou shalt go;
 And with Mine eyes upon thee set,
  I will direction show.

10 9 Then be not like the horse or mule
  Which do not understand;
 Whose mouth, that they may come to
  A bridle must command.   [thee,

11 10 Unto the man that wicked is,
  His sorrow shall abound;
 But him that in Jehovah trusts
  Shall mercy compass round.

12 11 Ye righteous, in the LORD be glad,
  In Him do ye rejoice;
 All ye that upright are in heart,
  For joy lift up your voice.

Psalm XXXIII. C. M.

1 YE righteous, in Jehovah sing
  For joy and give Him praise;
 A song of praise becoming is
  In men of upright ways.

2 2 Jehovah praise with harp ; to Him
   Sing with the psaltery ;
   Upon a ten-stringed instrument
   Make ye sweet melody.

3 3 A new song to Him sing, and play
   With loud noise skilfully ;
  4 Jehovah's word is right ; His works
   All done in verity.

4 5 To judgment and to righteousness
   A love He beareth still ;
   Jehovah's loving-kindness great
   The earth throughout doth fill.

5 6 The heavens by Jehovah's word
   Did their beginning take ;
   And by the breathing of His mouth,
   He all their hosts did make.

6 7 The waters of the seas He brings
   Together as a heap ;
   And in store-houses, as it were,
   He layeth up the deep.

7 8 Let all the earth with reverence
   Jehovah then adore ;
   Let all the world's inhabitants
   Tremble His face before.

8 9 For He did speak the word, and done
   It was without delay ;
   And it established firmly stood,
   Whatever He did say.

9 10 Jehovah surely brings to nought
   The counsel nations take,
   And what the peoples do devise
   Of no effect doth make.

10 11 The counsel of Jehovah doth
    For evermore stand sure;
  And of His heart the purposes
    From age to age endure.

11 12 That nation blessèd is, whose God
    Jehovah is, and those
  A blessèd people are, whom for
    His heritage He chose.

12 13 From heaven Jehovah looks; He sees
    All sons of men full well;
  14 He views all from His dwelling-place,
    That in the earth do dwell.

13 15 He forms their hearts alike, and all
    Their doings He observes.
  16 Great hosts save not a king; much
    No mighty man preserves. [strength

14 17 A horse for safety and defence
    Is a deceitful thing;
  And, by the greatness of his strength
    Can no deliv'rance bring.

15 18 Behold, on those that do Him fear
    Jehovah sets His eye;
  Even those who on His mercy do
    With confidence rely;

16 19 From death to free their soul, in dearth
    Life unto them to yield.
  20 Our soul upon Jehovah waits;
    He is our help and shield.

17 21 Since in His Holy Name we trust,
    Our hearts shall joyful be.
  22 LORD, let Thy mercy be on us,
    As we do hope in Thee.

Psalm XXXIV. C. M.

1 ALL times Jehovah I will bless,
    His praise my mouth employ;
2 My soul shall in Jehovah boast,
    The meek shall hear with joy

2 3 With me Jehovah magnify;
      Exalt His Name with me.
   4 I sought Jehovah; He me heard,
      And from all fears set free.

3 5 They looked to Him, and lightened
      Their faces were not shamed. [were;
   6 This poor man cried; Jehovah heard;
      Him from all straits redeemed.

4 7 The Angel of Jehovah camps,
      And round encompasseth
      All those about that do Him fear,
      And them delivereth.

5 8 O taste and see the LORD is good;
      Who trusts in Him He'll bless.
   9 Jehovah fear, His saints; none that
      Him fear shall want oppress.

6 10 The lions young may hungry be,
      And they may lack their food;
      But they that do Jehovah seek
      Shall not lack any good.

7 11 O children, hither do ye come,
      And unto me give ear;
      I unto you most carefully
      Will teach Jehovah's fear.

8 12 What man is he that life desires,
      To see good would live long?
   13 Thy lips refrain from speaking guile,
      And from ill words thy tongue.

9 14 Depart from ill, do good, seek peace,
Pursue it earnestly ;
15 Jehovah's eyes are on the just,
His ears attend their cry.

10 16 Jehovah's face is set against
Those that do wickedly ;
That He may quite out from the earth
Cut off their memory.

11 17 The righteous to Jehovah cry,
He unto them gives ear ;
And they out of their troubles all
By Him delivered are.

12 18 Jehovah unto them is nigh
That are of broken heart ;
To those of contrite spirit He
Salvation doth impart.

13 19 The just man's troubles many are,
Jehovah sets him free ;
20 He keepeth all his bones, not one
Of them can broken be.

14 21 Ill shall the wicked slay ; condemned
Shall be who hate the just.
22 Jehovah saves His servants' souls ;
None perish that Him trust.

Psalm XXXIV. L. M.

1 AT all times I 'll Jehovah bless,
My mouth His praises still express.
2 My soul boasts in the LORD ; my voice
Shall all the meek hear and rejoice.

2 3 Jehovah magnify with me,
    Let us to praise His name agree.
  4 I sought the LORD, He did me hear,
    And set me free from every fear.

3 5 They looked to Him and cheer received,
    Their faces were from shame relieved.
  6 This poor man on the LORD did call;
    He heard and saved from sorrows all.

4 7 Jehovah's angel camping near,
    Hath rescued all who did Him fear.
  8 The LORD is good; O taste and see,
    Who trusts in Him how blest is he!

5 9 O fear Jehovah, His saints all,
    Who fear Him can no want befall.
  10 Young lions hunger lacking food,
    Who seek the LORD shall want no good.

6 11 Ye children, come, to me give ear,
    I will you teach Jehovah's fear.
  12 Who is the man that life desires,
    And loving days to good aspires?

7 13 From evil let thy tongue refrain;
    Thy lips from speaking guile restrain;
  14 Do good; from wicked ways depart;
    Seek peace, pursue with all thy heart.

8 15 The LORD on just men keeps His eyes;
    His ears are open to their cries;
  16 The LORD on vile men sets His face
    From earth their mem'ry to erase.

9 17 They cry for help, Jehovah hears,
    And saves them from all ills and fears;
  18 On broken hearts the LORD attends,
    To spirits crushed salvation sends.

10 19 Though many ills the righteous see,
From all Jehovah sets him free;
20 Preserves his bones in every fall,
That none can broken be at all.

11 21 Their ills shall all the wicked slay;
Who hate the just, condemned be they;
22 The LORD His servants saves each one,
Who trust in Him condemned are none.

Psalm XXXV. C. M.

1 PLEAD, LORD, with those that plead and fight,
With those that fight with me.
2 Of shield and buckler take Thou hold;
Stand up my help to be.

2 3 Draw also out the spear, and do
Against them stop the way
That me pursue; unto my soul
I 'm thy salvation, say.

3 4 Let them confounded be, and shamed
That for my soul have sought;
Who plot my hurt, turned back be they
And to confusion brought.

4 5 Let them be like unto the chaff
That flies before the wind;
And let the angel of the LORD
Pursue them hard behind.

5 6 With darkness cover Thou their way,
And let it slipp'ry prove;
And let the angel of the LORD
Pursue them from above.

6 7 For they without a cause for me
    Have laid their secret snare ;
    And they a pit without a cause
    Did for my soul prepare.

7 8 At unawares shall ruin come,
    And then he shall be caught
    Within the net he hid for me,
    And to destruction brought.

8 9 I 'll in Jehovah joy, and glad
    In His salvation be ;
   10 And all my bones shall say, who is,
    Jehovah, like to Thee ?

9   Who dost the poor set free from him
    That is for him too strong,
    The poor and needy from the man
    That spoils and does him wrong ?

10 11 False witnesses against me rose,
    And unknown charges made ;
   12 They, to the spoiling of my soul,
    Me ill for good repaid.

11 13 But as for me, when they were sick,
    In sackcloth sad I mourned ;
    My humbled soul did fast ; my prayer
    Into my bosom turned.

12 14 I bore myself as for a friend,
    Or brother dear to me ;
    As one who for a mother mourns,
    I bowed down heavily.

13 15 But in my trouble they rejoiced,
    And they together met ;
    The abjects vile together did
    Themselves against me set.

14 I knew it not; they did me tear,
   And quiet would not be.
 16 With mocking hypocrites at feasts
   They gnashed their teeth at me.

15 17 How long, O Lord, wilt Thou look on?
   From ruins they intend
   Preserve my soul, from lions young
   My precious life defend.

16 18 I ever will give thanks to Thee,
   In the assembly great;
   And where much people gathered are
   Thy praises forth will set.

17 19 Let not my wrongful enemies
   In pride rejoice o'er me;
   Nor let them wink with scornful eye,
   Who hate me causelessly.

18 20 For peace they do not speak at all;
   But crafty plots prepare
   Against all those within the land
   That meek and quiet are.

19 21 Their mouths they open wide at me;
   They say, Ha, ha! we see.
 22 LORD, Thou hast seen, hold not Thy [peace;
   Lord, be not far from me.

20 23 Stir up Thyself; wake, that Thou [mayst
   Judgment to me afford,
   Even to my cause, O Thou that art
   My only God and Lord.

21 24 Jehovah, O my God, judge me
   In Thine own righteousness;
   And let them not their joy 'gainst me
   Triumphantly express.

22 25 Nor let them say within their hearts,
Ah, we would have it thus ;
Nor suffer them to say that he
Is swallowed up by us.

23 26 Shamed and confounded shall they be
That at my hurt are glad ; [all
And those who 'gainst me boast shall
With shame and scorn be clad.

24 27 Let them that love my righteous cause
Be glad, and shout, nor cease
To say, Jehovah be extolled,
Who loves His servant's peace.

25 28 And with my tongue I will proclaim
To all the world Thy praise,
And of Thy righteousness to speak
My voice each day I'll raise.

Psalm XXXVI. C. M.

1 THE trespass of the wicked man
To my heart testifies :
Undoubtedly the fear of God
Is not before his eyes.

2 2 Because himself he flattereth
In his own blinded eyes
The hatefulness shall not be found
Of his iniquities.

3 3 Words from his mouth proceeding are,
Fraud and iniquity ;
He to be wise, and to do good,
Hath left off utterly.

4 4 He mischief, lying on his bed,
Most cunningly doth plot ;
He sets himself in ways not good ;
Ill he abhorreth not.

5   5 Thy mercy, LORD, is in the heavens;
        Thy truth doth reach the clouds.
      6 Thy justice is like mountains great;
        Thy judgments deep as floods;

6   LORD, Thou preservest man and beast.
      7   How precious is Thy grace,
        O God! in shadow of Thy wings
        Men's sons their trust shall place.

7   8 They with the fatness of Thy house
        Shall be well satisfied;
        From rivers of Thy pleasures Thou
        Wilt drink to them provide.

8   9 Because of life the fountain pure
        Remains alone with Thee;
        And in that purest light of Thine
        We clearly light shall see.

9 10 Thy loving-kindness unto them
        Continue that Thee know;
        And still on men upright in heart
        Thy righteousness bestow.

10 11 Let not the foot of cruel pride
        Come, and against me stand;
        And let me never be removed
        By men of wicked hand.

11 12 There, fallen to the earth, are they
        That work iniquities;
        Cast down they are, and never shall
        Be able to arise.

Psalm XXXVII. C. M.

1   FOR evil-doers fret thou not
        Thyself unquietly;
        Nor do thou envy bear to them
        That work iniquity.

2 2 For, as the grass that groweth up,
  Soon be cut down shall they;
  And like the green and tender herb
  They wither shall away.

3 3 Upon Jehovah set thy trust,
  And be thou doing good,
  And so thou in the land shalt dwell
  And verily have food.

4 4 Joy in Jehovah, and He 'll give
  Thy heart's desire to thee.
  5 Thy way leave with the LORD, Him
  It bring to pass shall He.   [trust;

5 6 And like the morning light, He shall
  Thy righteousness display;
  And He thy judgment shall bring forth,
  Like noon-tide of the day.

6 7 Rest in Jehovah, wait for Him
  With patience; do not fret
  For him, who, prosp'ring in his way,
  Success in sin doth get.

7 8 Do thou from anger cease, and wrath
  See thou forsake also;
  Fret not thyself in any wise,
  That evil thou shouldst do.

8 9 For those that evil-doers are
  Shall be cut off and fall;
  But those that on Jehovah wait
  The earth inherit shall.

9 10 For yet a little while, and then
  The wicked shall not be;
  His place thou shalt consider well,
  But it thou shalt not see.

10 11 But by inheritance the earth
 The meek ones shall possess;
They also shall delight themselves
 In an abundant peace.

11 12 The wicked gnashes with his teeth,
 And plots the just to slay;
 13 The Lord shall laugh at him, because,
 At hand He sees his day.

12 14 The wicked have drawn out the sword,
 And bent their bow to slay
The poor and needy and to kill
 The men of upright way.

13 15 Their sword shall enter their own
 Their bows shall broken be. [heart;
 16 The just man's mite excels the wealth
 That many wicked see.

14 17 For sinners' arms shall broken be;
 The LORD the just sustains.
 18 Jehovah knows the upright's days;
 Their heritage remains.

15 19 They shall not be ashamed when they
 The evil time do see;
And when the days of famine are,
 They satisfied shall be.

16 20 But wicked men, Jehovah's foes,
 As fat of lambs decay;
They shall consume, yea, into smoke
 They shall consume away.

17 21 The wicked borrows, but the same
 Again he doth not pay;
Whereas the righteous mercy shows,
 And gives his own away.

18 22 For all such as be blessed of Him
  The earth inherit shall;
  And they that are accursed of Him
  Shall to destruction fall.

19 23 Man's footsteps by Jehovah are
  Established all aright;
  And in the way wherein he walks
  He greatly doth delight.

20 24 Although he fall, yet shall he not
  Be cast down utterly;
  Because Jehovah with His hand
  Upholds him mightily.

21 25 I have been young and now am old,
  Yet have I never seen
  The just man left, nor that his seed
  For bread have beggars been.

22 26 He's ever merciful, and lends;
  His seed is blessed therefore.
  27 Depart from evil, and do good,
  And dwell for evermore.

23 28 Jehovah judgment loves, His saints
  Leaves not in any case;
  They are kept ever; but cut off
  Shall be the sinner's race.

24 29 The just inherit shall the land,
  And ever in it dwell.
  30 The just man's mouth doth wisdom speak,
  His tongue doth judgment tell.

25 31 Within his heart is his God's law;
  His steps slide not away.
  32 The wicked man doth watch the just
  And seeketh him to slay.

26 33 Jehovah will not him forsake,
  Nor leave him in his hands;
 The righteous will He not condemn,
  When he in judgment stands.

27 34 Wait on Jehovah, keep His way,
  And thee exalt shall He
 Earth to inherit; when cut off
  The wicked thou shalt see.

28 35 I saw the wicked great in power,
  Spread like a green bay-tree.
 36 He passed, yea, was not; him I sought,
  But found he could not be.

29 37 Mark thou the perfect, and behold
  The man of uprightness;
 Because that surely of this man
  The latter end is peace.

30 38 But those that sinners are shall all
  Destroyed together be;
 The wicked's end shall be cut off
  Throughout eternity.

31 39 But the salvation of the just
  Is from the LORD above;
 And in the time of their distress
  Their stronghold He doth prove.

32 40 Jehovah helps and rescues them;
  He doth them free and save
 From wicked men; because in Him
  Their confidence they have.

Psalm XXXVIII. C. M.

1 JEHOVAH, in Thine anger great,
  Do Thou rebuke me not;
 Nor on me lay Thy chast'ning hand,
  In Thy displeasure hot.

2 2 For in me fast Thine arrows stick ;
Thy hand doth press me sore ;
3 Because of Thy wrath, in my flesh
No soundness have I more.

3 Nor in my bones is any rest,
For sin that I have done ;
4 My sins, a burden, weigh me down,
They 'bove my head are gone.

4 5 My wounds are putrid and corrupt,
My folly makes it so.
6 I troubled am, and much bowed down,
All day I mourning go.

5 7 For inflammation great so fills
My loins with burning pain,
That in my weak and weary flesh
No soundness doth remain.

6 8 So very feeble and infirm
And sorely crushed am I,
That through disquiet of my heart
I make loud moan and cry.

7 9 O Lord, before Thine eyes is all
That is desired by me,
And of my heart the secret groans
Not hidden are from Thee.

8 10 My heart doth pant incessantly,
My strength doth quite decay ;
As for mine eyes, their wonted light
Is from me gone away.

9 11 My lovers and my friends do stand
At distance from my sore ;
And those do stand aloof that were
Kinsmen and kind before.

10 12 Yea, they that seek my life lay snares;
   Who seek to do me wrong
Speak mischief, and deceitful things
   Imagine all day long.

11 13 But, as one deaf, that heareth not,
   I suffered all to pass;
I as a dumb man did become,
   Whose mouth not opened was;

12 14 As one that hears not, in whose mouth
   Are no replies at all.
   15 For, LORD, I hope in Thee; O Lord
   My God, Thou 'lt hear my call.

13 16 For I said, hear me, lest they should
   Rejoice o'er me with pride;
And o'er me magnify themselves,
   What time my foot doth slide.

14 17 Because I ready am to halt,
   My grief I ever see;
   18 For I 'll declare my sin, and grieve
   For mine iniquity.

15 19 But yet mine en'mies lively are,
   And strong are they beside;
And they that hate me wrongfully
   Are greatly multiplied.

16 20 And they for good that render ill,
   As en'mies, me withstood;
Yea, even for this, because that I
   Do follow what is good.

17 21 Jehovah, leave me not; my God,
   Far from me never be.
   22 O Lord, who my salvation art,
   Haste to give help to me.

Psalm XXXIX. C. M.

1 I SAID, my ways I'll guard with care,
  Lest with my tongue I sin ;
  In sight of wicked men my mouth
  With bridle I'll keep in.

2 2 With silence I as dumb became ;
  I did myself restrain
  From speaking good ; but then the
  Increasèd was my pain.   [more

3 3 My heart within me waxèd hot ;
  And while I musing was,
  The fire did burn ; and from my tongue
  These words I did let pass :

4 4 Mine end, and measure of my days,
  Jehovah, to me show
  What is the same ; that I thereby
  My frailty well may know.

5 5 Lo, Thou my days a hand-breadth
  Mine age is in Thine eye   [mad'st,
  As nothing ; sure each man at best
  Is wholly vanity.

6 6 Sure each man walks in a vain show ;
  They vex themselves in vain ;
  He heaps up wealth, and doth not
  To whom it shall pertain.   [know

7 7 And now, O Lord, what wait I for ?
  My hope is fixed on Thee.
  8 Free me from all my trespasses ;
  The fool's scorn make not me.

8 9 Dumb am I, op'ning not my mouth,
  Because this work is Thine.
  10 Thy stroke take from me ; by the blow
  Of Thy hand I do pine.

9 11 When with rebukes Thou dost correct
         Man for iniquity,
      Like moth Thou dost his beauty waste;
         Each man is vanity.

10 12 Regard my cry, LORD, at my tears
         And prayers not silent be ;
      I sojourn as my fathers all,
         And stranger am with Thee.

11 13 O spare Thou me, that I my strength
         Recover may again,
      Before from hence I do depart,
         And here no more remain.

Psalm XXXIX. 8s & 7s.

1 1 I WILL of my ways be heedful,
         That I sin not with my tongue ;
      For my mouth a curb is needful,
         While the wicked round me throng.

2 2 Thus I said, and dumb remainèd ;
         From my lips no sound was heard ;
      From good words I even refrainèd,
         But my inmost soul was stirred.

3 3 Long my heart was in me burning,
         Ere the smothered flames outbrake,
      And, th' enkindled words returning,
         Thus impatiently I spake :

4 4 Teach me, LORD, the number meting
         Of my days, how brief it is ;
      Make me see and know how fleeting,
         Vain and sad a life is this.

5 5 Life a span is at the longest ;
         Mine is nothing unto Thee ;

In his best estate and strongest
Man is only vanity.

6 6 Yea, he fleeting past us goeth
In a shadow brief and vain,
Heaping riches ; but none knoweth
Who shall gather them again.

7 7 And where, Lord, is my reliance?
All my hope is fixed on Thee.
8 From my sin and the defiance
Of the foolish, save Thou me.

8 9 I, because it was Thy pleasure,
Murmured not, nor silence broke ;
10 Yet remove Thy plague ; o'er measure
Is Thy hand's consuming stroke.

9 11 When for sin or slighted duty
Man corrected is by Thee,
But a moth-worn robe his beauty,
And but vanity is he.

10 12 See my tears, regard my danger ;
Hear, Jehovah, all my prayer ;
For a sojourner and stranger,
Am I, as my fathers were.

11 13 Spare me, yet a little spare me,
To recover strength, before
Thy dread summons hence shall bear
To be seen on earth no more. [me,

Psalm XL. C. M.

1 UPON Jehovah I did wait,
And patiently did bear ;
At length to me He did incline"
My voice and cry to hear.

2 2 He took me from a fearful pit,
   And from the miry clay,
 And on a rock He set my feet,
   Establishing my way.

3 3 He put a new song in my mouth,
   Our God to magnify;
 Many shall see it, and shall fear,
   And on the LORD rely.

4 4 O blessèd is the man who in
   Jehovah doth confide,
 Respecting not the proud, nor such
   As turn to lies aside.

5 5 My God, Jehovah, many are
   The wonders Thou hast done;
 Thy gracious thoughts to us-ward far
   Above all thoughts are gone.

6   In order none can reckon them
   To Thee; if them declare
 And speak of them I would, they more
   Than can be numbered are.

7 6 Mine ears Thou opened hast; and Thou
   No off'ring hast desired;
 Nor sacrifice; sin-off'ring Thou
   And burnt, hast not required.

8 7 Then unto Thee these were my words:
   I come; behold and see,
 Within the volume of the book
   It written is of me:

9 8 To do Thy will I take delight,
   O Thou my God that art;
 Yea, that most holy law of Thine
   I have within my heart.

10 9 Within the congregation great
    I righteousness did preach ;
  Lo ! Thou dost know, O LORD, that I
    Did not refrain my speech.

11 10 I never did within my heart
    Conceal Thy righteousness ;
  I Thy salvation have declared,
    And shown Thy faithfulness ;

12   Thy kindness, which most loving is,
    Concealèd have not I,
  Nor from the congregation great
    Have hid Thy verity.

13 11 Thy tender mercies, LORD, from me,
    O do Thou not restrain ;
  Thy loving kindness and Thy truth,
    Let them me still maintain.

14 12 For ills past reck'ning compass me,
    And mine iniquities
  Such hold upon me taken have,
    I cannot lift mine eyes.

15   They more than hairs are on my head,
    Thence is my heart dismayed.
  13 Be pleased, O LORD, to rescue me ;
    LORD, hasten to mine aid.

16 14 Shamed and confounded shall they be
    That seek my soul to kill ;
  Yea, they shall backward driven be,
    And shamed, that wish me ill.

17 15 For a reward of this their shame,
    Confounded they shall be,
  That in this manner scoffing say,
    Aha, aha ! to me.

18 16 In Thee let all be glad and joy,
   Who seeking Thee abide;
   Who Thy salvation love, say still,
   The LORD be magnified.

19 17 I'm poor and needy, yet the Lord
   Of me a care doth take;
   Thou who my help and Saviour art,
   My God, no tarrying make.

Psalm XLI. C. M.

1 BLESSED is the man that carefully
   Considereth the poor;
   Jehovah, in his day of ill,
   Deliv'rance will secure.

2 2 The LORD will guard, save him alive;
   On earth he blessed shall live;
   And to his enemies' desire
   Thou wilt him never give.

3 3 Upon his couch of languishing,
   The LORD will give him strength;
   And in his sickness sore, Thou wilt
   Make all his bed at length.

4 4 I said, Jehovah, O do Thou
   Thy mercy show to me;
   O do Thou heal my soul, because
   I have offended Thee.

5 5 Those that to me are enemies
   Of me do evil say;
   When shall he die, that so his name
   May perish quite away?

6 6 To see me if he comes, he speaks
   Vain words; but then his heart

Heaps mischief to it, which he tells,
When forth he doth depart.

7 7 My haters, jointly whispering,
'Gainst me my hurt devise.
8 Disease, say they, cleaves fast to him;
He lies, and shall not rise.

8 9 Yea, even mine own familiar friend,
On whom I did rely,
Who ate my bread, even he his heel
Against me lifted high.

9 10 But Thou, Jehovah, pity me,
And up again me raise,
That I may justly them requite
According to their ways.

10 11 By this I know that certainly
I favored am by Thee;
Because my hateful enemy
Triumphs not over me.

11 12 But as for me, Thou me uphold'st
In mine integrity ;
And me before Thy countenance
Thou sett'st continually.

12 13 Jehovah, God of Israel,
Be blessed for ever then,
From age to age eternally.
Amen, yea, and amen.

Psalm XLII. C. M.

1 AS for the water-brooks the hart
Doth pant exceedingly,
So, in its longing, O my God,
My soul pants after Thee.

2 2 My soul for God, the living God,
　　Doth thirst ; when shall I near
　Before Thy countenance approach,
　　And in God's sight appear?

3 3 My tears have unto me been meat
　　Both in the night and day,
　While unto me incessantly,
　　Where is thy God? they say.

4 My soul within me is poured out,
　　When this I think upon;
　Because that with the multitude
　　I heretofore had gone;

5 4 With them into God's house I went
　　With voice of joy and praise;
　Yea, with the multitude that kept
　　The solemn holy days.

6 5 O why art thou cast down, my soul?
　　Why in me so dismayed?
　Trust God, for I shall praise Him yet,
　　His count'nance is mine aid.

7 6 My God, my soul's cast down in me;
　　Remember Thee I will,
　From　Jordan-land,　the　Hermon-
　And from the Mizar-hill.　[mounts,

8 7 At sounding of Thy water-spouts
　　Deep unto deep doth call;
　Thy breaking waves pass over me,
　　Yea, and Thy billows all.

9 8 Jehovah yet His tender love
　　Command will in the day;
　His song is with me in the night;
　　To God, my life, I'll pray.

10 9 I 'll say to God, my rock, O why
    Dost Thou forget me so?
    And for oppression of my foes
    Why do I mourning go?

11 10 'T is as a sword within my bones,
    When my foes me upbraid;
    And when by them, Where is thy God?
    Is daily to me said.

12 11 O why art thou cast down, my soul?
    Why so disturbed in me?   [God,
    Trust God, I 'll praise Him yet; my
    Health of my face is He.

Psalm XLII. L. M.

1 AS pants the hart for water-brooks,
    So pants my soul, O God, for Thee,
  2 My soul for God has thirsty been,
    And longs the living God to see.

2   When shall I to God's presence come?
  3   My tears have fed me night and day,
    While all the day in mockery,
    O where is now thy God? they say.

3   When I with crowds to God's house go,
    I 'll this recall, my soul pour out;
  4 I 'll lead them on with voice of joy,
    In songs of praise and festal shout.

4 5 Why, O my soul, art thou cast down?
    Why in me art thou so dismayed?
    Wait thou for God, I will Him praise;
    His countenance shall be mine aid.

5 6 My God, my soul is still cast down;
    Remember Thee I therefore will
    In Jordan-land, in Hermon-mounts,
    And when upon the Mizar-hill.

6 7 Deep calls to deep at Thy floods' voice:
    Thy waves and billows passed o'er me.
  8 By day Jehovah grace commands,
    His song by night shall with me be.

7 9 I 'll pray to God who is my life;
    And unto God, my rock, I 'll say:
  Why me forget?   must I still mourn
    My foes' oppression every day?

8 10 My bones are pierced as by a sword,
    When enemies do me upbraid,
  And when to me, Where is thy God?
    By them in scorn is daily said.

9 11 Why, O my soul, art thou cast down?
    And what should so disquiet thee?
  Wait Thou for God, I will Him praise;
    My God and saving help is He.

Psalm XLIII. C. M.

1 AGAINST a cruel nation plead
    My cause, O God; judge me;
  From man deceitful and unjust
    O do Thou set me free.

2 2 For Thou the God art of my strength;
    Why thrust me then away?
  And for oppression of the foe
    Why mourn I all the day?

3 3 O send Thy light forth, and Thy truth;
    Let them be guides to me,
  And bring me to Thy holy hill,
    Even where Thy dwellings be.

4 4 Then will I to God's altar go,
To God, my chiefest joy;
Yea, God, my God, Thy name to praise
My harp I will employ.

5 5 O why art thou cast down, my soul?
Why so disturbed in me? [God,
Trust God, I 'll praise Him yet; my
Health of my face is He.

Psalm XLIV. C. M.

1 O GOD, we with our ears have heard,
Our fathers have us told,
The work that in their days Thou didst,
Even in the days of old.

2 2 Thy hand did drive the nations out,
And plant them in their place;
Thou didst afflict the peoples all,
But them Thou didst increase.

3 3 For neither got their sword the land,
Nor did their arm them save;
Thy right hand, arm, light of Thy face;
For Thy grace conquest gave.

4 4 Thou art my King; O mighty God
Deliv'rances command [crush
5 For Jacob; we through Thee shall
Those that against us stand.

5 We, through Thy name, shall tread down those
That risen against us have;
6 For in my bow I shall not trust,
Nor shall my sword me save.

6 7 But from our foes Thou hast us saved,
  Our haters put to shame.
 8 In God we all the day do boast,
  And ever praise Thy name.

7 9 But now we are cast off by Thee,
  And us Thou putt'st to shame ;
 And when our armies do go forth
  Thou go'st not with the same.

8 10 Thou mak'st us from the enemy,
  Faint-hearted, to turn back ;
 And they who hate us, for themselves
  Our spoils away do take.

9 11 Like sheep for meat Thou gavest us ;
  'Mong nations cast we be.
 12 Thou didst for nought Thy people sell;
  Their price enriched not Thee.

10 13 Thou makest us a vile reproach
  To all our neighbors near ;
 Derision and a scorn to them
  That round about us are.

11 14 A by-word also Thou dost us
  Among the nations make ;
 The peoples, in contempt and spite,
  At us their heads do shake.

12 15 Before me my confusion doth
  Abide continually ;
 And of my countenance the shame
  Doth wholly cover me.

13 16 For voice of him that doth reproach
  And speaketh blasphemy ;
 Because of the avenging foe,
  And cruel enemy.

14 17 All this is come on us, yet we
　　　Have not forgotten Thee ;
　　Nor falsely in Thy covenant
　　　Behaved ourselves have we.

15 18 Our heart is not turned back, nor have
　　　Our steps from Thy way strayed ;
　　19 Though us Thou break'st in dragon's
　　　　place,
　　And cover'dst with death's shade.

16 20 If we God's Name forgot, or stretched
　　　To a strange god our hands,
　　21 Shall not God search this out? for He
　　　Heart's secrets understands.

17 22 Yea, for Thy sake we're killed all day;
　　　Counted as slaughter-sheep ;
　　23 Rise, Lord, cast us not ever off ;
　　　Awake, why dost Thou sleep ?

18 24 O wherefore hidest Thou Thy face
　　　Forgett'st our case distressed,
　　25 And our oppression ? for our soul
　　　Is to the dust down pressed.

19　　Our body also on the earth
　　　Fast cleaving, hold doth take.
　　26 Rise for our help, and us redeem,
　　　Even for Thy mercy's sake.

Psalm XLV. C. M.

1 MY heart brings forth a goodly thing ;
　　　My words that I indite
　　Concern the King; my tongue 's a pen
　　　Of one that swift doth write.

2 2 Thou fairer art than sons of men;
　　Into Thy lips is store
　Of grace infused; God therefore Thee
　　Hath blessed for evermore.

3 3 O Thou that art the Mighty One,
　　Thy sword gird on Thy thigh;
　Even with Thy glory excellent,
　　And with Thy majesty.

4 4 For meekness, truth and righteousness,
　　In state ride prosp'rously,
　And Thy right hand shall Thee instruct
　　In things that fearful be.

5 5 Thine arrows sharply pierce the heart
　　Of en'mies of the King;
　And under Thy subjection they
　　The peoples down do bring.

6 6 For ever and for ever is,
　　O God, Thy throne of might;
　The sceptre of Thy kingdom is
　　A sceptre that is right.

7 7 Thou lovest right, and hatest ill;
　　For God, Thy God, even He
　Above Thy fellows hath with oil
　　Of joy anointed Thee.

8 8 Of aloes, myrrh and cassia
　　A smell Thy garments had;
　Out of the iv'ry palaces.
　　Harp strains have made Thee glad.

9 9 Among Thy women hon'rable,
　　Kings' daughters are at hand;
　Upon Thy right hand doth the queen
　　In gold of Ophir stand.

10 10 O daughter, hearken and regard,
  And do thine ear incline;
  Likewise forget thy father's house,
  And people that are thine;

11 11 Then of the King desired shall be
  Thy beauty more and more;
  Because He is thy Lord, do thou
  Him rev'rently adore.

12 12 The daughter there of Tyre shall be
  With gifts and off'rings great;
  Those of the people that are rich
  Thy favor shall entreat.

13 13 Behold, the daughter of the King
  All glorious is within;
  And with embroideries of gold
  Her garments wrought have been.

14 14 She shall be brought before the King
  In robes with needle wrought;
  Her fellow-virgins following
  Shall unto Thee be brought;

15 15 They shall be brought with gladness
  And mirth on every side,   [great
  Into the palace of the King,
  And there they shall abide.

16 16 Instead of those thy fathers dear,
  Thy children thou mayst take,
  And in all places of the earth
  Them noble princes make.

17 17 Thy name remembered I will make,
  Through ages all to be;
  The peoples therefore evermore
  Shall praises give to Thee.

Psalm XLV. S. M.

1 MY heart inditing is
  Good matter in a song;
   I speak the things that I have made,
    Which to the King belong.

2   My tongue shall be as quick
     His honor to indite,
    As is the pen of any scribe
     That useth fast to write.

3 2 Thou 'rt fairest of all men;
     Grace in Thy lips doth flow;
    And therefore blessings evermore
     On Thee doth God bestow.

4 3 Thy sword gird on Thy thigh,
     Thou that art most of might;
    Appear in dreadful majesty,
     And in Thy glory bright.

5 4 For meekness, truth and right,
     Ride prosp'rously in state;
    And Thy right hand shall teach to Thee
     Things terrible and great.

6 5 Thy shafts shall pierce their hearts
     That foes are to the King;
    Whereby into subjection Thou
     The people down shalt bring.

7 6 Thy royal seat, O God,
     For ever shall remain;
    The sceptre of Thy kingdom doth
     All righteousness maintain.

8 7 Thou lovest right, hat'st ill;
     For God, Thy God, even He,
    Above Thy fellows hath with oil
     Of joy anointed Thee.

9   8 Of myrrh and spices sweet
   A smell Thy garments had
   Out of the iv'ry palaces
   Harp strains have made Thee glad.

10 9 And in Thy glorious train
   Kings' daughters waiting stand ;
   And Thy fair queen, in Ophir gold,
   Doth stand at Thy right hand.

11 10 O daughter, take good heed,
   Incline and give good ear ;
   Thou must forget thy kindred all,
   And father's house most dear.

12 11 Thy beauty to the King
   Shall then delightful be ;
   And do thou humbly worship Him,
   Because thy Lord is He.

13 12 The daughter then of Tyre
   There with a gift shall be ;
   And all the wealthy of the land
   Shall make their suit to thee.

14 13 The daughter of the King
   All glorious is within ;
   And with embroideries of gold
   Her garments wrought have been.

15 14 She cometh to the King
   In robes with needle wrought ;
   The virgins that do follow her
   Shall unto Thee be brought.

16 15 They shall be brought with joy
   And mirth on every side,
   Into the palace of the King,
   And there they shall abide.

17 16 And in thy father's stead,
   Thy children thou mayst take,
And in all places of the earth
   Them noble princes make.

18 17 I will show forth Thy name
   To generations all ;
The peoples therefore evermore
   To Thee give praises shall.

Psalm XLVI. C. M.

1 GOD is our refuge and our strength,
   In straits a present aid ;
2 Therefore, although the earth remove,
   We will not be afraid ;

2   Though hills amidst the seas be cast,
3   Though waters roaring make,
And troubled be ; yea, though the hills
   By swelling seas do shake.

3 4 A river is, whose streams make glad
   The city of our God ;
The holy place, where the Most High
   Hath made His own abode.

4 5 God in the midst of her doth dwell ;
   Nothing shall her remove ;
Yea, God to her a helper will,
   And that right early, prove.

5 6 The nations raged, the kingdoms moved ;
   His voice came, earth did melt ;
7 The LORD of hosts, yea, Jacob's God,
   Our refuge, with us dwelt.

6 8 Come, and behold what wondrous
   Jehovah here hath wrought ; [works

Come, see what desolations He
   Upon the earth hath brought.

7 9 And to the ends of all the earth
   Wars into peace He turns ;
   The bow He breaks, the spear He cuts,
   In fire the chariot burns.

8 10 Be still, and know that I am God !
   Among the nations I
   Will be exalted ; I on earth
   Will be exalted high.

9 11 The mighty LORD of hosts with us
   Our safety doth maintain ;
   The God of Jacob doth for us
   A refuge high remain.

Psalm XLVI. 8, 7 ; 8, 7 ; 8, 8, 7.

1 GOD is our Refuge and our Rock,
   Our Help in tribulation—
 2 Therefore we will not fear the shock
     That moves the world's foundation.
     Let mountains be
     Sunk in the sea ;
 3   Its waters roar,
     And shake the shore—
   Our hearts shall ne'er be shaken.

2 4 There is a river whose pure streams
     Make glad the Holy City ;
   Hard by the hill it glides and gleams,
     Where dwells the God of Pity.
 5   Where God abides
     No danger hides ;
     Seems He withdrawn,
     At break of dawn
   His help will be extended.

3 6 The nations raged, the kingdoms were
   In turmoil and commotion ;
   He spake, earth melted ; ceased the stir
   And madness of the ocean.
  7   The Lord of Hosts
      Defends our coasts ;
      In perils high
      To Him we fly,
   And Jacob's God protects us.

4 8 Come, see Jehovah's works of peace—
   Who wrought earth's desolations,
  9 Now causing wars and strifes to cease
   Among all tribes and nations ;
      He breaks the bow,
      The spear also ;
      The chariot burns ;
      To ashes turns
   The engines of destruction.

5 10 Be still, and know that I am God !
   My name shall be exalted—
   I 'll stretch my peace-restoring rod
   O'er nations that revolted.
  11 The Lord of Hosts
      Defends our coasts ;
      In perils high
      To Him we fly,
   And Jacob's God protects us.

Psalm XLVII. C. M.

1 ALL peoples clap your hands ; to God
   With voice of triumph shout ;
  2 For dreadful is the LORD Most High,
   Great King the earth throughout.

2 3 He 'll peoples under us subdue,
   And nations 'neath our feet ;

  4 Choose Jacob's glory, whom He loved,
   Our heritage most meet.

8 5 God is with shouts gone up, the LORD
   With trumpets sounding high.
  6 Sing praise to God, sing praise, sing
   Praise to our King, sing ye. [praise,

4 7 For God is King of all the earth ;
   With knowledge praise express.
  8 God rules the nations. God sits on
   His throne of holiness.

5 9 The people's princes gathered are
   With Abram's God to be ;
  Because earth's shields to God belong
   Exalted high is He.

Psalm XLVII. 7s & 6s.

1 O CLAP the hand, all peoples !
   Shout triumph's voice to God ;
  2 The LORD Most High is dreadful,
   Great King o'er earth abroad.

   Because the earth's defenders
    Belong to God alone ;
   They all belong to Jesus ;
    He 's the Exalted One.

2 3 For us He 'll rule the peoples,
   Put nations under feet,
  4 And choose loved Jacob's glory,
   Our heritage most meet.

   Because the earth's, etc.

3 5 God has with shout ascended,
　　The LORD with trumpet's sound;
　6 Praise God, sing praise, sing praises,
　　To our King praise resound.
　　　Because the earth's, etc.

4 7 For God, earth's King, is reigning,
　　In psalms His praise make known;
　8 God ever rules the nations,
　　God sits on holy throne.
　　　Because the earth's, etc.

5 9 The people's chiefs assemble,
　　Who Abram's God obey;
　Earth's shields their God are owning,
　　Exalt Him high do they.
　　　Because the earth's, etc.

Psalm XLVIII. C. M.

1 GREAT is Jehovah, worthy He
　　Is to be praisèd still,
　Within the city of our God,
　　Upon His holy hill.

2 2 Mount Zion is most beautiful,
　　The joy of all the lands;
　The city of the mighty King
　　Upon the north side stands.

3 3 God in her palaces hath made
　　Himself a refuge known.
　4 For, lo, the kings assembled; they
　　Together by have gone.

4 5 But when they did behold the same,
　　They, wond'ring would not stay;
　But being troubled at the sight
　　They thence did haste away.

5 6 Then, seized with fear, they were as
      Whom travail-pain o'ertakes ; [one
    7 As stricken by the eastern wind
      That ships of Tarshish breaks.

6 8 In city of the LORD of Hosts
      We see, as we were told ;
      In our God's city, that our God
      Will ever her uphold.

7 9 We on Thy goodness thought, O God,
      Within Thy holy place.
    10 As is Thy name, O God, so is
      To ends of earth Thy praise ;

8   Thy hand is full of righteousness.
    11   Let Zion mount be glad ;
      Make Judah's daughters joy, because
      Thy judgments are displayed.

9 12 Walk about Zion, and go round ;
      The high towers thereof tell ;
    13 Consider ye her palaces,
      And mark her bulwarks well ;

10   That ye may tell posterity.
    14   For this God doth abide
      Our God for evermore ; He will
      Even unto death us guide.

Psalm XLIX. C. M.

1 HEAR this, all people, and give ear,
      All in the world that dwell ;
    2 Both low and high, both rich and poor,
    3   My mouth shall wisdom tell ;

2   My heart shall knowledge meditate.
    4   I will incline mine ear
      To parables ; and on the harp
      My sayings dark declare.

3 5 Amidst those days that evil be,
　　Why should I fearing doubt,
　When crime of my supplanters doth
　　Encompass me about?

4 6 Whoe'er they be that in their wealth
　　Their confidence do pitch,
　And boast themselves, because they are
　　Become exceeding rich;

5 7 Yet none of these his brother can
　　Redeem in any way;
　Nor can he unto God for him
　　Sufficient ransom pay;

6 8 For their soul's purchase costly is;
　　And it can never be
　9 That still he should for ever live,
　　And not corruption see.

7 10 Because he sees that wise men die,
　　And brutish fools also
　Do perish, and their wealth, when dead,
　　To others they let go.

8 11 Their inward thought is that their
　　And dwelling places shall　　[house
　Forever stand; and they their lands
　　By their own names do call.

9 12 But man in honor dwelleth not,
　　He's like the beasts that die;
　13 Their way their folly is, though praised
　　By their posterity.

10 14 Like sheep they in the grave are laid,
　　And death shall them devour;
　And in the morning upright men
　　Shall over them have power;

11 Their beauty from their dwelling shall
Consume within the grave.
15 But from death's hand God will me
For He shall me receive. [free,

12 16 Be not afraid when one gains wealth,
Whose house in glory grows;
17 For dying he takes nothing hence;
No glory with him goes.

13 18 Although he his own soul did bless,
While he on earth did live,
(And when thou to thyself do'st well,
Men will thee praises give,)

14 19 He to his fathers' race shall go;
They never shall see light.
20 Man honored, wanting knowledge, is
Like beasts that perish quite.

Psalm L. C. M.

1 JEHOVAH, God of gods, did speak,
And called the earth upon,
Even from the rising of the sun
Unto the going down.

2 2 From out of Zion, His own hill,
Where the perfection high
Of beauty is, from thence hath God
Shined forth most gloriously.

3 3 Our God assuredly shall come,
Keep silent shall not He; [storms
Before Him fire shall waste, great
Shall round about Him be.

4 4 He to the heavens above shall call,
And to the earth below;
That of His people He to all
His judgment just may show.

5 5 Now unto Me let all My saints
　　Together gathered be;
　Those that by sacrifice have made
　　A covenant with Me.

6 6 And then the heavèns shall declare
　　His righteousness abroad,
　Because He judgment executes,
　　None else is Judge but God.

7 7 Hear, O My people, and I'll speak;
　　O Israel, by name,
　Against thee I will testify;
　　God, thine own God, I am.

8 8 Not for thy sacrifices will
　　I blame upon thee lay;
　Nor for burnt-offerings of thine,
　　Before Me every day.

9 9 I'll take no bullock nor he-goats
　　From house or folds of thine;
　10 For beasts of forests, cattle all
　　On thousand hills are Mine.

10 11 The fowls are all to Me well known,
　　That mountains high do yield;
　And I do challenge as Mine own
　　The wild beasts of the field.

11 12 If I were hungry, I would not
　　To thee for need complain;
　For earth, and all its fulness, doth
　　To Me of right pertain.

12 13 Will I the flesh of bullocks eat?
　　Or goats' blood drink will I?
　14 Thanks offer thou to God, and pay
　　Thy vows to the Most High.

13 15 And, in the day of trouble great,
   See that thou call on Me ;
I will deliver thee and thou
   My Name shalt glorify.

14 16 But to the wicked man God saith,
   How is it thou dost dare
My cov'nant in thy mouth to take,
   My statutes to declare ?

15 17 And yet all good instruction thou
   Perversely hated hast ;
Likewise My words behind thy back
   Thou in contempt dost cast.

16 18 When thou a thief didst see, with him
   Thou didst consent to sin,
And with the vile adulterers
   Thou hast partaker been.

17 19 Thy mouth to evil thou dost give,
   Thy tongue deceit doth frame.
   20 Thou sitt'st thy brother to revile,
   Thy mother's son defame.

18 21 Because I silence have preserved,
   While thou these things hast
That I was altogether like   [wrought,
   Thyself, hath been thy thought ;

19   Yet I will sharply thee reprove,
   And set before thine eyes,
Arrayed in order, thy misdeeds,
   And thine iniquities.

20 22 O now consider this, all ye
   Who God forgotten have,
Lest I should you in pieces tear
   And there be none to save.

21 23 Who offers sacrifice of praise,
  Great glory yields to Me;
And he who orders right his way,
  Shall God's salvation see.

Psalm L. S. M.

1 JEHOVAH, God of gods,
    Hath spoken, and did call
  The earth, from rising of the sun,
    To where he hath his fall.

2 2 From out of Zion hill,
    Where the perfection high
  Of beauty is, from thence hath God
    Shined forth most gloriously.

3 3 Our God shall surely come,
    Keep silence shall not He;
  Before Him fire shall waste, great
      storms
  Shall round about Him be.

4 4 He to the heavens above
    Shall then send forth His call,
  And to the earth likewise, that He
    May judge His people all.

5 5 To Me let all My saints
    Together gathered be;
  Those that by sacrifice have made
    A covenant with Me.

6 6 And then the heavens shall show
    His righteousness abroad,
  Because He judgment executes,
    None else is Judge but God.

7 7 My people Isr'el, hear,
    Speak will I from on high,
  Against thee I will testify;
    God, thine own God am I.

8 8 I, for thy sacrifice,
     No blame will on thee lay,
  Nor for burnt-offerings of thine
     Before Me every day.

9 9 I 'll take no calf nor goats
     From house or folds of thine;
  10 For beasts of forests, cattle all
     On thousand hills, are Mine.

10 11 The fowls on mountains high
     Are all to Me well known;
  Wild beasts which in the fields do lie,
     Even they are all Mine own.

11 12 Then, if I hungry were,
     I would not tell it thee;
  Because the world, and fulness all
     Thereof belongs to Me.

12 13 Will I eat flesh of bulls?
     Or goats' blood drink will I?
  14 Thanks offer thou to God, and pay
     Thy vows to the Most High.

13 15 And call upon Me when
     In trouble thou shalt be;
  I will deliver thee, and thou
     My Name shalt glorify.

14 16 But to the wicked man
     God saith, How dost thou dare
  Take in thy mouth My covenant?
     My statutes to declare?

15 17 Yet thou instruction wise
     Perversely hated hast,
  Likewise My words behind thy back
     Thou in contempt dost cast.

16 18 Thou didst to him consent,
    When thou a thief hast seen;
And with the vile adulterers
    Thou hast partaker been.

17 19 Thy mouth to ill is given,
    Thy tongue deceit doth frame;
 20 Thou sitt'st thy brother to revile,
    Thy mother's son defame.

18 21 Because I silence kept,
    While thou these things hast wrought,
That I was altogether like
    Thyself, hath been thy thought;

19 Yet I will thee reprove,
    And set before thine eyes,
Arrayed in order, thy misdeeds,
    And thine iniquities.

20 22 Now ye that God forget,
    Consider this with care,
Lest I, when there is none to save,
    Do you in pieces tear.

21 23 He honors Me who brings
    His sacrifice of praise;
I'll God's salvation show to him
    Who orders right his ways.

Psalm LI. C. M.

1 O GOD, according to Thy love,
    Be merciful to me;
For Thy compassions great, blot out
    All mine iniquity.

2 2 Me cleanse from sin, wash thoroughly
    From mine iniquity:
 3 For my transgressions I confess;
    My sin I ever see.

3 4 'Gainst Thee, Thee only have I sinned,
   In Thy sight done this ill;
   That when Thou speak'st Thou mayst be just,
   And clear in judging still.   [

4 5 Behold, I in iniquity
   My being did receive;
   Yea, me in guiltiness and sin
   My mother did conceive.

5 6 Behold, Thou in the inward parts
   With truth delighted art;
   And wisdom Thou shalt make me know
   Within the hidden part.   [

6 7 Do Thou with hyssop sprinkle me,
   I shall be cleansèd so;
   Yea, wash Thou me, and then I shall
   Be whiter than the snow.

7 8 Of gladness and of joyfulness
   Make me to hear the voice;
   That so these very bones which Thou
   Hast broken, may rejoice.

8 9 All mine iniquities blot out,
   Thy face hide from my sin.
  10 Clean heart create, O God, renew
   Right spirit me within.

9 11 And from before Thy gracious face,
   Cast Thou me not away;
   Thy Holy Spirit utterly
   Take not from me, I pray.

10 12 The joy which Thy salvation brings
   Again to me restore;
   With willing spirit do Thou me
   Uphold for evermore.

11 13 Then will I teach Thy ways unto
    Those that transgressors be;
  And those that sinners are, shall then
    Converted be to Thee.

12 14 O God, of my salvation God,
    Me from blood-guiltiness
  Set free; then shall my tongue aloud
    Sing of Thy righteousness.

13 15 My closèd lips, O Lord, let them
    Be opened wide by Thee,
  And then Thy praises by my mouth
    Abroad shall published be.

14 16 For Thou desir'st not sacrifice,
    Else would I give it Thee;
  Nor wilt Thou with burnt-offering
    At all delighted be.

15 17 A broken spirit is to God
    A pleasing sacrifice;
  A broken and a contrite heart,
    O God, Thou 'lt not despise.

16 18 In Thy good pleasure kindness show
    To Zion, Thine own hill;
  The walls of Thy Jerusalem
    Build up of Thy good will.

17 19 Then righteous off'rings shall Thee
      please,
    And off'rings burnt, which they
  With whole burnt-off'rings and with
      calves
    Shall on Thine altar lay.

Psalm LI. 7s.

1 ME, O God, compassion show,
As Thy tender mercies flow;
In Thy vast and boundless grace,
My transgressions all erase;
2 Wash me wholly from my sins,
Cleanse me from my guilty stains.

2 3 For my great transgression lies
Ever present to mine eyes;
4 I have sinned 'gainst Thee alone,
In Thy sight this evil done;
That Thy judgment may be clear,
And Thy speaking just appear.

3 5 Lo, I came to birth unclean,
Mother me conceived in sin;
6 Lo, Thou dost desire to find
Truth sincere within the mind;
And Thou wilt within my heart
Wisdom unto me impart.

4 7 Wash from every guilty stain,
Cleanse with hyssop, make me clean;
Then, from all pollution free,
Whiter than the snow I'll be.
8 Let me hear joy's cheering tones,
Making glad these broken bones.

5 9 From my sins hide Thou Thy face,
Blot them out in Thy rich grace;
10 Free my heart, O God, from sin,
Spirit right renew within.
11 Cast me not away from Thee,
Nor Thy Spirit take from me.

6 12 Give salvation's joy again,
With free spirit me sustain.

13 Then shall sinners, taught by me,
　　Learn Thy ways and turn to Thee.
14 Free me from the guilt of blood,
　　God, of my salvation God.

7　　Freed from guilt, my tongue shall raise
　　Songs Thy righteousness to praise;
15 Open Thou my lips, O Lord,
　　Then my mouth shall praise accord;
16 Sacrifice Thou wilt not take,
　　Else would I the off'ring make.

8　　Off'rings burnt in sacred rite
　　Can to Thee bring no delight;
17 But a spirit crushed for sin,
　　Contrite, broken heart within,
　　God's accepted sacrifice,
　　Thou, O God, wilt not despise.

9　18 Zion favor in Thy grace,
　　Yea, Jerus'lem's ramparts raise;
19 Then shall sacrifices right,
　　Whole burnt-off'rings Thee delight
　　So shall men, their vows to pay,
　　Bullocks on Thine altar lay.

Psalm LII. C. M.

1　WHY dost thou boast, O mighty man,
　　　Of mischief and of ill?
　　The loving-kindness of our God
　　　Endureth ever still.

2　2 Thy tongue doth slanders mischievous
　　　Devise in subtlety,
　　And like a razor, sharp to cut,
　　　It works deceitfully.

3　3 Ill more than good, and more than
　　　Thou lovest to speak wrong; [truth

4 Thou lovest all devouring words,
  O thou deceitful tongue.

4 5 So God shall thee destroy for aye,
     Remove thee, pluck thee out
  Quite from thy house, out of the land
     Of life He shall thee root.

5 6 The righteous shall it see, and fear,
     And laugh at him they shall;
  7 Lo, this the man is, that did not
     Make God his strength at all;

6   But he in his abundant wealth
     His confidence did place;
    And he took strength unto himself
     From his own wickedness.

7 8 But I am in the house of God
     Like to an olive green;
    My confidence forever hath
     Upon God's mercy been.

8 9 And I forever will Thee praise,
     Because Thou hast done this;
    I on Thy name will wait; for good
     Before Thy saints it is.

Psalm LIII. C. M.

1 THAT there is not a God, the fool
    Doth in his heart conclude;
  They are corrupt, their works are vile,
    Not one of them do'th good.

2 2 Upon the sons of men did God
     From heaven cast His eyes,
    To see if any one there was
     That sought God, and was wise.

3 3 They altogether filthy are,
  They all are backward gone;
 And there is none that doeth good,
  No, not so much as one.

4 4 These workers of iniquity,
  Do they not know at all,
 That they My people eat as bread,
  And on God do not call?

5 5 They had great fear, where no fear was;
  His bones who camps 'gainst thee
 God scattered; thou didst them defeat;
  Despised of God they flee.

6 6 Let Isr'el's help from Zion come!
  When God again shall bring
 His captives, Jacob shall rejoice,
  And Israel shall sing.

Psalm LIV. C. M.

1 SAVE me, O God, by Thy great Name,
   And judge me by Thy strength.
 2 My prayer regard, O God; give ear
   To all my words at length.

2 3 For strangers do against me rise;
   My soul oppressors sought,
 Who set not God before their eyes.
 4   But, lo, God help hath brought;

3   The Lord is with them who uphold
  5 My soul. He shall requite
 Their evil to mine enemies;
   In Thy truth crush their might.

4 6 I will a sacrifice to Thee
   Give with free willingness;
 Thy Name, Jehovah, for 't is good,
   With praise I will confess.

5 7 Because He hath delivered me
      From all adversities ;
      And its desire mine eye hath seen
      Upon mine enemies.

Psalm LV. C. M.

1 O GOD, my prayer hear; hide Thee not
      From my entreating voice.
   2 Attend and hear me ; in my plaint
      I mourn and make a noise ;

2 3 For voice of foes, for wicked men
      In their oppression great,
      Who on me cast iniquity,
      And who in wrath me hate.

3 4 Sore pained within me is my heart ;
      Death's terrors on me fall ;
   5 On me comes trembling, fear and dread
      Me overwhelmed withal.

4 6 O that I, like a dove, had wings,
      Said I, then would I flee
      Far hence, that I might find a place
      Where I at rest might be.

5 7 Lo, then far off I wander would,
      And in the desert stay ;
   8 From windy storm and tempest I
      Would haste to 'scape away.

6 9 O Lord, on them destruction bring,
      And do their tongues divide ;
      For in the city, violence
      And strife I have espied.

7 10 They day and night go round her walls;
      Vain rites and sorrow meet
   11 In her, and crimes ; deceit and wrong
      Depart not from her street.

8 12 He was no foe that me reproached;
　　　Then that endure I could;
　　Nor hater that did 'gainst me boast;
　　　From him me hide I would;

9 13 But, thou, man, who mine equal, friend,
　　　And my companion wast.
　　14 We took sweet counsel, to God's house
　　　In company we passed.

10 15 Death shall them seize, and to the grave
　　　Alive they shall depart;
　　For wickedness is in their house,
　　　And also in their heart.

11 16 I'll call on God; Jehovah will
　　17　Me save; I'll grieve and sigh
　　At ev'ning, morning, and at noon;
　　　And He shall hear my cry.

12 18 He hath in love my soul redeemed,
　　　That it in peace might be
　　From battle that against me was;
　　　For many strove with me.

13 19 God shall them hear, and answer them,
　　　(Of old abideth He,)
　　Even them who have no fear of God,
　　　And changes never see.

14 20 'Gainst those who were at peace with
　　　He hath put forth his hand;　[him
　　The covenant that he had made,
　　　By breaking he profaned.

15 21 More smooth than butter were his
　　　　words,
　　　While in his heart was war;
　　His speeches were more soft than oil,
　　　And yet drawn swords they were.

16 22 Thy burden on Jehovah cast,
And He shall thee sustain ;
Yea, He shall cause the righteous man
Unmovèd to remain.

17 23 But Thou, God, shalt to ruin's pit
Them cast ; the men of guile
And blood shall not live half their days;
But trust in Thee I will.

Psalm LVI. C. M.

1 O PITY me, my God, for man
Would swallow me outright ;
He me oppresseth, while he doth
Against me daily fight.

2 2 They daily would me swallow up
That en'mies are to me,
For they that proudly 'gainst me fight
In number many be.

3 3 When I 'm afraid, I 'll trust in Thee.
4 In God His word I 'll praise ;
I will not fear what flesh can do,
In God I 'll trust always.

4 5 Each day they wrest my words ; their
'Gainst me are all for ill. [thoughts
6 They meet, they lurk, they mark my
Who wait my soul to kill. [steps,

5 7 But shall they by iniquity
Escape Thy judgments so ?
O God, with indignation down
Do Thou the peoples throw.

6 8 Thou tellest all my wanderings,
Not one dost overlook ;
Into Thy bottle put my tears ;
Are they not in Thy book ?

7 9 What day I cry, my foes shall flee;
    I know God for me is;
  10 In God His word I 'll praise; His word
    I 'll in Jehovah praise.

8 11 In God I trusted; I 'll not fear;
    What can man do to me?
  12 Thy vows upon me are, O God,
    I 'll render thanks to Thee.

9 13 Wilt Thou not, who from death me
    My feet from falls keep free, [saved,
    To walk before God in the light
    Of those that living be?

Psalm LVII. C. M.

1 BE merciful to me, O God;
    Be merciful to me;
    My soul Thee trusts; to Thy wings'
    For refuge I will flee, [shade

2   Until calamities be past.
  2 I 'll cry to God Most High;
    To God, who doth all things for me
    Perform most perfectly.

3 3 From heaven He shall send down, and
    From his reproach defend [me
    That would devour me; God His truth
    And mercy forth shall send.

4 4 My soul among fierce lions is;
    I firebrands live among,
    Men's sons, whose teeth are spears and
    A sharp sword is their tongue. [darts,

5 5 Be Thou exalted very high
    Above the heavens, O God;

Let Thou Thy glory be advanced
O'er all the earth abroad.

6 6 My soul's bowed down ; for they a net
Have laid, my steps to snare ;
But in the pit which they have digged
For me they fallen are.

7 7 My heart is fixed, O God, my heart
Is fixed ; I 'll sing and praise.
8 My glory, wake ; wake, psalt'ry, harp ;
Myself I 'll early raise.

8 9 I 'll praise Thee 'mong the peoples,
'Mong nations sing will I ; [Lord,
10 For great to heaven Thy mercy is
Thy truth is to the sky.

9 11 O God, exalted be Thy name
Above the heavens to stand ;
Do Thou Thy glory far advance
Above both sea and land.

Psalm LVIII. C. M.

1 DO ye, O congregation, now
Indeed speak righteousness ?
O ye that are the sons of men,
Judge ye with uprightness ?

2 2 Yea, wrongs in heart ye work, your
Weigh violence on earth. [hands
3 The wicked, from their birth estranged,
Speak lies and stray from birth.

3 4 And as the poison of a snake
Their poison doth appear ;
Yea, they are like the adder deaf,
That closely stops her ear ;

4 5 That so she may not hear the voice
    Of one that charm her would,
No, not though he most cunning were,
    And charm most wisely could.

5 6 Their teeth, O God, within their mouth,
    Break Thou in pieces small ;
The great teeth, O Jehovah, break
    Of those young lions all.

6 7 Let them like waters melt away,
    Which downward still do flow ;
In pieces cut his arrows all,
    When he shall bend his bow.

7 8 And like a snail that melts away,
    Let each of them be gone ;
That as a birth untimely, they
    May never see the sun.

8 9 He shall them take away before
    Your pots the thorns can heat,
Both living, and in dreadful wrath
    As with a whirlwind great.

9 10 The righteous, when he vengeance sees,
    Shall be most joyful then ;
The righteous one shall wash his feet
    In blood of wicked men.

10 11 So men shall say, The righteous man
    Reward shall never miss ;
And verily upon the earth
    A God to judge there is.

Psalm LIX. C. M.

1 MY God, deliver me from those
    That are mine enemies ;
And do Thou me defend from those
    That up against me rise.

2 2 Do Thou deliver me from them
        That work iniquity ;
     And give me safety from the men
        Of bloody cruelty.

3 3 For, lo, they for my soul lay wait ;
        The mighty do combine
     Against me, LORD, and for no fault,
        Nor any sin of mine.

4 4 They run, and without fault in me,
        Themselves do ready make ;
     Awake to meet me with Thy help,
        And do Thou notice take.

5 5 Awake, Jehovah, God of Hosts,
        Thou God of Israel,
     To visit nations all ; spare none
        That wickedly rebel.

6 6 At eve they turn, howl like a dog,
        And round the city stray ;
     7 Lo, they belch out, swords in their
        For who doth hear ? they say.   [lips,

7 8 Jehovah, Thou shalt laugh at them
        And all the nations mock.
     9 O Thou my Strength, I 'll wait on Thee;
        For God is my high rock.

8 10 He of my mercy that is God
        Will early succor me ;
     God my desire upon my foes
        Will cause mine eyes to see.

9 11 Them slay not, lest my people should
        Forget Thy favor soon ;
     But by Thy power, O Lord, our Shield,
        Disperse and bring them down.

10 12 For their mouth's sin, and for the words
  That from their lips do fly,
 Let them be taken in their pride,
  Because they curse and lie.

11 13 In wrath consume them, them consume,
  That so they may not be;
 And that in Jacob God doth rule
  To earth's ends let them see.

12 14 At eve they'll turn, howl like a dog,
  And round the city stray;
 15 Go to and fro for food, all night
  Unsatisfied shall stay.

13 16 But of Thy power I'll sing aloud,
  At morn Thy mercy praise;
 For Thou to me my refuge wast,
  And tower in troublous days.

14 17 O Thou who art my strength, I will
  Sing praises unto Thee;
 For God is my defence, a God
  Of mercy unto me.

Psalm LX. C. M.

1 1 O GOD, Thou hast rejected us,
  And scattered us afar;
 Thou justly hast offended been;
  Restore us to Thy care.

2 2 The earth to tremble Thou hast made,
  Therein didst breaches make;
 Do Thou thereof the breaches heal,
  Because the land doth shake.

3 3 To Thine own people Thou hard things
  Hast showed, and on them sent;

Thou also hast caused us to drink
  Wine of astonishment.

4 4 And yet a banner Thou hast given
    To them who Thee do fear,
  That for the sake of truth, by them
    Displayed it may appear.

5 5 In order that Thy saints beloved
    May all delivered be,
  Save with the power of Thy right hand
    And answer give to me.

6 6 God in His holiness hath said :
    In this exult I will ;
  I Shechem will divide, and I
    Will mete out Succoth's vale.

7 7 I Gilead claim as Mine by right ;
    Manasseh Mine shall be ;
  Of My head Ephraim's the strength,
    Judah gives laws for Me ;

8 8 Moab 's My washing pot ; My shoe
    I 'll over Edom throw ;
  And o'er Philistia My shout
    Of triumph forth shall go.

9 9 O who is he will bring me to
    The city fortified ?
  O who is he that to the land
    Of Edom will me guide ?

10 10 Is it not Thou, O God, who hast
    Cast us from Thee afar ?
  Yea, with our armies Thou dost not
    Go forth, O God, to war.

11 11 Help us from trouble; for the help
　　　Is vain which man bestows.
　　12 Through God we shall do valiantly;
　　　He shall tread down our foes.

Psalm LXI. C. M.

1 O GOD, give ear unto my cry,
　　　And to my prayer attend.
　2 From utmost corner of the land
　　　My cry to Thee I 'll send.

2　　What time my heart is overwhelmed,
　　　And in perplexity,
　　Do Thou me lead unto the Rock
　　　That higher is than I.

3 3 For Thou hast for my refuge been
　　　A shelter by Thy power;
　　And for defence against my foes
　　　Thou hast been my strong tower.

4 4 Within Thy tabernacle I
　　　For ever will abide;
　　And under covert of Thy wings
　　　With confidence I 'll hide.

5 5 Because the vows that I did make,
　　　O Thou, my God, didst hear;
　　Thou hast me given the heritage
　　　Of those Thy name that fear.

6 6 A life prolonged for many days,
　　　Thou to the king shalt give;
　　Like many generations be
　　　The years which he shall live.

7 7 He in God's presence his abode
　　　For evermore shall have;
　　O do Thou truth and mercy both
　　　Prepare, that may him save.

8 8 And so will I for evermore
　　Sing praises to Thy name,
　That, having made my vows, I may
　　Each day perform the same.

Psalm LXII. C. M.

1 1 MY soul waits only upon God;
　　My saving strength is He;
　2 My only Saviour, Rock, High Tower;
　　Much moved I shall not be.

2 3 How long will ye assail a man,
　　That all of you may slay
　One who is like a bowing wall,
　　Or fence that giveth way?

3 4 They only plot to cast him down
　　From his high dignity;
　They joy in lies; with mouth they bless,
　　But they curse inwardly.

4 5 My soul, wait thou on God alone;
　　Because my hope is He;
　6 My only Saviour, Rock, High Tower;
　　And moved I shall not be.

5 7 In God alone my glory is,
　　And my salvation sure;
　In God the Rock is of my strength,
　　My refuge most secure.

6 8 On Him, ye people, evermore,
　　With confidence rely;
　Before Him pour ye out your heart;
　　God is our refuge high.

7 9 Surely mean men are vanity,
　　And great men are a lie;

      In balance laid, they wholly are
        More light than vanity.

8 10 Then do not in oppression trust,
        In robb'ry be not vain;
      And if your riches are increased,
        Set not your hearts on gain.

9 11 God hath it spoken once to me,
        Yea, this I heard again,
      That power to the mighty God
        Alone doth appertain.

10 12 Yea, mercy also unto Thee
        Belongs, O Lord, alone;
      For Thou according to his work
        Rewardest every one.

Psalm LXIII. C. M.

1 THEE, God, my God, I'll early seek;
        My soul doth thirst for Thee;
      My flesh longs in a dry, parched land,
        Wherein no waters be;

2 2 That I Thy power may behold,
        And brightness of Thy face,
      As I have seen Thee heretofore
        Within Thy holy place.

3 3 Since better is Thy love than life,
        My lips Thee praise shall give.
    4 I in Thy name will lift my hands,
        And bless Thee while I live.

4 5 Even as with marrow and with fat
        My soul supplied shall be;
      Then shall my mouth with joyful lips
        Sing praises unto Thee;

5   6 When I do Thee upon my bed
       Remember with delight,
     And when on Thee I meditate
       In watches of the night.

6   7 In shadow of Thy wings I 'll joy ;
       For Thou my help hast been.
     8 My soul Thee follows hard ; and me
       Thy right hand doth sustain.

7   9 Who seek my soul to spill shall sink
       Down to earth's lowest room.
    10 They by the sword shall be cut off,
       And jackals' prey become.

8 11 Yet shall the king in God rejoice ;
       And each one glory shall
     That swears by Him ; but stopped shall
       The mouth of liars all.   [be

Psalm LXIII. 6s & 4s.

1 O GOD, Thou art my God ;
       I 'll now seek Thee ;
     My soul and flesh desire
       With Thee to be.
     In thirsty land and dry,
     Where waters come not nigh,
     Thy glory and Thy power,
       O let me see.

2   2 As in Thy holy place
       Thee oft I 've seen,
     3 And Thy dear love than life
       Has better been ;
     Thee praise my lips shall give,
     4 I 'll bless Thee while I live,
     In Thy name lift my hands
       With soul serene.

3 5 As with fat meats my soul
　　　Well filled shall be;
　　My mouth with joyful lips
　　　Shall then praise Thee.
　　6 When I am on my bed,
　　　To Thee is mem'ry led;
　　And in night watch Thou giv'st
　　　Sweet thoughts to me.

4 7 Because Thou oftentimes
　　　Hast been mine aid,
　　I therefore will be glad
　　　In Thy wings' shade;
　　8 My soul cleaves after Thee;
　　　Thy right hand holdeth me;
　　9 Who would me kill shall in
　　　Earth's depths be laid.

5 10 By sword they 'll fall, a prey
　　　Of jackals be;
　　11 And then the King in God
　　　Shall gladness see.
　　And all who by Him swear,
　　　Shall glory in Him there;
　　But mouth of liars all
　　　Soon stop shall He.

Psalm LXIV. C. M.

1 To voice of my complaint and cry
　　　O God, give Thou an ear;
　　My life save from the enemy
　　　Of whom I stand in fear.

2 2 Me from their secret counsel hide
　　　Who do live wickedly;
　　From insurrection of those men
　　　That work iniquity.

3 3 Who do their tongues with malice
whet,
And make them cut like swords;
In whose bent bows are arrows set,
Even sharp and bitter words;

4 4 That they may at the perfect man
In secret aim their shot;
Yea, suddenly they dare at him
To shoot, and fear it not.

5 5 In ill encourage they themselves,
And their snares close do lay;
Together conference they have;
Who shall them see? they say.

6 6 They have searched out iniquities,
A perfect search they keep;
. Of each of them the inward thought,
And very heart, is deep.

7 7 God shall an arrow shoot at them,
And wound them suddenly.
8 So their own tongue shall them con-
All who them see shall fly. [found;

8 9 And on all men a fear shall fall,
God's works they shall declare;
For they shall wisely notice take
What these His doings are.

9 10 The just shall in Jehovah joy,
And trust upon His might;
Yea, they shall greatly glory all
In heart that are upright.

Psalm LXV. C. M.

1 IN Zion, God, praise waits for Thee,
To Thee vows paid shall be.
2 O Thou that Hearer art of prayer,
All flesh shall come to Thee.

2 3 Iniquities, I must confess,
　　Prevail against me do;
　But as for our transgressions all,
　　Them purge away shalt Thou.

3 4 Blessed is the man whom Thou dost choose,
　　And bringest near to Thee,
　That he within Thy temple courts
　　May still a dweller be.

4　We surely shall be satisfied
　　With Thine abundant grace,
　And with the goodness of Thy house,
　　Even of Thy holy place.

5 5 O God, our Saviour, by dread deeds
　　In right Thou 'lt answer prayer;
　All ends of earth shall trust in Thee,
　　And those on seas afar.

6 6 Who, being girt with power, sets fast
　　By His great strength the hills;
　 7 Who noise of seas, noise of their waves,
　　And peoples' tumult stills.

7 8 Those in the utmost parts that dwell
　　Are at Thy signs afraid;
　The goings out of morn and eve
　　By Thee are joyful made.

8 9 Thou earth dost visit, wat'ring it;
　　Thou mak'st it rich to grow
　With God's full flood; Thou givest corn
　　For Thou prepar'st it so.

9 10 Its ridges Thou dost water well,
　　Its furrows down are pressed;
　Thou dost with showers soften it,
　　Its fruits by Thee are blessed.

10 11 With goodness Thou dost crown the
   Thy paths drop fatness still.   [year;
   12 They drop on desert pastures so
   That gladness girds each hill.

11 13 The meadows all are clothed with
     flocks,
   The vales with corn are clad ;
   And now they shout and sing to Thee,
   For Thou hast made them glad.

Psalm LXVI. C. M.

1 ALL lands to God, in joyful sounds,
     Aloft your voices raise ;
   2 Sing forth the honor of His name,
     Make glorious His praise.

2 3 Say unto God, How terrible
     In all Thy works art Thou !
   Through Thy great power Thy foes to
   Shall be constrained to bow.   [Thee

3 4 All earth shall worship Thee, and sing;
     Their songs Thy name shall own.
   5 Come, see God's works, His dealings
     dread,
     That are to men's sons known.

4 6 He into dry land turned the sea,
     And they a passage had,
   Even marching through the flood on
   There we in Him were glad.   [foot;

5 7 He ruleth ever by His might ;
     His eyes the nations see ;
   O let not those that rebels are
     Exalt themselves on high.

6 8 Ye peoples, bless our God ; aloud
　　　The voice speak of His praise ;
　　9 Our soul in life who safe preserves,
　　　Our feet from sliding stays.

7 10 For as men silver try, O God,
　　　Thou didst us prove and try ;
　　11 Brought'st us into the net, and mad'st
　　　Bands on our loins to lie.

8 12 Thou hast made men ride o'er our heads ;
　　　Through fire and flood we passed ;
　　But yet into abundance great
　　　Thou hast us brought at last.

9 13 I'll bring burnt-off'rings to Thy house;
　　　To Thee my vows I'll pay,
　　14 Which my lips uttered, my mouth spake,
　　　When trouble on me lay.

10 15 Fat sheep in sacrifices burnt,
　　　With incense, I will bring ;
　　Of bullocks and of goats I will
　　　Present an offering.

11 16 All that fear God, come, hear, I'll tell
　　　What He did for my soul.
　　17 I with my mouth cried unto Him,
　　　My tongue did Him extol.

12 18 If in my heart I sin regard,
　　　The Lord me will not hear ;
　　19 But surely God me heard, and did
　　　To my prayer's voice give ear.

13 20 I'll therefore say with grateful heart,
　　　O let God blessèd be,
　　Who did not turn my prayer from Him,
　　　Nor yet His grace from me.

Psalm LXVII. C. M.

1 O GOD, be merciful, us bless;
    Shine on us with Thy face;
2 That earth Thy way and nations all
    May know Thy saving grace.

2 3 Let peoples give Thee praise, O God;
    Let peoples all Thee praise.
4 O let the nations joyful be,
    In songs their voices raise;

3 For Thou shalt justly peoples judge,
    On earth rule nations all.
5 Let peoples give Thee praise, O God;
    All peoples praise Thee shall.

4 6 The earth her increase yielded hath;
    God, our God, bless us shall.
7 God shall us bless; and of the earth
    The ends shall fear Him all.

Psalm LXVII. S. M.

1 GOD bless and pity us,
    Shine on us with Thy face;
2 That earth Thy way, and nations all
    May know Thy saving grace.

2 3 Let peoples praise, O God;
    Let peoples all Thee praise.
4 O let the nations all be glad,
    In songs their voices raise;

3 Thou 'lt justly people judge,
    On earth rule nations all.
5 Let peoples give Thee praise, O God,
    All peoples praise Thee shall.

4 6 The earth her fruit did yield;
    God, our God, bless us shall;

7 God shall us bless; and of the earth
   The ends shall fear Him all.

Psalm LXVIII. C. M.

1 LET God arise, and let His foes
   Abroad all scattered be;
   And let all those that do Him hate
   Before His presence flee.

2 2 As smoke is driven, so drive Thou
   As fire melts wax away,   [them;
   Before God's face let wicked men,
   So perish and decay.

3 3 But let the righteous all be glad;
   Let them before God's sight
   Be very joyful; yea, let them
   Exult with all their might.

4 4 To God sing, to His Name sing praise;
   Extol Him with your voice,
   That rides on heaven, by His name Jah,
   Before His face rejoice.

5 5 Because He is a Father kind
   To children fatherless;
   God is the widow's Judge within
   His place of holiness.

6 6 God sets the solitary ones
   In families; from bands
   He pris'ners frees; but rebels do
   Inhabit desert lands.

7 7 O God, when Thou wast going forth
   Before Thy people's face,
   And when through the great wilderness
   Thy glorious marching was;

8 8 Then shook the earth before God's face;
   Great drops from heaven fell;
   This Sinai at God's presence shook,
   The God of Israel.

9 9 O God, Thou to Thy heritage
   Didst send a plenteous rain,
   Whereby Thou, when it weary was,
   Didst it refresh again.

10 10 Thy congregation then did make
   Their habitation there;
   Of Thine own goodness for the poor,
   O God, Thou didst prepare.

11 11 The Lord the word gives, a great host
   Of women it declare;
   12 Kings of hosts flee, they flee; their
   At home the women share.   [spoil

12 13 When ye shall lie among the folds,
   Like doves ye shall appear,
   Whose wings with silver, and with gold
   Whose feathers covered are.

13 14 When there th' Almighty scattered
   Like Salmon's snow 't was   [kings,
   white.
   15 A mount of God is Bashan hill,
   Mount Bashan, peaks of height!

14 16 Why look askance, ye mountains high?
   This is the hill where God
   Desires to dwell; Jehovah here
   Will ever make abode.

15 17 God's chariots twenty thousand are,
   Thousands of angels strong;
   Sinai is in the holy place,
   The Lord is them among.

16 18 Thou didst ascend on high, and lead
    Captive captivity;   [LORD,
Take gifts for men, that God the
    Might dwell where rebels be.

17 19 Blessed be the Lord, who is to us
    Of our salvation God;
Who daily with His benefits
    Us plenteously doth load.

18 20 He of salvation is the God,
    Who is our God most strong;
And to the Lord Jehovah do
    Escapes from death belong.

19 21 But surely God shall wound the head
    Of those that are His foes;
The hairy scalp of him that still
    On in his trespass goes.

20 22 The Lord hath said, I will them bring
    Again from Bashan hill;
Yea, from the sea's devouring depths
    Them bring again I will;

21 23 That in the blood of enemies
    Thy foot imbrued may be;
And of thy dogs dipped in the same
    The tongues thou mayest see.

22 24 Thy goings they have seen, O God;
    The steps of majesty
Of my God, and my mighty King,
    Into the sanctuary.

23 25 Before went singers, after them
    The minstrels took their way,
Within the midst of damsels who
    Upon their timbrels play.

24 26 Within the congregations great
   Bless God with one accord ;
   From Isr'el's fountains do ye bless
   And praise the mighty Lord.

25 27 Their prince is there, young Benjamin,
   And Judah's princes high ;
   The chiefs of Zebulun are there,
   And chiefs of Naphtali.

26 28 Thy God commands thy strength ; O
   Make strong Thy work for us ; [God,
   29 For to Jerus'lem kings shall bring
   Rich presents for Thy house.

27 30 The beasts of reeds, the multitude
   Of bulls, which fiercely look,
   Those calves which people have in pride
   Sent forth do Thou rebuke,

28   Till all submit and tribute bring
   Of silver from afar ;
   He hath the people scattered, who
   Delight themselves in war.

29 31 Those that be princes great shall then
   Come out of Egypt lands ;
   And Ethiopia to God
   Shall soon stretch out her hands.

30 32 O all ye kingdoms of the earth,
   Sing praise to God, sing praise ;
   The praises of our sovereign Lord
   In sweet psalms do ye raise.

31 33 To Him who rides on heavens of
       heavens
   Which He of old did found ;
   Lo, He sends out His voice—a voice
   In might that doth abound.

32 34 Strength unto God do ye ascribe,
  Because His majesty
  Is over Israel, His strength
  Is in the clouds most high.

33 35 Thou, God, art dreadful from Thy
  Isr'el's own God is He,   [house;
  Who gives His people strength and
  O let God blessèd be.   [power;

Psalm LXIX. C. M.

1 SAVE me, O God, because the floods
    Come in unto my soul;
 2 I sink in mire, no standing have;
    In deeps, floods o'er me roll.

2 3 I weary with my crying am,
    My throat is also dried;
    Mine eyes do fail, while for my God
    I waiting do abide.

3 4 My causeless haters are far more
    Than hairs upon my head;
    False foes, who slay me, mighty are;
    What I took not I paid.

4 5 Thou, God, dost know my faults; my
    Not covered are from Thee; [sins
   6 Lord, LORD of Hosts, let none who
      wait
    On Thee, be shamed through me;

5   O God of Israel, let none
    Of those who search do make,
    And seek Thee, be at any time
    Confounded for my sake.

6 7 For I have borne reproach for Thee;
    My face is hid with shame.

8 To brethren strange, to mother's sons,
 An alien I became.

7 9 Because the zeal did eat me up
 Which to Thy house I bear ;
 And the reproaches cast at Thee
 Upon me fallen are.

8 10 With tears and fasting mourned my
 And that was made my shame. [soul,
 11 I put on sackcloth, and to them
 A by-word I became.

9 12 The men who in the gate do sit
 Against me evil spake ;
 They also who vile drunkards were,
 Of me their song did make.

10 13 But in a time accepted, LORD,
 I make my prayer to Thee ;
 In Thy salvation's truth, O God,
 And mercy great, hear me.

11 14 Deliver me out of the mire,
 From sinking do me keep ;
 Free me from those that do me hate
 And from the waters deep.

12 15 Let not the flood on me prevail,
 Whose water overflows ;
 Nor deep me swallow ; nor the pit
 Her mouth upon me close.

13 16 Hear me, Jehovah ; for Thy love
 And kindness are most good ;
 Turn unto me, according to
 Thy mercies' multitude.

14 17 Nor from Thy servant hide Thy face;
 I 'm troubled, soon attend.

18 Draw near my soul, and it redeem ;
　　Me from my foes defend.

15 19 To Thee is my reproach well known,
　　My shame and my disgrace.
　Those that mine adversaries be
　　Are all before Thy face.

16 20 Reviling broke my heart ; I 'm full
　　Of grief ; I looked for one
　To pity me, but none there was,
　　To comfort me found none.

17 21 They also bitter gall to me
　　Did give to be my meat ;
　They gave me vinegar to drink,
　　When as my thirst was great.

18 22 Their table shall become a snare,
　　A trap their joys attend ;　　[sight ;
　23 Their darkened eyes shall lose their
　　Make Thou their loins to bend.

19 24 On them Thine indignation pour ;
　　Them seize in anger great ;
　25 And in their tents let no one dwell,
　　Their homes be desolate.

20 26 Because they persecute the man
　　Whom Thou didst smite before ;
　They talk unto the grief of those
　　Whom Thou hast wounded sore.

21 27 Add sin unto their sin, let them
　　Not share Thy righteousness ;
　28 Blot from life's book, and write them
　　With men of uprightness.　　[not

22 29 But now become exceeding poor
　　And sorrowful am I ;

By Thy salvation, O my God,
Let me be set on high.

23 30 The name of God I with a song
Most cheerfully will praise;
And I, in giving thanks to Him,
His Name shall highly raise.

24 31 This to Jehovah better far
Than sacrifice shall prove,
Than bullock, ox, or any beast
That hath both horn and hoof.

25 32 When this the humble men shall see,
It joy to them shall give;
All ye that after God do seek,
Your hearts shall ever live.

26 33 Jehovah hears the poor; nor does
His prisoners contemn.
34 Let heaven, and earth, and seas **Him**
And all that move in them. [praise,

27 35 For God will Judah's cities build,
And He will Zion save;
That they may dwell therein, and it
In sure possession have.

28 36 And they that are His servants' seed
Inherit shall the same;
So shall they have their dwelling there
That love His blessèd Name.

Psalm LXX. C. M.

1 DELIVER me, O God; make haste,
Jehovah, succor me.
2 And they that seek my soul shall all
Shamed and confounded be;

2   They shall be backward turned, and
        That in my hurt delight. [shamed
    3 Turned back shall be, Ha, ha! that say,
        Their shaming to requite.

3   4 In Thee shall all be glad and joy
        Who truly seek for Thee;
        Who Thy salvation love shall say,
        God praised for ever be.

4   5 But I both poor and needy am;
        O God, come, haste, I pray;
        Jehovah, who my Saviour art
        And help, make no delay.

Psalm LXX. S. M.

1 SAVE me, O God; with speed,
       Jehovah, succor me.
    2 And they that seek my soul shall all
        Shamed and confounded be;

2   Turned back shall be, and shamed,
        That in my hurt delight.
    3 Turned back shall be, Ha, ha! that say,
        Their shaming to requite.

3   4 In Thee shall all be glad
        And joy that seek for Thee;
        Who Thy salvation love shall say,
        God praised for ever be.

4   5 I poor and needy am,
        O God, come, haste, I pray;
        Jehovah, who my Saviour art
        And help, make no delay.

Psalm LXXI. C. M.

1 JEHOVAH, all my confidence
       Is placed in Thee alone;
       Then let Thy servant never be
       Into confusion thrown.

PSALM LXXI.

2 2 And let me, in Thy righteousness,
From Thee deliv'rance have ;
Cause me escape, incline Thine ear
To me, and do me save.

3 3 Be Thou my dwelling-rock, to which
I ever may resort ;
Thou gav'st commandment me to save,
For Thou 'rt my rock and fort.

4 4 Free me, my God, from wicked hands,
Hands cruel and unjust ;
5 For, Lord Jehovah, Thou 'rt my hope,
And from my youth my trust.

5 6 Thou from my birth hast held me up ;
Thou art the same that me
Out of my mother's womb didst take ;
I ever will praise Thee.

6 7 To many I a wonder am ;
Thou art my refuge strong.
8 Filled let my mouth be with Thy praise
And honor all day long.

7 9 O do not cast me off, when me
Old age doth overtake ;
And in the time of failing strength
Do Thou not me forsake.

8 10 For those that are mine enemies
Against me speak with hate ;
And they together counsel take
That for my soul lay wait.

9 11 They say, God leaves him ; him pursue,
And take ; there's none to save.
12 Be near to me, O God ; my God,
Thy speedy help I crave.

10 13 They shall be shamed, consumed, that
My soul are enemies; [to
Clothed be they with reproach and
That do my hurt devise. [shame

11 14 But I will hope continually,
And more and more Thee praise.
15 Thy justice and salvation shall
My mouth tell all my days;

12 16 For I know not the count; but in
The Lord Jehovah's might
I'll go and tell Thy righteousness,
And Thine alone will write.

13 17 For even from my youth, O God,
By Thee I have been taught;
And hitherto I have declared
The wonders Thou hast wrought.

14 18 Now leave me not, O God, when I
Old and gray-headed grow;
Till to this age Thy strength and power
To all to come I show.

15 19 O God, Thy justice is most high,
Thou, God, hast great things done.
20 Who is like Thee? Thou, who sore ills
And many hast me shown,

16 Thou shalt me quicken, and from
Of earth bring up again; [depths
21 My greatness shalt increase, and turn
To comfort me in pain.

17 22 Thee, even Thy truth, I'll also praise,
My God, with psaltery;
Thou Holy One of Israel,
With harp I'll sing to Thee.

18 23 My lips shall much rejoice in Thee,
When I Thy praises sound ;
My soul, which is redeemed by Thee,
In joy shall much abound.

19 24 My tongue Thy justice shall proclaim,
Yea, utter all day long ;
For they confounded are and shamed,
That seek to do me wrong.

Psalm LXXI. S. M.

1 JEHOVAH, Thee I trust,
Ashamed let me not be ;
2 But in Thy righteousness provide
Escape ; O save Thou me.

2   Incline Thine ear, me save ;
3   My dwelling rock be Thou,
Where I may always come ; Thou hast
My safety ordered now.

3   Since Thou 'rt my rock and fort,
4   My God, from wicked hand·
Me free, from hand of men perverse,
Who vi'lent me withstand.

4 5 For, Lord Jehovah, Thou,
From youth my hope and stay,
6 At birth did'st me uphold, bring forth;
Thee I will praise for aye.

5 7 Crowds me their wonder make ;
But Thou 'rt my refuge strong.
8 Filled let my mouth be with Thy
And honor all day long.   [praise

6 9 Cast me not off when old,
Nor when strength fails forsake ;
10 For foes revile, who for my soul
Lay wait and counsel take.

7 11 They cry: Pursue and take,
       God leaves him, none will save.
    12 O God, be near to me; my God,
       Thy speedy help I crave.

8 13 They shall be shamed, consumed,
       Who 'gainst my soul arise;
       Be covered with reproach and shame,
       That do my hurt devise.

9 14 But I will ever hope,
       And add to all Thy praise.
    15 Thy justice and salvation shall
       My mouth tell all my days,

10   For I know not the count.
    16 In Lord Jehovah's might,
       I 'll go and tell Thy righteousness,
       And Thine alone will write.

11 17 O God, from early youth
       By Thee I have been taught;
       And hitherto I have declared
       The wonders Thou hast wrought.

12 18 Now leave me not, O God,
       When old and gray I grow;
       Till to this age Thine arm and power
       To all to come I show.

13 19 Thou art more just than all,
       O God; what God has done
    20 Great deeds like Thee? Who many ills
       And sore to me hast shown,

14   Thou shalt revive, and me
       From earth's depths bring again;
    21 My greatness shalt increase and turn
       To comfort me in pain.

15 22 Thee, O my God, Thy truth,
   I'll praise with psaltery;
   Thou Holy One of Israel,
   With harp I'll sing to Thee.

16 23 My lips and soul shall joy
     To praise Thee, who redeemed;
   24 My tongue all day Thy justice tells;
     Who wrong me blush, are shamed.

Psalm LXXII. C. M.

1 O GOD, Thy judgments give the king,
   His son Thy righteousness.
  2 With right He shall Thy people judge,
   Thy poor with uprightness.

2 3 The lofty mountains shall bring forth
   To all the people peace;
   The little hills shall also yield
   The same by righteousness.

3 4 The people's poor ones He shall judge,
   The needy's children save;
   And those shall He in pieces break
   Who them oppressèd have.

4 5 They shall Thee fear while sun and
   Do last through ages all.   [moon
  6 Like rain on mown grass He'll descend,
   Or showers on earth that fall.

5 7 The just shall flourish in His days,
   And prosper in His reign;
   He shall, while doth the moon endure,
   Abundant peace maintain.

6 8 His large and great dominion shall
   From sea to sea extend;
   It from the river shall reach forth
   To earth's remotest end.

7   9 They in the wilderness that dwell
        Bow down before Him must;
      And they that are His enemies
        Shall lick the very dust.

8 10 The kings of Tarshish, and the isles,
        To Him shall presents bring;
      And unto Him shall offer gifts
        Sheba's and Seba's king.

9 11 Yea, kings shall all before Him bow;
        All nations serve Him shall.
     12 He'll save the poor who cries, the weak
        Who hath no help at all.

10 13 He shall the weak and needy spare,
        Save needy souls, and free
     14 From violence and fraud; to Him
        Their blood shall precious be.

11 15 Yea, He shall live, and given to Him
        Shall be of Sheba's gold;
      For Him still shall they pray, and He
        Shall daily be extolled.

12 16 Of corn a handful in the earth
        On tops of mountains high,
      With prosp'rous fruit shall shake, like
        On Lebanon that be.   [trees

13   The city shall be flourishing;
        Her citizens abound
      In number shall, like to the grass
        That grows upon the ground.

14 17 His name for ever shall endure,
        Last like the sun it shall;
      Men shall be blessed in Him, and
        All nations shall Him call.   [blessed

15 18 O blessèd be Jehovah, God,
  The God of Israel ;
  For He alone do'th wondrous works,
  In glory that excel.

16 19 And also let His glorious Name
  Be blessed for ever then ;
  The whole earth let His glory fill ;
  Amen, yea and Amen.

Psalm LXXII. L. M.

1 O GOD, Thy judgments give the king,
  His royal son Thy righteousness ;
 2 He to Thy people right shall bring,
  By justice shall Thy poor redress.

2 3 The mountains high shall peace secure,
  And little hills by means of right ;
 4 He 'll save the needy, judge the poor,
  And crush the proud oppressor's might.

3 5 Till sun and moon no more are known,
  They shall Thee fear in ages all ;
 6 He 'll come as rain on meadows mown,
  And showers upon the earth that fall.

4 7 The just shall flourish in His day,
  While lasts the moon shall peace extend ;
 8 From sea to sea shall be His sway,
  And from the river to earth's end.

5 9 To Him shall bow who dwell in wilds,
  Down to the dust His foes shall bend;
 10 The kings of Tarshish, and the isles,
  Sheba and Seba, gifts shall send.

6 11 All kings before Him down shall fall ;
      All nations shall His laws obey ;
   12 He 'll save the needy when they call,
      The poor, and him who has no stay.

7 13 The poor and needy spare shall He,
      The needy's soul save by His might;
   14 From fraud and violence set free,
      Dear shall their blood be in His sight.

8 15 He 'll live ; before Him shall be laid
      Of Sheba's gold an offering ;
   For Him shall constant prayer be made,
      His praises they shall daily sing.

9 16 On hill-tops sown a little corn,
      Like Lebanon with fruit shall bend ;
   New life the city shall adorn ;
      She shall like grass grow and extend.

10 17 Long as the sun His name shall last,
      It shall endure through ages all ;
   And men shall still in Him be blessed,
      Blessed all the nations shall Him call.

11 18 Blessed be Jehovah, God, the One,
      Who is sole God of Israel,
   For He alone hath wonders done,
      His deeds in glory far excel.

12 19 And blessed be His all-glorious name,
      Long as the ages shall endure.
   O'er all the earth extend His fame.
      Amen, amen, for evermore.

Psalm LXXIII. C. M.

1 YEA, God is good to Israel,
      To each pure-hearted one ;
   2 But as for me, my steps near slipped,
      My feet were almost gone.

2 3 I envied foolish ones when I
    Saw wicked men succeed ;
  4 Because their strength continues firm,
    Their death from bands is freed.

3 5 They are not troubled as men are,
    Nor plagued as men are they ;
  6 So pride doth as a chain them gird,
    And violence array.

4 7 Their eyes stand out with fat; they have
    More than their heart could seek.
  8 They mock, and loftily of wrong
    And of oppression speak.

5 9 They set their mouth against the heavens,
    Their tongue walks earth about ;
  10 His people, therefore, hither turn,
    Full waters they wring out.

6 11 And thus they say, How can it be
    That God these things doth know ?
  Or, can there in the Highest be
    Knowledge of things below ?

7 12 Lo, these the wicked are, and yet
    They prosper at their will
  In worldly things ; they do increase
    In wealth and riches still.

8 13 I, verily, have sought in vain
    My heart to purify ;
  And vainly also washed my hands
    In innocence have I.

9 14 For daily, and all day throughout,
    Great plagues I suffered have ;
  Yea, every morning I of new
    Did chastisement receive.

10 15 If in this manner foolishly
  To speak I would intend,
The generation of Thy sons,
  Behold, I should offend.

11 16 When I this thought to know, it was
  Too hard a thing for me;
17 Till to God's holy place I went;
  Then I their end did see.

12 18 Upon a slipp'ry place them set
  Assuredly Thou hast;
And down into destruction deep
  Thou dost them quickly cast.

13 19 How in a moment suddenly
  To ruin brought are they!
With fearful terrors utterly
  They are consumed away.

14 20 Even like unto a dream, when one
  From sleeping doth arise;
So Thou, O Lord, when Thou awak'st,
  Their image shalt despise.

15 21 Thus grieved within me was my heart,
  And me my reins opprest;
22 So rude was I, and ignorant,
  And in Thy sight a beast.

16 23 But I am still with Thee; Thou dost
  By my right hand me hold.
24 Thy counsel guides me, and Thou wilt
  In glory me enfold.

17 25 Whom have I in the heavens but Thee,
  None else on earth beside.
26 Flesh fails and heart; God, my heart's
  And portion will abide.   [strength

18 27 For, lo, they that are far from Thee
    For ever perish shall ;
    Them that forsake Thee faithlessly
    Thou hast destroyèd all.

19 28 But surely it is good for me
    That I to God draw near ;
    Jehovah, Lord, I trust that all
    Thy works I may declare.

Psalm LXXIV. C. M.

1   O GOD, why hast Thou cast us off ?
        Is it for evermore ?
    Against Thy pasture-sheep why doth
        Thine anger smoke so sore ?

2 2 The congregation of Thy choice
        In Thy remembrance hold ;
    The people who have purchased been
        By Thee in days of old ;

3   The rod of Thine inheritance,
        Which Thou redeemèd hast ;
    This Zion hill, wherein Thou hadst
        Thy dwelling in times past.

4 3 To these long desolations lift
        Thy feet, and tarry not,
    For all the ills Thy foes within
        Thy holy place have wrought.

5 4 In midst of Thine own meeting place
        Thine enemies do roar ;
    Their ensigns they set up for signs
        Of triumph Thee before.

6 5 They seemed as one who lifted up
        The axe thick trees upon ;

6 For now with axe and hammers they
   Do break the carved work down.

7 7 Thy holy place they set on fire,
   And have defiled the same,
   By casting down unto the ground
   The place where dwelt Thy name.

8 8 Thus said they in their hearts, Let us
   Destroy them out of hand;
   They burnt up all the synagogues
   Of God within the land.

9 9 Our signs we do not now behold;
   There is not us among
   A prophet more, nor any one
   That knows the time how long.

10 10 How long thus shall the foe, O God,
   Reproachfully exclaim?
   And shall the adversary thus
   Always blaspheme Thy Name?

11 11 Thy hand, even Thy right hand of
      might,
   To stretch forth why delay?
   O from Thy bosom pluck it out,
   And sweep them quite away.

12 12 For certainly God is my King,
   Even from the times of old;
   He works in midst of all the earth
   Salvation manifold.

13 13 The sea, by Thy great power, to part
   Asunder Thou didst make;
   And Thou the great sea-monsters'
   Didst in the waters break.   [heads,

14 14 The heads of the leviathan
  Thou breakest and didst give
  Him to be meat unto the folk
  In wilderness that live.

15 15 Thou clav'st the fountain and the
    Didst dry the rivers great ; [flood,
  16 Both day and night are Thine ; Thou
    The light and sun create. [didst

16 17 By Thee the borders of the earth
  Were settled everywhere ;
  The summer and the winter both
  By Thee created were.

17 18 Remember that the enemy
  Jehovah did defame ;
  And that the foolish people have
  Blasphemed Thy holy Name.

18 19 O do not to the multitude
  Thy turtle's soul give o'er ;
  The congregation of Thy poor
  Forget not evermore.

19 20 Now to the cov'nant have respect ;
  For in the earth are found
  Dark places, full of shadowed homes,
  Where cruelties abound.

20 21 O let not those that be oppressed
  Return again with shame ;
  Let those that poor and needy are
  Give praises to Thy Name.

21 22 Do Thou, O God, arise and plead
  The cause that is Thine own ;
  Remember how Thou art reproached
  Still by the foolish one.

22 23 Do not forget the voice of those
    That are Thine enemies;
    Of those the tumult ever grows
    That do against Thee rise.

Psalm LXXV. C. M.

1 TO Thee, O God, we render thanks,
    We render thanks to Thee;
    Because Thy wondrous works declare
    Thy great Name near to be.

2 2 When the appointed time I find,
    In righteousness I 'll reign;
  3 Earth and its dwellers are dissolved,
    The pillars I sustain.

3 4 I said to boastful fools, Boast not;
    To sinners said, Your horn
  5 Lift not; lift not your horn on high,
    Nor speak with neck of scorn.

4 6 For not from east, nor west, nor south,
    Comes exaltation nigh;
  7 But God is Judge; He puts down one,
    Another lifts on high.

5 8 A cup is in Jehovah's hand;
    Red wine, full mixed withal,
    He pours; earth's wicked all wring out
    Its dregs, and drink them shall.

6 9 But I forever will declare,
    I Jacob's God will praise.
  10 All horns of lewd men I 'll cut off;
    But just men's horns will raise.

Psalm LXXVI. C. M.

1 IN Judah God is known ; His name
In Israel is great.
2 In Salem His pavilion is,
In Zion is His seat.

2 3 There arrows of the bow He brake,
The shield, the sword, the war.
4 More glorious Thou than hills of prey,
More excellent art far.

3 5 Those that were stout of heart are spoiled,
They slept their sleep outright ;
And none of those their hands did find
That were the men of might.

4 6 When Thy rebuke, O Jacob's God,
Had forth against them passed,
Their horses and their chariots both
Were in a dead sleep cast.

5 7 Thou, evèn Thou, art He that should
Be feared ; and who is he
That may stand up before Thy sight,
If once Thou angry be ?

6 8 From heaven Thou sentence didst pro-
The earth was still with fear; [claim,
9 When God to judgment rose, to save
All meek on earth that were.

7 10 Because the very wrath of man
Unto Thy praise redounds ;
Thou to the remnant of his wrath
Wilt set restraining bounds.

8 11 Vow to the LORD your God, and pay;
All ye that near Him be,

Bring gifts and presents unto Him,
For to be feared is He.

9 12 For He the spirit shall cut off
Of those that princes be;
To kings that are upon the earth
Most terrible is He.

Psalm LXXVII. C. M.

1 1 WITH my voice cried unto God,
I unto God did cry,
Even with my voice; and unto me
His ear He did apply.

2 2 In day of woe I sought the Lord;
My hand was stretched by night,
And not withdrawn; but yet my soul
Refused the cheering light.

3 3 I to remembrance God do call,
Yet trouble doth remain;
And overwhelmed my spirit is,
Whilst I do sore complain.

4 4 Mine eyes debarred from rest and sleep
Thou makest still to wake;
My trouble is so great, that I
Unable am to speak.

5 5 I thought on days and years of old,
Recalled my songs by night;
6 I with my heart communed, my soul
Made earnest search for light.

6 7 For ever will the Lord cast off,
And gracious be no more?
8 For ever is His mercy gone?
Fails His word evermore?

7 9 Oh, is it so, that all His grace
    Our God forgotten hath?
    And that His tender mercies He
    Hath shut up in His wrath?

8 10 Then did I say, that surely this
    Is mine infirmity;
    But oh, the years of the right hand
    Of Him that is Most High.

9 11 Jehovah's deeds I will recount;
    Thy wonders old relate;
  12 On all Thy doings I will muse,
    On Thy works meditate.

10 13 O God, in holiness Thy way!
    What god is great like God?
  14 Thou, wonder working God, Thy strength
    'Mong peoples show'st abroad.

11 15 To Thine own people with Thine arm
    Thou didst redemption bring;
    To Jacob's sons, and to the tribes
    Of Joseph that do spring.

12 16 The waters Thee perceived, O God,
    The waters saw Thee well;
    And they for fear aside did flee;
    The depths on trembling fell.

13 17 The clouds in water forth were poured;
    Sound loudly did the sky;
    And swiftly through the world abroad
    Thine arrows fierce did fly.

14 18 Thy thunder's voice along the heaven
    A mighty noise did make;
    By lightnings lightened was the world;
    Earth trembled and did shake.

15 19 Thy way was in the sea, and in
　　　The waters great Thy path ;
　　Yet there Thy footsteps hidden are ;
　　　None knowledge thereof hath.

16 20 Thy people Thou didst safely lead,
　　　Like to a flock of sheep ;
　　By Moses' hand, and Aaron's, Thou
　　　Didst them conduct and keep.

Psalm LXXVIII. C. M.

1　ATTEND, my people, to my law ;
　　　Thereto give thou an ear ;
　　The words that from my mouth pro-
　　　Attentively do hear.　　　　[ceed,

2　2 My mouth shall speak a parable,
　　　And sayings dark of old ;
　　3 The same which we have heard and
　　　And us our fathers told.　[known,

3　4 We will not from their children hide,
　　　But to their sons make known
　　Jehovah's praises, and His strength,
　　　And wonders He hath done.

4　5 He Jacob testimony gave
　　　In Isr'el law did place,
　　And charged our fathers them to show
　　　To their succeeding race ;

5　6 That so the race which was to come
　　　Might well them learn and know ;
　　And sons unborn who should arise,
　　　Might to their sons them show ;

6　7 That they might set their hope in God,
　　　And suffer not to fall

God's mighty works out of their mind,
   But keep His precepts all ;

7 8 And might not, like their fathers, be
   A stubborn rebel race ;
   A race not right in heart ; with God
   Whose spirit faithless was.

8 9 The sons of Ephr'im, armed, with
   In day of battle fled ;   [bows,
   10 Kept not God's cov'nant, and refused
   By His law to be led.

9 11 His works and wonders, He them
   They did forget outright ;   [shewed
   12 Marvels in Egypt, Zoan's field,
   He did in fathers' sight.

10 13 He clave a pathway in the sea,
   He led them through the deep ;
   The waters on each side He raised,
   They stood up as a heap.

11 14 With cloud by day, with light of fire
   All night, He did them guide.
   15 He in the desert clave the rocks,
   And drink as floods supplied.

12 16 He from the rock brought streams, as
   Made waters down to run.   [floods
   17 Yet, sinning more, in desert they
   Provoked the Highest One.

13 18 For in their heart they tempted God,
   And speaking with mistrust,
   They greedily did meat require
   To satisfy their lust.

14 19 Moreover they against God spake,
  And, murmuring, they said :
Can God in such a wilderness
  For us a table spread ?

15 20 Behold, He smote the rock, and thence
  Came streams and waters great ;
But can He give His people bread?
  And send them flesh to eat ?

16 21 Jehovah therefore heard, was wroth ;
  So kindled was a flame
In Jacob, yea, on Israel
  His burning anger came.

17 22 For they believed not God, nor trust
  In His salvation had ;
23 Though clouds above He did command
  And heavens' doors open made ;

18 24 And manna rained on them, and gave
  Them corn of heaven to eat.
25 Man angels' food did eat ; to them
  He to the full sent meat.

19 26 He in the heaven also caused
  An eastern wind to blow,
And by His power did direct
  The southern wind to go.

20 27 Then flesh He rained on them like
    dust,
  Winged fowl like sand of sea ;
28 Within their camp He made them fall,
  Around their tents to be.

21 29 So they did eat and were well filled ;
  For what they did require,
30 He brought to them ; yet unappeased
  Was their corrupt desire ;

22 Then, while the meat was in their mouths
  31 God's wrath upon them fell ;
He slew their fat ones, yea, smote [down
The flower of Israel.

23 32 Yet still they sinned, did not believe
His wondrous works ; so He
33 With terror great consumed their [years,
Their days in vanity.

24 34 But when He slew them, then they did
To seek Him show desire ;
Yea, they returned, and after God
Right early did inquire.

25 35 And that this God had been their Rock
They did remember then ;
That He who is the Most High God
Had their Redeemer been.

26 36 Yet with their mouth they flattered Him,
And with their tongues they lied ;
37 Their heart not steadfast was, they [from
His cov'nant turned aside.

27 38 But, full of pity, He forgave
Their sin, them did not slay ;
Nor stirred up all His wrath, but oft
His anger turned away.

28 39 For that they were but fading flesh
He did remember then ;
A breath that passeth soon away,
And cometh not again.

29 40 How oft in wilds they Him withstood!
Grieved Him in desert lone!

41 Yea, turned and tempted God, pro-
　　Isr'el's own Holy One.　　　[voked

30 42 They did not call to mind His power,
　　　Nor yet the day when He
　　Delivered them out of the hand
　　　Of their fierce enemy.

31 43 How wonders He in Egypt wrought
　　　And signs in Zoan's field;
　　44 Their rivers into blood He turned,
　　　Their streams no drink did yield.

32 45 He sent the fly which them devoured,
　　　The frog which did them spoil;
　　46 He gave the worm their increase all,
　　　The locust all their toil.

33 47 Their vines with hail, their sycamores
　　　He with the frost did blast.
　　48 Their beasts to hail He gave, their
　　　Hot thunderbolts did waste.　[flocks

34 49 Fierce anger He let loose on them,
　　　And indignation strong,
　　Distress and trouble, angels sent
　　　Of evil them among.

35 50 He for His wrath made way, their soul
　　　From death He did not save;
　　But over to the pestilence
　　　Their living ones He gave.

36 51 In Egypt land the first-born all
　　　He smote down everywhere;
　　Among the tents of Ham, even these
　　　Chief of their strength that were.

37 52 But His own people, like to sheep,
　　　Thence to go forth He made;

And He, amidst the wilderness,
    Them as a flock did lead.

38 53 And He them safely on did lead,
    So that they did not fear ;
    But by the sea's returning waves
    O'erwhelmed their en'mies were.

39 54 To borders of His holy place
    His people thus He brought ;
    To this same mountain which for them
    His own right hand had bought.

40 55 For them He nations did expel,
    Their lands by lot divide,
    That so the tribes of Israel
    Might in their tents abide.

41 56 Yet God Most High they did provoke
    And Him they tempted still ;
    His testimonies to observe
    Did not incline their will ;

42 57 But, like their fathers, they turned
    And dealt with treachery ;   [back,
    Aside they turned, like to a bow
    That shoots deceitfully.

43 58 For they to anger did provoke
    Him with their places high ;
    And with their graven images
    Moved Him to jealousy.

44 59 God heard, was wroth, and much
    His people Isr'el then ;   [abhorred
  60 So Shiloh's tent He left, the tent
    Which He had placed with men.

45 61 And He His strength delivered up
   To sore captivity;
  He left His glory in the hand
   Of His proud enemy.

46 62 His people also He gave o'er
   Unto the sword's fierce rage;
  And hotly did His anger burn
   Against His heritage.

47 63 The fire consumed their choice young
   Their maids no marriage had; [men;
  64 And when their priests fell by the
    sword,
   Their wives no mourning made.

48 65 The Lord then woke, as one from
    sleep,
   Strong one whom wine doth cheer;
  66 He smote His en'mies' backs, and gave
   Them endless shame and fear.

49 67 And He rejected Joseph's tent,
   Ephr'im was not approved;
  68 But He selected Judah's tribe,
   The Zion mount He loved.

50 69 His Holy place He built like heights,
   Like earth to stand for aye;
  70 And He His servant David chose,
   From sheep folds took away.

51 71 From following the ewes with young,
   He brought him forth to feed
  Isr'el, His own inheritance,
   His people, Jacob's seed.

52 72 And so in His integrity
   Of heart He did them feed;
  And by His skilfulness of hand
   He did them safely lead.

Psalm LXXIX. C. M.

1 O GOD, into Thy heritage
   The nations entrance made ;
Thy Holy temple they defiled,
   On heaps Jerus'lem laid.

2 2 Thy servants' bodies they have thrown
   To fowls of heaven for meat ;
And Thy saints' flesh they have cast
   To beasts of earth to eat.   [out

3 3 All round about Jerusalem
   Like water they have shed
Their blood ; and there was none to
   Them burial when dead.   [give

4 4 Thus to our neighbors a reproach
   Most base become are we ;
A scorn and laughing-stock to them
   That round about us be.

5 5 How long, Jehovah ? evermore
   Wilt Thou still keep Thine ire ?
And shall Thy fervent jealousy
   Forever burn like fire ?

6 6 Thy wrath upon the nations pour,
   That have Thee never known,
And on those kingdoms which Thy
   Have never called upon.   [Name

7 7 For these are they who have devoured
   Thy servant Jacob's race ;
And they all waste and desolate
   Have made his dwelling place.

8 8 Against us count not former sins ;
   Thy tender mercies show,
Let them relieve us speedily ;
   For we 're brought very low.

9 9 For Thy Name's glory help, O God,
   Who hast our Saviour been;
 Yea, free us, and for Thy Name's sake,
   O cover Thou our sin.

10 10 Why say the nations, Where's their
   'Mong nations in our sight [God?
 Make known, for Thy saints' blood
     poured out,
   Thine own avenging might.

11 11 Before Thy presence, O do Thou
   Let come the pris'ner's sigh;
 In greatness of Thy power preserve
   Those that are doomed to die.

12 12 And to our neighbors' bosom let
   Be seven-fold repaid,
 The same reviling which, O Lord,
   They have upon Thee laid.

13 13 So we, Thy folk, and pasture-sheep,
   Shall give Thee thanks always;
 And unto generations all
   We will show forth Thy praise.

Psalm LXXX. C. M.

1 HEAR, Isr'el's Shepherd, like a flock
   Thou that dost Joseph guide;
 Shine forth, O Thou that dost above
   The cherubim abide.

2 2 In Ephraim's, and Benjamin's,
   And in Manasseh's sight,
 Come Thou, for our salvation come;
   Stir up Thy strength and might.

3 3 O God, in Thine abundant grace
   Restore us unto Thee;

O cause Thy face to shine on us,
And saved we then shall be.

4 4 O Thou, Jehovah, God of Hosts,
How long shall kindled be
Thy wrath against the earnest prayer
Thy people make to Thee ?

5 5 Thou tears of sorrow givest them
Instead of bread to eat ;
Thou givest tears instead of drink
To them in measure great.

6 6 Thou makest us to neighbors all
A strife on every side ;
Our enemies among themselves
With laughter us deride.

7 7 O God of hosts, in Thine own grace
Restore us unto Thee ;
O cause Thy face to shine on us,
And saved we then shall be.

8 8 A vine from Egypt Thou hast brought
By Thine almighty hand ;
And Thou didst cast the nations out
To plant it in their land.

9 9 Before it Thou a place didst make,
And give it room to stand ;
Thou causedst it deep root to take,
And it did fill the land.

10 10 It covered hills with shade, its boughs
The goodly cedars hide ;
11 It sent its branches to the sea,
Its shoots to river's side.

11 12 Why hast Thou broken down its
So passers pluck at will ?   [hedge,

13 The boar out of the wood it wastes,
 The field beasts eat their fill.

12 14 O God of hosts, we Thee beseech,
 Return now unto Thine ;
 Look down from heaven in love ; be-
 And visit this Thy vine ; [hold,

13 15 This vine-tree, which Thine own right
 Hath planted us among ; [hand
 And that same branch, which for Thy-
  self
 Thou hast made to be strong.

14 16 Burnt up it is with flaming fire,
 It also is cut down ;
 And perished utterly are they
 Because Thy face doth frown.

15 17 O let Thy hand be still upon
 The man of Thy right hand,
 The Son of man, whom for Thyself
 Thou hast made strong to stand.

16 18 So henceforth we will not go back,
 Nor turn from Thee at all ;
 O do Thou quicken us, and we
 Upon Thy name will call.

17 19 Jehovah, God of hosts, in grace
 Restore us unto Thee ;
 O cause Thy face to shine on us,
 And saved we then shall be.

Psalm LXXXI. C. M.

1 SING loud to God our strength ; with
  To Jacob's God shout ye. [joy
 2 Take up a psalm, the timbrel bring,
 Sweet harp and psaltery.

2 3 Blow trumpet at new moon, full moon,
On our solemnities ;
4 For charge to Isr'el, and a law
Of Jacob's God was this.

3 5 In Joseph this an ordinance
He made, when Egypt land
He travelled through, where speech I
I did not understand. [heard

4 6 His shoulder I from burdens took,
His hands from pots did free.
7 Thou didst in trouble on Me call,
And I delivered thee ;

5 In secret place of thunder I
To thee did answer make ;
And at the streams of Meribah
Of thee a proof did take.

6 8 O thou, My people, give an ear,
I 'll testify to thee ;
To thee, O Isr'el, if thou wilt
But hearken unto Me.

7 9 In midst of thee there shall not be
Any strange god at all ;
Nor unto any god unknown
Thou bowing down shalt fall.

8 10 I am thy God, Jehovah, who
From Egypt did thee guide ;
I 'll fill thy mouth abundantly,
Do thou it open wide.

9 11 My people would not hear My voice,
Isr'el My presence spurned ;
12 So I them left to their hard heart,
To their own ways they turned.

10 13 O that My people would Me hear,
    Isr'el My ways would choose!
  14 I would their en'mies soon subdue,
    My hand turn on their foes.

11 15 Jehovah's haters unto Him
    Submission then should feign;
  But as for them, their time should still
    For evermore remain.

12 16 He also should them ever feed
    With finest of the wheat;
  Of honey from the rock, thy fill
    I still should make thee eat.

Psalm LXXXII. C. M.

1   GOD stands in council of the great
    'Mong gods the Judge is He;
  2 How long for persons vile, will ye
    The unjust judges be?

2 3 Defend the weak and fatherless;
    To poor oppressed do right.
  4 The weak and needy ones set free;
    Save them from ill men's might.

3 5 They know not, nor will understand;
    In darkness they walk on;
  All the foundations of the earth
    Out of their course are gone.

4 6 I said that ye are gods, and are
    Sons of the Highest all;
  7 But ye shall die like men, and as
    One of the princes fall.

5 8 O God, do Thou raise up Thyself,
       The earth to judgment call ;
    For Thou, as Thine inheritance,
       Shalt take the nations all.

Psalm LXXXII. L. M.

1 GOD stands in council of the great ;
       Among the gods the Judge is He;
   2 How long will ye unjustly judge?
       The face of wicked persons see?

2 3 Judge for the fatherless and weak ;
       To sufferers and poor do right ;
   4 Deliver weak and needy ones,
       And save them from the wicked's might.

3 5 They know not, will not learn, will walk
       In darkness, tho' earth's pillars shake.
   6 I did exalt you, called you gods,
       Sons of the Highest did you make ;

4 7 But ye shall die like other men,
       Like any princes ye shall fall.
   8 Arise, O God, and judge the earth ;
       For Thou shalt take the nations all.

Psalm LXXXIII. C. M.

1 O GOD, not silent be, nor mute;
       Rest not, O God, we said ;
   2 For, lo, Thy foes a tumult make,
       Thy haters lift the head.

2 3 They 'gainst Thy people, hidden ones,
       With crafty counsel plot ;
   4 They said, Come, we 'll their nation raze,
       Be Isr'el's name forgot.   [raze,

3 5 For they with one consent conspire,
   In league 'gainst Thee combine.
  6 The tents of Edom, Ishmaelites;
   Moab and Hagar's line.

4 7 Gebal, and Ammon, Amalek,
   Philistines, those of Tyre;
  8 And Assur joined with them; to help
   Lot's children they conspire.

5 9 To them do as to Midian;
   Jabin at Kison strand;
  10 And Sis'ra who at Endor fell;
   They fertilize the land.

6 11 Like Oreb, and like Zeeb, make
   Their noble men to fall;
   To Zeba, and Zalmunna like
   Make Thou their princes all.

7 12 Who said, For our inheritance
   Let us God's dwellings take.
  13 Like dust or chaff whirled by the blast,
   My God, do Thou them make.

8 14 As fire the forest burns, as flame
   The mountains sets on fire,
  15 Chase and affright them with the
   And tempest of Thine ire.   [storm

9 16 Jehovah, fill with shame their face,
   That they may seek Thy Name.
  17 They shall confounded be, and vexed,
   And perish in their shame;

10 18 That men may know that Thou, to
   Alone doth appertain   [whom
   The name Jehovah, dost Most High
   O'er all the earth remain.

Psalm LXXXIV. C. M.

1 HOW lovely is Thy dwelling-place
  O Lord of hosts, to me !
  The tabernacles of Thy grace
  How pleasant, Lord, they be !

2 2 My thirsty soul longs veh'mently,
  Yea faints, Thy courts to see :
  My very heart and flesh cry out,
  O living God, for Thee.

3 3 Behold, the sparrow findeth out
  A house wherein to rest ;
  The swallow also for herself
  Hath purchasèd a nest ;

4 Even Thine own altars, where she safe
  Her young ones forth may bring,
  O Thou almighty LORD of hosts,
  Who art my God and King.

5 4 Blessed are they in Thy house that
  They ever give Thee praise. [dwell;
  5 Blessed is the man whose strength
  Thou art,
  In whose heart are Thy ways.

6 6 Who, passing through the vale of tears,
  Make it a place of springs ;
  Also the rain that falleth down
  Rich blessing to it brings.

7 7 So they from strength unwearied go
  Still forward unto strength,
  Until in Zion they appear
  Before God's face at length.

8 8 LORD, God of hosts, O hear my
  O Jacob's God, give ear ;   [prayer ;

    9 See, God, our Shield, look on the face
        Of Thine Anointed dear.

9   10 For in Thy courts one day excels
        A thousand; rather in
     My God's house will I keep a door,
        Than dwell in tents of sin.

10 11 For God the LORD 's a sun and
        Jehovah grace will give   [shield;
     And glory; good will not withhold
        From them who rightly live.

11 12 O Thou that art the LORD of hosts,
        That man is truly blest,
     Who, by a confidence assured,
        On Thee alone doth rest.

Psalm LXXXIV. 7s & 6s.

1   O LORD of hosts, most glorious,
        How lovely are Thy tents!
     2 Jehovah's courts to enter,
        My soul with longing faints.

2   My heart and flesh still crying
        For Thee, O Living God,
     3 The sparrow found a dwelling,
        The swallow her abode,

3   Wherein are safely sheltered
        The young she forth may bring;
     Thine altars, LORD of armies,
        Who art my God and King.

4   4 Blest who Thy house inhabit,
        They ever give Thee praise;
     5 Blest man whom Thou dost strengthen,
        In whose heart are Thy ways.

5   6 The vale of tears while passing
      They make a place of springs;
      And there the rain descending
      Rich blessing to it brings.

6   7 So they from strength unwearied
      Go forward unto strength,
      Till they appear in Zion
      Before God's face at length.

7   8 Hear me, LORD God of armies;
      O Jacob's God, give ear;
    9 Thy Christ's own face beholding,
      See, God, our Shield, be near.

8 10 One day excels a thousand,
      If spent Thy courts within;
      I 'll choose God's threshold rather
      Than dwell in tents of sin.

9 11 The LORD God 's Sun, Protector,
      The LORD will glory give
      And grace; nor good deny them
      That uprightly do live.

10 12 O Thou, the LORD of armies,
      How blest is every one
      Who confidently places
      His trust in Thee alone!

Psalm LXXXV. C. M.

1 JEHOVAH, Thou hast favor shown
      To Thy belovèd land;
      And Jacob's captive state Thou hast
      Recalled with mighty hand.

2   2 Thou to Thy people all their sins
      Most freely pardoned hast;

And over all their trespasses
  Thou hast a cov'ring cast.

3 3 Thou all Thine anger hast removed;
    From wrath hast turned to peace;
  4 O God, our Saviour, turn Thou us,
    And make Thy wrath to cease.

4 5 Shall Thy displeasure thus endure
    Against us without end?
  Wilt Thou to generations all
    Thine anger forth extend?

5 6 That in Thee may Thy people joy,
    Wilt Thou not us revive?
  7 Jehovah, us Thy mercy show,
    And Thy salvation give.

6 8 I'll hear what God, Jehovah speaks;
    To His folk He'll speak peace,
  And to His saints; but let them not
    Return to foolishness.

7 9 For His salvation surely is
    Nigh them that do Him fear;
  That as a dweller in our land
    True glory may appear.

8 10 Truth meets with mercy, righteousness
    And peace kiss mutually;
  11 Truth springs from earth, and right-
    eousness
    Looks down from heaven high.

9 12 Yea, good Jehovah shall bestow;
    Our land shall yield increase;
  13 Justice, to set us in His steps,
    Shall go before His face.

Psalm LXXXV. L. P. M.

1 1 THOU, LORD, hast favor shown Thy land,
And brought back Jacob's captive band;
2 Thy people's sins Thou pardoned hast,
And all their guilt has covered o'er,
3 Thou hast removed Thine anger sore,
All Thy fierce wrath behind Thee cast.

2 4 Turn us, O God our Saviour, turn,
Nor longer let Thine anger burn.
5 Wilt Thou for ever angry be?
Through ages shall Thy wrath survive?
6 Wilt Thou not us again revive,
That so we may rejoice in Thee?

3 7 Jehovah, us Thy mercy show,
And Thy salvation now bestow;
8 I'll hear what God, the LORD, will say;
Peace to His people He will speak,
And to His saints, but let them seek
No more in folly's path to stray.

4 9 His saving help is surely near
To those His holy Name that fear;
Thus glory dwells in all our land.
10 Now heavenly truth unites with grace,
And righteousness and peace embrace;
In full accord they ever stand.

5 11 Truth, springing forth, the earth shall crown,
And righteousness from heaven look down.
12 Jehovah shall His goodness shed;

Our land shall then with plenty flow.
13 Before Him righteousness shall go,
 And cause us in His steps to tread.

Psalm LXXXVI. C. M.

1
O THOU, Jehovah, bow Thine ear,
 And hear me graciously;
Because I sore afflicted am,
 And am in poverty.

2
2 Because I'm holy, let my soul
 By Thee delivered be;
O Thou my God, Thy servant save
 That puts his trust in Thee.

3
3 Since unto Thee I daily cry,
 Be gracious, Lord, to me.
4 Rejoice Thy servant's soul; for, Lord,
 I lift my soul to Thee.

4
5 For Thou, O Lord, most gracious art,
 And ready to forgive;
And rich in mercy, all that call
 Upon Thee to relieve.

5
6 Jehovah, hear my prayer; the voice
 Of my requests attend;
7 In day of straits I'll call on Thee;
 For Thou wilt answer send.

6
8 Among the many gods, O Lord,
 Like Thee there is not one;
Nor are their works to be compared
 With works which Thou hast done.

7
9 All nations Thou hast made shall
 And worship rev'rently   [come
Before Thy face, O Lord; and they
 Thy name shall glorify.

8 10 Because Thou art exceeding great,
    And works by Thee are done
Which are to be admired ; and Thou
    Art God Thyself alone.

9 11 Jehovah, teach to me Thy way ;
    In Thy truth walk will I ;
Unite my heart, that I Thy Name
    May fear continually.

10 12 O Lord my God, with all my heart
    I will Thy praise proclaim ;
I also glory will ascribe
    Forever to Thy name ;

11 13 Because Thy mercy unto me
    In greatness doth excel ;
And Thou delivered hast my soul
    Out from the lowest hell.

12 14 O God, the proud against me rise ;
    The violent have met,
That for my soul have sought ; and
    Before them have not set.   [Thee

13 15 But Thou, Lord, art a God of grace,
    In whom compassions flow ;
Thy mercy and Thy truth abound,
    Thou art to anger slow.

14 16 O turn to me Thy countenance,
    And mercy on me have ;
Thy servant strengthen, and the son
    Of Thine own handmaid save.

15 17 Show me a sign for good, which they
    Who do me hate may see,
And be ashamed ; for Thou, O LORD,
    Didst help and comfort me.

Psalm LXXXVI. S. M.

1 1 JEHOVAH, give Thine ear;
　　I 'm poor oppressed, hear me;
　2 Keep me, I 'm holy; my God, save
　　Thy servant trusting Thee.

2 3 Be gracious, Lord, to me,
　　All day to Thee I cry;
　4 Give joy unto Thy servant, Lord,
　　My soul to Thee comes nigh.

3 5 For Thou, O Lord, art good
　　And ready to forgive;
　　Art rich in mercy all that call
　　Upon Thee to relieve.

4 6 Jehovah, hear my prayer,
　　My pleading voice attend;
　7 When in distress I 'll call on Thee,
　　For Thou wilt answer send.

5 8 'Mong gods none is like Thee,
　　O Lord, nor works like Thine;
　9 All nations Thou hast made shall bow,
　　Jehovah, at Thy shrine;

6　　They honor will Thy Name;
　10　For Thou 'rt the Greatest One,
　　Who doest things most wonderful;
　　Thyself art God alone.

7 11 Teach me Thy way, O LORD,
　　I 'll walk in Thy truth's way;
　　Unite my heart that rev'rently
　　Thy Name regard I may.

8 12 O Lord my God, Thee praise
　　With all my heart will I;
　　And evermore Thy Holy Name
　　I 'll seek to glorify.

9 13 Because Thy grace to me
    In greatness doth excel,
  And Thou my soul delivered hast
    Out from the lowest hell.

10 14 O God, the proud 'gainst me
    Rose up ; in council met,
  Oppressors sought my soul, and Thee
    Before them have not set.

11 15 But Thou, Lord, art a God
    Compassionate, most good,
  Long suffering. of richest grace,
    Thy truth has ever stood.

12 16 O turn to me Thy face,
    Have mercy me upon ;
  Strength unto me, Thy servant give,
    O save Thy handmaid's son.

13 17 Good token to me show ;
    My haters then shall see
  With shame that Thou, Jehovah, still
    Dost help and comfort me.

Psalm LXXXVII. C. M.

1 UPON the hills of holiness
    He His foundation sets,
  2 Jehovah 'bove all Jacob's tents
    Delights in Zion's gates.

2 3 Things glorious are said of thee,
    Thou city of our God.
  4 Rahab and Babel, knowing Me,
    I will proclaim abroad ;

3   Behold Philistia, and with it
    Land of the Tyrian,

        And likewise Ethiopia ;
          This man was born therein.

4 5 Of Zion shall be said, This man
        And that man born was there ;
      And He that is Himself Most High,
        Shall surely stablish her.

5 6 Jehovah, when He peoples writes,
          Will count : This born was there.
    7 The singers, as the players, say,
        My well-springs in thee are.

Psalm LXXXVIII. C. M.

1 JEHOVAH, Saviour-God, to Thee,
        Both day and night cried I.
    2 My prayer let to Thy presence come ;
        Give ear unto my cry ;

2 3 For troubles great do fill my soul ;
        My life draws nigh the grave.
    4 I 'm counted with those that go down
        To death, and no strength have.

3 5 Set free among the dead, like slain
        That in the grave do lie ;
    Cut off from Thy hand, whom no
        Thou hast in memory.   [more

4 6 Thou hast me laid in lowest pit,
        In deeps and darksome caves.
    7 Thy wrath lies hard on me, Thou hast
        Me pressed with all Thy waves.

5 8 Thou hast put far from me my friends,
        Made me their scorn to know ;
    And I am so shut up, that I
        No longer forth can go.

6 9 By reason of affliction sore,
   Mine eye doth waste away;
   Upon Jehovah I do call
   And stretch my hands each day.

7 10 Wilt Thou show wonders to the dead?
   Shall they rise, and Thee bless?
   11 Shall in the grave Thy love be told?
   In death Thy faithfulness?

8 12 Shall Thy great wonders in the dark,
   Or shall Thy righteousness,
   Be known to any in the land
   Of deep forgetfulness?

9 13 But I to Thee, Jehovah, cried;
   At morn I'll pray to Thee.
   14 Jehovah, why cast off my soul?
   Why hide Thy face from me?

10 15 Distressed am I, and from my youth
   I ready am to die;
   Thy terrors I have borne, and am
   Distracted fearfully.

11 16 By Thy fierce wrath I'm overwhelmed,
   Cut off by dread of Thee;
   17 Like floods Thy terrors round me close,
   All day they compass me.

12 18 My friends Thou hast put far from me,
   And him that did me love;
   And those that mine acquaintance
   To darkness didst remove.   [were

Psalm LXXXIX. C. M.

1 JEHOVAH'S mercies ever sing
   Will I; with mouth I shall
   Thy faithfulness make to be known
   To generations all.

2 2 For mercy shall be built, said I,
      For ever to endure;
   Thy faithfulness, even in the heavens
      Thou wilt establish sure.

3 3 I with my chosen one have made
      A cov'nant graciously;
   And to my servant, whom I loved,
      To David sworn have I;

4 4 That I thy seed establish shall
      For ever to remain;
   And will to generations all
      Thy throne build and maintain.

5 5 Jehovah, of Thy wonders all
      The heavens shall praise express;
   The congregation of Thy saints
      Shall praise Thy faithfulness.

6 6 For with Jehovah in the heavens
      Who can at all compare?
   Who like Jehovah is 'mong sons
      Of those that mighty are?

7 7 In council of the saints a God
      Most terrible is He;
   And more than all that round Him are
      He ever feared should be.

8 8 Jehovah, God of hosts, who is
      A mighty LORD like Thee?
   9 Truth girds Thee; stilling all her
      Thou rulest the proud sea. [waves,

9 10 In pieces Thou didst Rahab break,
      Like one that slaughtered is;
   And with Thy mighty arm Thou hast
      Dispersed Thine enemies.

10 11 The heavens are Thine, Thou for
    Thine own
    The earth dost also take ;
    The world, and fulness of the same,
    Thy power did found, and make.

11 12 The north and south from Thee alone
    Their first beginning had ;
    Both Tabor mount and Hermon hill
    Shall in Thy name be glad.

12 13 Thou hast an arm that's full of power;
    Thy hand is great in might,
    And Thy right hand exceedingly
    Exalted is in height.

13 14 Justice and judgment of Thy throne
    Are made the dwelling-place ;
    Yea, mercy in accord with truth,
    Shall go before Thy face.

14 15 O greatly blessed the people are
    The joyful sound that know ;
    In light, Jehovah, of Thy face,
    They ever on shall go.

15 16 They in Thy name shall all the day
    Rejoice exceedingly ;
    And in Thy righteousness shall they
    Exalted be on high.

16 17 Because the glory of their strength
    Doth only stand in Thee ;
    And in Thy favor shall our horn
    And power exalted be.

17 18 Because our covering shield belongs
    Unto the LORD alone ;
    And He who is our King belongs
    To Isr'el's Holy One.

18 19 In vision then Thou to Thy saints
　　Didst speak, I'll help impose
　On one that's mighty, whom I raised,
　　And from the people chose.

19 20 Even David, I have found him out
　　A servant unto Me,
　And with My holy oil My King
　　Anointed him to be;

20 21 With whom My hand established is;
　　Mine arm shall make him strong.
　22 On him the foe shall not exact,
　　Nor son of mischief wrong.

21 23 I will beat down before his face
　　All his malicious foes;
　I will them greatly plague, who do
　　With hatred him oppose.

22 24 My mercy and My faithfulness
　　With him yet still shall be;
　And in My name his horn and power
　　Men shall exalted see.

23 25 His hand and power shall reach afar,
　　I'll set it in the sea;
　And his right hand established shall
　　Upon the rivers be.

24 26 Thou art my Father and my God
　　He unto Me shall cry;
　Thou also art the Rock on which
　　For safety I rely.

25 27 I'll make him My first born, supreme
　　O'er kings of every land,
　28 My love I'll ever keep for him,
　　My cov'nant fast shall stand.

26 29 His seed I by My power will make
    For ever to endure ;
    And, as the days of heaven, his throne
    Shall stable be and sure.

27 30 But if his children shall forsake
    My law and go astray,
    And in My judgments shall not walk,
    But wander from My way ;

28 31 If they My statutes break, and My
    Commands do not obey ;
  32 I 'll visit then their sins with rods,
    Their guilt with stripes repay ;

29 33 Yet I 'll not take My love from him,
    Nor false My promise make ;
  34 My cov'nant I 'll not break, nor change
    What with My mouth I spake.

30 35 Once by My holiness I sware,
    To David I 'll not lie ;
  36 His seed and throne shall, as the sun,
    Before Me last for aye.

31 37 It like the moon shall ever be,
    Established steadfastly ;
    And like to that which in the heaven
    Doth witness faithfully.

32 38 Yet Thou hast cast off and abhorred ;
    Art wroth with Christ, Thine own ;
  39 Thy servant's cov'nant hast made void,
    To earth profaned his crown.

33 40 Thou all his hedges broken hast,
    His strongholds down hast torn ;
  41 He to all passers-by a spoil,
    To neighbors is a scorn.

34 42 Thou hast set up his foes' right hand;
  Made all his en'mies glad;
  43 Turned his sword's edge, and him to
  In battle hast not made. [stand

35 44 His glory Thou hast made to cease,
  His throne to ground down cast;
  45 Shortened his days of youth, and him
  With shame Thou covered hast.

36 46 How long, Jehovah, wilt Thou hide?
  For ever, in Thine ire?
  And shall Thine indignation hot
  Burn like a flaming fire?

37 47 Remember, Thou, how short a time
  I shall on earth remain;
  O wherefore is it so that Thou
  Hast made all men in vain?

38 48 What man is he that liveth here,
  And death shall never see?
  Or from the power of the grave
  What man his soul shall free?

39 49 Thy former loving-kindnesses,
  O Lord, where be they now?
  Those which in truth and faithfulness
  To David sworn hast Thou?

40 50 Remember, Lord, Thy saint's re-
  What I in heart have borne [proach,
  51 From mighty peoples all; Thy foes,
  Jehovah, who Thee scorn;

41 Yea, how the footsteps of Thy Christ
  Reproached by them have been.
  52 Blessed be Jehovah evermore;
  Amen, yea, and amen.

Psalm XC. C. M.

1 THOU, Lord, hast been our dwelling-
 In generations all. [place
2 Before Thou ever hadst brought forth
 The mountains great or small;

2 Ere ever Thou hadst formed the earth
 And all the world abroad;
 Even Thou from everlasting art
 To everlasting God.

3 3 And yet Thou to destruction dost
 Man that is mortal turn;
 Thou unto them dost say, Again,
 Ye sons of men return.

4 4 Because a thousand years appear
 No more before Thy sight
 Than yesterday, when it is past,
 Or than a watch by night.

5 5 As with an overflowing flood
 Thou sweepest them away;
 They like a sleep are, like the grass
 That grows at morn are they.

6 6 At morn it flourishes and grows,
 Cut down at eve doth fade.
 7 For by Thine anger we 're consumed,
 Thy wrath makes us afraid.

7 8 All our iniquities Thou dost
 Before Thy presence place,
 And set our secret faults before
 The brightness of Thy face.

8 9 For in Thine anger all our days
 Do pass on to an end;
 And as a tale that hath been told,
 So we our years do spend.

9 10 Threescore and ten years do sum up
   Our days and years, we see;
   Or if, by reason of more strength,
   In some fourscore they be;

10 Yet doth the strength of such old men
   But grief and labor prove;
   For it is soon cut off, and we
   Fly hence, and soon remove.

11 11 Who knows Thine anger's power, and
   Thy fear before his eyes?   [keeps
   12 So teach Thou us to count our days
   That our hearts may be wise.

12 13 Return, Jehovah, unto us;
   How long thus shall it be?
   Let it repent Thee now for those
   That servants are to Thee.

13 14 O with Thy tender mercies, do
   Us early satisfy;
   So we rejoice shall all our days,
   And still be glad in Thee.

14 15 According as the days have been
   Wherein we grief have had,
   And years wherein we ill have seen,
   So do Thou make us glad.

15 16 O let Thy work and power appear
   Thy servants' face before;
   And unto their dear children show
   Thy glory evermore.

16 17 And let the beauty of the LORD
   Our God be us upon;
   Our handy works establish Thou,
   Establish them each one.

Psalm XC. 7s.

1 1 LORD, our dwelling Thou hast been,
In all ages men have seen.
2 Ere the mountains had their birth,
Ere Thou mad'st the worlds or earth,
Thou from dateless ages gone
Art forever God alone.

2 3 Soon Thou turnest man to dust;
Say'st to all, Return ye must.
4 For a thousand years to Thee,
Yesterday, a night-watch be.
5 Men, as floods, Thou sweep'st away;
Like a sleep, like grass, are they.

3 6 In the morn they grow and bloom,
Mown at eve they fade in gloom;
7 For Thine anger us devours,
Thy wrath gives us fearful hours;
8 All our guilt to Thee is known,
Secret sins Thy light has shown.

4 9 In Thy wrath our days we spend;
Like a tale our years soon end.
10 Life is threescore years and ten,
Fourscore years the strong may gain;
Yet their strength gives toil and sighs,
Soon is gone, O quickly flies!

5 11 Who knows all Thine anger's power?
Duly fears thy wrathful hour?
12 So teach us to count our days,
We 'll our hearts to wisdom raise.
13 Turn, Jehovah, why delay?
Now repent, Thy servants pray.

6 14 Satisfy us every morn
With Thy mercy to us borne;

So we shall exultant be
All our days made glad in Thee.
15 Give glad days, as Thou hast grieved,
Long as years we ill received.

7 16 To Thy servants Thy works show;
Make their sons Thy glory know.
17 Let Jehovah's beauty be,
Our own God's, on us from Thee;
Stay our hands' work on us now,
Our hands' work establish Thou.

Psalm XCI. C. M.

1 HE that doth in the secret place
    Of the Most High reside,
Beneath the shade of Him that is
    Almighty shall abide.

2 2 I of Jehovah now will say,
    He is my refuge still;
He is my fortress, and my God,
    In whom confide I will.

3 3 Assuredly He shall thee save,
    And give deliverance
Both from the fowler's snare and from
    The noisome pestilence.

4 4 His feathers shall thee hide; thy trust
    Beneath His wings shall be;
His faithfulness shall be a shield
    And buckler unto thee.

5 5 Thou shalt not need to be afraid
    For terrors of the night;
Nor for the arrow that doth fly
    By day while it is light.

PSALM XCI.

6 6 Nor for the pestilence that walks
In darkness secretly;
Nor for destruction that doth waste
At noon-day openly.

7 7 A thousand at thy side shall fall,
On thy right hand shall lie
Ten thousand dead; yet unto thee
It shall not once come nigh.

8 8 Thou with thine eyes shalt only look,
And a beholder be;
And thou the merited reward
Of wicked men shalt see.

9 9 For Thou, Jehovah, art alone
A refuge unto me.
Thou hast Him made, who is Most
Thy dwelling place to be. [High,

10 10 No plague shall near thy dwelling
No ill shall thee befall; [come;
11 For thee to keep in all thy ways
His angels charge He shall.

11 12 They in their hands shall bear thee up,
Still waiting thee upon;
Lest thou at any time shouldst dash
Thy foot against a stone.

12 13 Upon the adder thou shalt tread,
And on the lion strong;
Thy feet the dragon trample shall,
And on the lion young.

13 14 Because on Me he set his love,
Deliver him will I;
Because My great name he hath known
I will him set on high.

14 15 He 'll call on Me, I 'll answer him ;
I will be with him still
In trouble, to deliver him,
And honor him I will.

15 16 With length of days unto his mind
I will him satisfy ;
Moreover, My salvation I
Will cause his eyes to see.

Psalm XCII. C. M.

1 1 TO thank Jehovah every day
Is a becoming thing ;
And to Thy Name, O Thou Most High,
Due praise aloud to sing ;

2 2 Thy loving-kindness to show forth
When shines the morning light ;
And to declare Thy faithfulness
With pleasure every night,

3 3 Upon the ten-stringed instrument,
And on the psaltery,
Upon the harp with solemn sound
And grave sweet melody.

4 4 For Thou, Jehovah, by Thy works,
Hast gladness to me brought ;
And I will triumph in the works
Which by Thy hands are wrought.

5 5 How great, Jehovah, are Thy works,
A deep Thine every thought.
6 A brutish person doth not know,
Fools understand it not.

6 7 When quickly, like the growing grass,
Springs up the wicked race,
And workers of iniquity
Do flourish all apace ;

7   Yet surely they for evermore
       Shall be destroyed and slain.
    8 But Thou, Jehovah, art Most High
       For ever to remain.

8   9 For lo, Thy foes, Jehovah, lo,
       Thine en'mies perish shall ;
    The workers of iniquity
       Shall soon be scattered all.

9   10 But like the unicorn's, my horn
       Exalted is by Thee ;
    Anointed also with fresh oil
       I am abundantly.

10 11 Mine eye shall also my desire
       See on mine enemies ;
    Mine ears shall of the wicked hear,
       That do against me rise.

11 12 But like the palm-tree flourishing
       Shall be the righteous one ;
    He shall like to the cedar grow
       That is in Lebanon.

12 13 Those that within Jehovah's house
       Are planted by His grace,
    Shall flourish all within the courts
       Of our God's holy place.

13 14 And in old age, when others fade,
       They fruit still forth shall bring ;
    They shall be fat and full of sap,
       And ever flourishing ;

14 15 To snow Jehovah upright is,
       He is a Rock to me ;
    And He from all unrighteousness
       Is altogether free.

Psalm XCIII. C. M.

1 JEHOVAH reigns; enrobed is He
      With majesty most bright;
   Jehovah is enrobed, Himself
      He girded hath with might.

2 Established also is the world,
      That it cannot depart.
   2 Thy throne is fixed of old, and Thou
      From everlasting art.

3 3 The floods, Jehovah, lifted up,
      They lifted up their voice;
   The floods have lifted up their waves,
      And made a mighty noise.

4 4 Than noise of many waters is,
      Or great sea-billows are,
   Jehovah in His place on high
      Is mightier by far.

5 5 Thy testimonies every one
      In faithfulness excel;
   And holiness for ever, LORD,
      Thy house becometh well.

Psalm XCIII. S. M.

1 JEHOVAH reigns; He 's clothed
      With majesty most bright;
   Jehovah is enrobed, and girds
      Himself about with might.

2 The world is firmly fixed,
      That it cannot depart.
   2 Thy throne is fixed of old, and Thou
      From everlasting art.

3   3 O LORD, the floods lift up,
       The floods lift up their voice,
     The floods have lifted up their waves
       And made a mighty noise.

4   4 But yet the LORD on high
       Is mightier by far
     Than noise of many waters is,
       Or great sea-billows are.

5   5 Thy testimonies all
       In faithfulness excel ;
     And holiness for ever, LORD,
       Thy house becometh well.

Psalm XCIV. C. M.

1   JEHOVAH, God to whom alone
      All vengeance doth belong ;
    Thou, who the God of vengeance art,
      Shine forth, avenging wrong.

2   2 Lift up Thyself, Thou of the earth
      The Judge supreme that art ;
    And unto those that haughty are
      A recompense impart.

3   3 How long, Jehovah, shall the men
      Who evil-doers be,
    How long shall they who wicked are
      Thus triumph haughtily ?

4   4 How long shall grievous things by
      Still uttered be and told ?   [them
    And all that work iniquity
      To boast themselves be bold ?

5   5 Jehovah, they Thy people smite,
      Thy heritage oppress ;
    6 The widow and the stranger slay,
      And kill the fatherless ;

PSALM XCIV.

6 7 They say: Jehovah doth not see,
   Nor God of Jacob know.
 8 Ye brutish people! understand;
   Fools! when wise will ye grow?

7 9 He is the planter of the ear,
   And hear then shall not He?
   He is the former of the eye,
   And shall He then not see?

8 10 He who the nations doth correct,
   Shall He reproof not show?
   He that doth knowledge teach to man,
   Shall He Himself not know?

9 11 Man's thoughts to be but vanity
   Jehovah doth discern.
 12 Blessed is the man Thou chast'nest, LORD,
   And mak'st Thy law to learn.

10 13 That Thou mayst give him rest from [days
   Of sad adversity,
   Until the pit be digged for those
   That work iniquity.

11 14 Because the LORD will not cast off
   Those that His people be,
   Nor yet His own inheritance
   Forsake at all will He.

12 15 But judgment unto righteousness
   Shall yet return again;
   And all shall follow after it
   That are right-hearted men.

13 16 Who will rise up for me against
   Those that do wickedly?
   Who will stand up for me 'gainst those
   That work iniquity.

14 17 Had not Jehovah helped, my soul
  In silence had remained.
  18 When I said, My foot slips, Thy love,
  Jehovah, me sustained.

15 19 Amidst the multitude of thoughts
  Which in my heart do fight,
  Thy consolations manifold
  Afford my soul delight.

16 20 Shall of iniquity the throne
  Have fellowship with Thee,
  Which mischief, cunningly contrived,
  Doth by a law decree?

17 21 Against the righteous souls they join,
  They guiltless blood condemn.
  22 Jehovah is my tower, my God,
  My refuge-rock from them.

18 23 On them their own iniquity
  He causeth back to fall;
  In their sin cuts them off; our God,
  Jehovah, slay them shall.

Psalm XCV. C. M.

1 COME, let us to Jehovah now
  In songs our voices raise;
  With joyful shout let us the rock
  Of our salvation praise.

2 2 Let us before His presence come
  With praise and thankful voice;
  Let us sing psalms to Him with grace,
  And make a joyful noise.

3 3 A great God is the LORD; great King
  Above all gods He is.
  4 Depths of the earth are in His hand,
  The strength of hills is His.

4 5 To Him the spacious sea belongs,
  For He the same did make;
 The dry land also from His hands
  Its form at first did take.

5 6 O come and let us worship Him,
  Let us bow down withal,
 Before Jehovah on our knees,
  Before our Maker fall.

6 7 For He's our God, the people we
  Of His own pasture are,
 And of His hand the sheep; to-day,
  If ye His voice will hear;

7 8 O give not, as at Meribah,
  Your hearts to stubbornness,
 Even as it was in Massah's day
  Within the wilderness.

8 9 When Me your fathers tempted,
  And did My working see. [proved,
 10 Even for the space of forty years
  This race hath grievèd Me.

9 I said, This people errs in heart,
  My ways they do not know;
 11 So in My wrath I sware that they
  To My rest should not go.

Psalm XCVI. C. M.

1 A NEW song to Jehovah sing,
  The LORD praise, all the earth.
 2 The LORD praise, bless His Name;
  each day
  His saving power show forth.

2 3 Among the nations of the earth
  His glory do declare;

  And unto all the peoples show
  His works that wondrous are.

3   4 For great Jehovah is, and He
  Is to be magnified ;
  Yea, worthy to be feared is He
  Above all gods beside.

4   5 For all the gods are idols dumb
  Which blinded nations fear ;
  But by Jehovah's mighty hands
  The heavens created were.

5   6 Great honor is before His face,
  And majesty divine ;
  Strength is within His holy place,
  And there doth beauty shine.

6   7 O do ye to Jehovah give,
  Of people every tribe,
  Yea, to Jehovah majesty
  And mighty power ascribe.

7   8 The glory to Jehovah give
  That to His name is due ;
  Come ye into His courts, and bring
  An offering with you.

8   9 In beauty of His holiness
  Jehovah now adore ;
  Likewise let all the earth bow down
  With awe His face before.

9   10 'Mong nations say, Jehovah reigns ;
  The world shall steadfast be,
  So that it move not ; He shall judge
  The people righteously.

10 11 O let the heavens exultant be,
    And let the earth rejoice ;
    Let seas and all their fulness roar,
    And make a mighty noise.

11 12 Let fields rejoice, and everything
    That springeth of the earth ;
    Then of the forest all the trees
    Shall shout aloud with mirth—

12 13 Before Jehovah ; for He comes,
    To judge the earth comes He ;
    He 'll judge the world with righteous-
    The people faithfully.   [ness,

Psalm XCVII. C. M.

1   JEHOVAH reigns, let earth be glad,
      And isles rejoice each one.
    2 Dark clouds Him compass; and on right
      And judgment rests His throne.

2   3 Fire goes before Him, and His foes
      It burns up round about ;
    4 His lightnings lighten did the world ;
      Earth saw, and shook throughout.

3   5 Before the LORD, earth's Lord, like
      The mountains melted are ;   [wax
    6 Skies show His righteousness, all men
      Behold His glory there.

4   7 Ye, who carved image serve, and boast
      Of idols, blush with shame ;
      To Him in humble worship bow,
      Ye gods of every name.

5   8 Mount Zion heard and joyful was,
      Glad Judah's daughters were ;

Jehovah, glad were they, because,
Thy judgments did appear.

6   9 For Thou, Jehovah, art Most High
O'er all on earth that are ;
Above all other gods Thou art
Exalted very far.

7   10 Hate ill, ye who Jehovah love ;
His saints' souls keepeth He ;
And from the hands of wicked men
. He sets them safe and free.

8   11 For every one that righteous is
Sown is a joyful light,
And gladness sown is for all those
That are in heart upright.

9   12 Ye righteous in Jehovah joy ;
Your thankfulness express,
When into memory again
Ye call His holiness.

Psalm XCVIII. C. M.

1   A NEW song to Jehovah sing,
For wonders He hath done ;
His right hand and His holy arm
Him victory have won.

2   2 Jehovah His salvation hath
Made to be clearly known ;
His justice in the nations' sight
He openly hath shown.

3   3 He mindful of His grace and truth
To Isr'el's house hath been ;
The great salvation of our God
All ends of earth have seen.

4 4 O to Jehovah, all the earth,
      Send forth a joyful noise;
   Lift up your voice aloud to Him,
      Sing praises, and rejoice.

5 5 With harp, with harp, and voice ot
      Sing to Jehovah, sing;   [psalms
   6 With trumpets, cornets, gladly sound
      Before the LORD, the King.

6 7 Let seas and all their fulness roar;
      The world, and dwellers there;
   8 Let floods clap hands, and let the hills
      Together joy declare—

7 9 Before Jehovah; for He comes,
      To judge the earth comes He;
   He'll judge the world with righteous-
      The nations uprightly.   [ness,

Psalm XCVIII. 7s.

1 SING a new song to the LORD;
      Mighty wonders He hath done;
   His right hand and holy arm
      Him the victory have won.

2 2 Lo, Jehovah far and wide
      His salvation hath made known;
   To the nations of the earth
      He His righteousness hath shown.

3 3 Mindful unto Isr'el He
      Of His love and truth hath been;
   The salvation of our God
      All the ends of earth have seen.

4 4 To Jehovah shout aloud,
      Let the earth with gladness ring;

Break ye forth with mighty voice,
Break ye forth, rejoice and sing.

5 5 Praise Jehovah with the harp,
Harp and psalm together bring;
6 With the trump and cornet sound,
Shout ye to Jehovah, King.

6 7 Sea and all its fulness, roar;
Earth and dwellers, lift the voice;
8 Floods and rivers, clap your hands;
Hills, with one accord rejoice—

7 9 Now before Jehovah all;
For to judgment cometh He;
Justly He the earth will judge,
And the people uprightly.

Psalm XCIX. C. M.

1 JEHOVAH is enthroned as King,
Let all the nations quake;
He dwells between the cherubim,
Let earth be moved and shake.

2 2 In Zion is Jehovah great,
Above all people high;
3 Thy great, dread Name, which holy is,
O let them magnify.

3 4 The king's strength also judgment loves,
Thou settlest equity;
Just judgment Thou dost execute
In Jacob righteously.

4 5 Exalt Jehovah, our own God,
And rev'rently do ye
Before His footstool bow yourselves;
The Holy One is He.

5 6 Even Moses, Aaron, Samuel,
   His priests, with all who prayed ;
 These on Jehovah called, and He
   To them an answer made.

6 7 Within the pillar of the cloud
   He unto them did speak ;
 His testimonies they observed,
   His statute did not break.

7 8 O LORD our God, Thou wast a God
   Who didst them answer send ;
 And punishing their deeds, to them
   Thou pardon didst extend.

8 9 Exalt Jehovah, our own God,
   And at His holy hill
 Do ye Him worship ; for the LORD
   Our God is holy still.

Psalm C. C. M.

1 UNTO Jehovah, all ye lands,
   O make a joyful noise ;
 2 With joy Jehovah serve, before
   Him come with cheerful voice.

2 3 Know that the LORD is God indeed ;
   Not we, but He us made ;
 We are His people, and the sheep
   Within His pasture fed.

3 4 O enter then His gates with thanks,
   His courts with voice of praise ;
 Give thanks to Him with joyfulness,
   And bless His name always.

4 5 Because Jehovah is most good,
   His mercy never ends ;

  And unto generations all
   His faithfulness extends.

Psalm C. L. M.

1 ALL people that on earth do live,
  Jehovah praise with cheerful voice ;
2 Glad service to Jehovah give ;
  Come ye before Him and rejoice.

2 3 Know that Jehovah 's God indeed,
  Without our aid He did us make ;
  We are His flock, He doth us feed,
  And for His sheep He doth us take.

3 4 O enter then His gates with praise,
  His courts with songs of loud acclaim ;
  With grateful hearts your voices raise,
  To bless and magnify His name.

4 5 Because Jehovah is most good,
  His mercy is for ever sure ;
  His truth at all times firmly stood,
  And shall from age to age endure.

Psalm C. L. M.

1 ALL people that on earth do dwell,
  Sing to the LORD with cheerful voice.
2 Him serve with mirth, His praise forth tell,
  Come ye before Him and rejoice.

2 3 Know that the Lord is God indeed ;
  Without our aid He did us make ;
  We are His flock, He doth us feed,
  And for His sheep He doth us take.

3 4 O enter then His gates with praise,
Approach with joy His courts unto ;
Praise, laud, and bless His name
For it is seemly so to do.   [always,

4 5 Because the LORD our God is good,
His mercy is for ever sure ;
His truth at all times firmly stood,
And shall from age to age endure.

Psalm C.   8s.

1 ALL people that dwell on the earth,
Your songs to Jehovah now raise ;
2 O worship Jehovah with mirth,
Approach Him with anthems of praise.

2 3 Know ye that Jehovah is God,
We are His, our Maker is He ;
His people who bow to His rod,
And sheep of His pasture are we.

3 4 O enter His temple with praise,
His portals with thankful acclaim ;
Your voices in thanksgiving raise,
And bless ye His glorious name.

4 5 For ever Jehovah is good,
His mercy to us never ends ;
His faithfulness true to His word,
Through ages unending extends.

Psalm CI.   C. M.

1 I MERCY will and judgment sing,
LORD, I will sing to Thee ;
2 With wisdom in a perfect way
Shall my behavior be.

2   O when in kindness unto me
    Wilt Thou be pleased to come?
    I with a perfect heart will walk
    Within my house at home.

3   3 I will endure no wicked thing
      Before mine eyes to be;
    I hate their work that turn aside,
      It shall not cleave to me.

4   4 A stubborn and a froward heart
      Depart quite from me shall;
    A person given to wickedness
      I will not know at all.

5   5 I'll cut him off that slandereth
      His neighbor privily;
    The haughty heart I will not bear,
      Nor him whose look is high.

6   6 Upon the faithful of the land
      Mine eyes shall be, that they
    May dwell with me; he shall me serve
      That walks in perfect way.

7   7 Who of deceit a worker is
      In my house shall not dwell;
    And in my presence shall he not
      Remain that lies doth tell.

8   8 Yea, all the wicked of the land
      Each morn destroy I shall,
    From city of the LORD cut off
      The wicked workers all.

Psalm CII. C. M.

1   JEHOVAH, to my prayer attend,
      My cry let come to Thee;

PSALM CII.

    2 And in the day of my distress
       Hide not Thy face from me.

2   Give ear to me what time I call,
       To answer me make haste ;
   3 For as a hearth my bones are burnt,
       My days, like smoke, do waste.

3   4 My smitten heart like grass doth fade,
       To eat bread I forget ;
   5 From voice of endless groans, my
       Fast to my skin are set.   [bones

4   6 Like pelican in wilderness,
       Like desert owl, I moan ;
   7 I watch, and like a sparrow am
       That sits on house-top lone.

5   8 All day my foes have taunted me ;
       Enraged they 'gainst me swear ;
   9 For ashes I like bread did eat ;
       With drink tears mingled were.

6 10 Thine indignation and Thy wrath
       Did cause this grief and pain ;
    For Thou hast lifted me on high,
       And cast me down again.

7 11 My days are like unto a shade
       Which doth declining pass ;
    And I am dry and withered am,
       Even like unto the grass.

8 12 But Thou, Jehovah, art enthroned
       To all eternity ;
    And unto generations all
       Shall Thy memorial be.

9 13 Thou shalt arise and mercy have
       Upon Thy Zion yet ;
    The time to favor her is come,
       The time that Thou hast set.

10 14 For in her rubbish and her stones
    Thy servants pleasure take ;
    Yea, they the very dust thereof
    Do favor for her sake.

11 15 So shall the heathen people fear
    Jehovah's holy name ;
    And all the kings upon the earth
    Thy glory and Thy fame.

12 16 For Zion by Jehovah's might
    Built up again shall be.
    And in His glorious majesty
    To men appear shall He.

13 17 The prayer of those who are in need
    He surely will regard ;
    Their prayer He never will despise,
    By Him it shall be heard.

14 18 For generations yet to come
    Shall men these things record ;
    So shall a people yet to be
    Created praise the LORD.

15 19 For from His sanctuary's height
    He downward cast His eye,
    Jehovah on the earth beneath
    Did look from heaven high ;

16 20 That of the mournful prisoner
    The groanings He might hear,
    To set them free that unto death
    By men appointed are.

17 21 That they in Zion may declare
    Jehovah's holy Name,
    And publish in Jerusalem
    The praises of the same ;

18 22 When all the people gathered are
  In troops with one accord,
  And kingdoms are assembled all
  To serve the highest LORD.

19 23 My strength He weakened in the way,
  My days a brief span made;
  24 My God, in mid-time of my days,
  Cut me not off, I said;

20   Thy years through generations last;
  25   Of old-time Thou hast laid
  The firm foundation of the earth;
  Thy hands the heavens arrayed.

21 26 Thou shalt endure; they perish shall,
  Like garments soon decay;
  Thou as a vesture shalt them change,
  And they shall pass away.

22 27 But Thou the same art, and Thy years
  Shall never ended be.
  28 Thy servants' children shall abide,
  Their seed still dwell with Thee.

Psalm CII. L. M.

1 JEHOVAH, hear my prayer in grace;
  And let my cry come unto Thee;
  2 In day of grief hide not Thy face,
  Thine ear incline Thou unto me.

2   Hear when I call to Thee; that day
  An answer speedily return.
  3 My days like smoke consume away,
  And as a hearth my bones do burn.

3 4 My smitten heart like grass is dried,
  To eat bread I 've forgetful been;
  5 Since with my groaning voice I cried,
  My bones are cleaving to my skin.

4 6 The pelican of wilderness,
   The owl of ruins drear, I match ;
 7 And, like a bird companionless
   Upon the housetops, I keep watch.

5 8 All day my foes with taunts me greet,
   And in mad rage against me swear ;
 9 For I like bread did ashes eat
   And in my drink tears mingled were.

6 10 I by Thy wrath and anger pine,
   Thou hast me raised and cast away ;
 11 My days, a shadow, swift decline,
   Like grass I wither every day.

7 12 But Thou, Jehovah, shalt endure
   From age to age eternally ;
   And to all generations sure
   Shall Thy memorial ever be.

8 13 Thou shalt arise and mercy yet
   Thou to Mount Zion shalt extend ;
   The time is come, the time that's set,
   When Thou wilt favor to her send.

9 14 Thy saints take pleasure in her stones,
   Her very dust to them is dear ;
 15 Earth's nations and all kingly thrones
   Jehovah's glorious Name shall fear.

10 16 The LORD in glory shall appear
   When Zion He builds and repairs ;
 17 He shall regard and lend His ear
   To all the needy's humble prayers.

11   The needy's prayer He will not scorn,
 18   On record this shall always be,
   And generations yet unborn
   The LORD shall praise and magnify.

12 19 He from His holy height looked down,
    Jehovah earth from heaven did see,
 20 To hear the pris'ner's mourning groan,
    From death the doomed ones to set free.

13 21 That Zion may Jehovah's Name,
    Jerusalem His praise record,
 22 When peoples and the kings of fame
    Assemble all to praise the LORD.

14 23 My strength He weakened in the way;
    My days of life a span He made;
 24 My God, O take me not away
    In mid-time of my days, I said.

15   Thy years throughout all ages last;
 25   In the beginning Thou hast laid
    The earth's foundations firm and fast;
    Thy mighty hands the heavens have made.

16 26 They perish shall as garments do,
    But Thou shalt evermore endure;
    As vestures Thou shalt change them so,
    And they shall all be changèd sure.

17 27 But from all changes Thou art free,
    Thy countless years do last for aye;
 28 Thy servants and their seed who be
    Established shall before Thee stay.

Psalm CIII. C. M.

1 BLESS thou Jehovah, O my soul,
    And all that in me is,
    Be lifted up His holy name
    To magnify and praise.

PSALM CIII.

2 2 Bless thou Jehovah, O my soul,
And not forgetful be
Of all His gracious benefits
He hath bestowed on thee.

3 3 All thine iniquities who doth
Most graciously forgive;
Who thy diseases all and pains
Doth heal and thee relieve.

4 4 Who doth redeem thy life, that thou
To death mayst not go down;
Who thee with loving kindness doth,
And tender mercies, crown.

5 5 Who with abundance of good things
Doth satisfy thy mouth,
So that, even as the eagle's age,
Renewèd is thy youth.

6 6 Jehovah justice executes
For all oppressèd ones;
7 His way to Moses He made known,
His acts to Isr'el's sons.

7 8 Jehovah is compassionate,
And gracious He is found;
To anger is He very slow,
In mercy doth abound.

8 9 He will not chide continually,
Nor keep His anger still;
10 With us He dealt not as we sinned,
Nor did requite our ill.

9 11 For as the heavèn in its height
The earth surmounteth far,
So great to those that do Him fear
His tender mercies are.

10 12 As far as east is distant from
    The west, so far hath He
From us removed in tender love
    All our iniquity.

11 13 Like as a father pity hath
    To his own children dear,
Jehovah pity shows to those
    Who worship Him in fear.

12 14 For He remembers we are dust,
    And He our frame well knows.
15 Frail man, his days are like the grass,
    As flower in field he grows.

13 16 For over it the wind doth pass,
    And it away is gone;
And of the place where once it was
    It shall no more be known.

14 17 But unto them that do Him fear
    The LORD'S grace never ends.
And to their children's children still
    His righteousness extends;

15 18 To such as keep His covenant,
    With strict integrity,
And His commandments bear in mind
    To do them faithfully.

16 19 Jehovah hath His throne prepared
    Firm in the heavens to stand;
And every thing that being hath
    His kingdom doth command.

17 20 O ye His angels, that excel
    In strength, bless ye the LORD,
Ye who obey what He commands,
    And hearken to His word.

18 21 Jehovah bless and magnify,
Ye glorious hosts of His ;
Ye ministers that do fulfil
Whate'er His pleasure is.

19 22 Jehovah bless, all ye His works
Wherewith the world is stored
In His dominions everywhere :
My soul, bless thou the LORD.

Psalm CIII. 8s, 7s.

1 1 O MY soul, bless thou Jehovah
All within me bless His name ;
2 Bless Jehovah, and forget not
All His mercies to proclaim.

2 3 Who forgives all thy transgressions,
Thy diseases all who heals,
4 Who redeems thee from destruction,
Who with thee so kindly deals.

3 Who with tender mercies crowns thee,
5 Who with good things fills thy mouth,
So that evèn like the eagle
Thou hast been restored to youth.

4 6 In His righteousness Jehovah
Will deliver those distressed ;
He will execute just judgment
In the cause of all oppressed.

5 7 He made known His ways to Moses,
And His acts to Isr'el's race ;
8 Tender, loving, is Jehovah,
Slow to anger, rich in grace.

6 9 He will not for ever chide us,
Nor keep anger in His mind ;
10 Hath not dealt as we offended,
Nor rewarded as we sinned.

7 11 For as high as is the heavèn,
    Far above the earth below,
Ever great to them that fear Him.
    Is the mercy He will show.

8 12 Far as east from west is distant
    He hath put away our sin ;
13 Like the pity of a father
    Hath Jehovah's pity been.

9 14 Well He knows our frame, rememb'ring
    We are dust, our days like grass.
15 Man is like the flower blooming,
    Till the hot winds o'er it pass ;

10 16 Then 'tis gone, and is remembered
    No more by its former place ;
17 But on them that fear Jehovah
    Comes from age to age His grace.

11   Ever unto children's children
    Is His righteousness, if they
18 Keep His cov'nant and remember
    All His precepts to obey.

12 19 In the heavens high Jehovah
    For Himself prepared a throne,
And throughout His vast dominion
    All His works His power shall own.

13 20 Bless Jehovah, ye His angels,
    Spirits that excel in might,
Ye who hear what He commands you,
    Ye that do it with delight.

14 21 Bless and magnify Jehovah,
    All ye hosts that do His will ,
Ye His servants ever ready
    All His pleasure to fulfil.

15 22 Bless Jehovah all His creatures,
Ever under His control,
All throughout His vast dominion :
Bless Jehovah, O my soul.

Psalm CIV. C. M.

1 MY soul, Jehovah bless ; O LORD,
My God, Thou 'rt very great ;
With honor and with majesty
Thou clothèd art in state.

2 2 With light as with a robe, Thyself
Thou coverest about ;
And, like unto a curtain, Thou
The heavèns stretchest out.

3 3 Who of His chambers doth the beams
Within the waters lay ;
Who doth the clouds His chariot make
On wings of wind make way.

4 4 Who flaming fire His ministers,
His angels spirits doth make ;
5 Who earth's foundations firm did lay,
That it should never shake.

5 6 Thou didst it cover with the deep,
As with a garment spread ;
The waters rising high did stand,
Above the mountains' head.

6 7 But at the voice of Thy rebuke
They fled and would not stay ;
They at Thy thunder's dreadful voice
Did haste them fast away.

7 8 O'er hills they rise, and by the vales
Flow down to their fixed place ;
9 They shall not earth o'erflow, Thou
Set bounds they cannot pass. [hast

8 10 He through the valleys sendeth springs,
   'Mong hills their course they take ;
   11 Beasts of the field all drink of them,
   Their thirst wild asses slake.

9 12 Above them there the birds of heaven
   Do dwell, and from among
   The leafy branches of the trees
   Give voice to pleasant song.

10 13 He from His chambers watereth
   The hills when they are dried ;
   With fruit and increase of Thy works
   The earth is satisfied.

11 14 For cattle He makes grass to grow,
   He makes the herb to spring
   For use of man, that food to him
   He from the earth may bring.

12 15 And wine that to the heart of man
   Doth cheerfulness impart,
   Oil that his face makes shine, and bread
   That strengtheneth his heart.

13 16 Jehovah's trees are full of sap ;
   The cedars that do stand
   On Lebanon, which planted were
   By His almighty hand.

14 17 And here the sparrows build their nests;
   Storks in the firs abide ;
   18 The mountains high are for wild goats;
   In rocks the conies hide.

15 19 He sets the moon in heaven, thereby
   The seasons to discern ;
   From Him the sun his certain time
   Of going down doth learn.

16 20 Thou darkness mak'st, 'tis night, then
   Of forest creep abroad,   [beasts
   21 The lions young roar for their prey,
   And seek their meat from God.

17 22 The sun doth rise, and home they
   Down in their dens they lie ;   [flock,
   23 Man goes to work, his labor he
   Doth to the evening ply.

18 24 Jehovah, manifold Thy works !
   In wisdom wonderful
   Thou every one of them hast made ;
   Earth 's of Thy riches full.

19 25 So is this great and spacious sea,
   Wherein things creeping are,
   Which numbered cannot be; and beasts
   Both great and small are there.

20 26 There ships go, there 's leviathan,
   Which Thou mad'st there to play ;
   27 All wait on Thee, that in due time
   Their food receive they may.

21 28 That which Thou givest unto them
   They gather for their food ;
   Thy gracious hand Thou openest,
   And they are filled with good.

22 29 Thou hid'st Thy face, they troubled are,
   Their breath Thou tak'st away ;
   Then do they die, and to their dust
   Return again do they.

23 30 Thy Spirit then Thou sendest forth,
   And they created are ;
   The face of earth Thou dost revive,
   And all things new appear.

24 31 The glory of Jehovah shall
  Last to eternity;
 Jehovah shall in His own works
  Rejoice exceedingly.

25 32 Earth, as affrighted, trembleth all,
  If He on it but look;
 And if the mountains He but touch,
  They presently do smoke.

26 33 I 'll to Jehovah sing with joy,
  So long as I shall live;
 And while I being have, I shall
  To my God praises give.

27 34 Of Him my meditation shall
  Sweet thoughts to me afford;
 And as for me, I will rejoice
  And triumph in the LORD.

28 35 From earth let sinners be consumed,
  Let ill men no more be;
 O thou my soul, Jehovah bless,
  Praise to the LORD give ye.

Psalm CV. C. M.

1 JEHOVAH praise, call on His Name,
  To men His deeds make known;
 2 Sing ye to Him, sing psalms; proclaim
  His wondrous works each one.

2 3 To glory in His holy Name,
  Your tongues in praise employ;
 And let the heart of those that seek
  Jehovah sing for joy.

3 4 Jehovah and His strength seek ye;
  Still seek His face aright;
 5 Think on the judgments of His mouth,
  His wondrous deeds, and might.

4 6 Ye sons of Jacob, Abr'ham's seed,
      His servant, chosen friend,
   7 He is the LORD our God ; through
      His judgments do extend.   [earth.

5 8 His cov'nant He remembered hath,
      That it may ever stand ;
      To thousand generations He
      The promise did command.

6 9 Which covenant He firmly made
      With faithful Abraham ;
      And unto Isaac by His oath
      He did renew the same ;

7 10 And unto Jacob, for a law,
      He made it firm and sure,
      A covenant to Israel,
      Which ever should endure ;

8 11 He said, I will give Canaan's land
      For heritage to you ;
  12 While they were strangers there, and
      In number very few.   [few,

9 13 While yet they went from land to land,
      Through sundry kingdoms roved ;
  14 He suffered none to do them wrong,
      For them He kings reproved.

10 15 Thus did He say : Touch ye not those
      That Mine anointed be,
      Nor do the prophets any harm
      That do pertain to Me.

11 16 He famine on the land did call,
      The staff of bread withhold ;
  17 But He a man before them sent,
      Joseph a slave was sold ;

12 18 His feet with fetters they did hurt,
  In irons he was laid ;
 19 Until His word had been fulfilled,
  Jehovah's word him tried.

13 20 The king, the people's ruler, sent
  To loose and set him free ;
 21 He made him ruler of his house,
  Lord of his wealth to be.

14 22 That he might at his pleasure bind
  The princes of the land ;
  And also teach his senators
  Wisdom to understand.

15 23 The people then of Israel
  Down into Egypt came ;
  And Jacob also sojourned there
  Within the land of Ham.

16 24 And He did greatly by His power
  Increase His people there ;
  And stronger than their enemies
  They by His blessing were.

17 25 Their heart He turned about to hate
  His people bitterly,
  With those that His own servants
  To deal in subtlety.   [were

18 26 His servant Moses He did send,
  And Aaron, chosen one ;
 27 By these His signs and wonders great
  In Ham's land were made known.

19 28 Darkness He sent, and made it dark ;
  His word they did obey.
 29 He turned their waters into blood,
  And He their fish did slay.

20 30 The land in plenty brought forth
   In chambers of their kings. [frogs
   31 His word all sorts of flies and lice
   In all their borders brings.

21 32 Hailstones for rain, and flaming fire,
   He into their land sent;
   33 And He their vines and fig-trees smote,
   Trees of their coasts He rent.

22 34 He spake, and caterpillars came,
   Locusts did much abound;
   35 Which in their land all herbs consumed
   And all fruits of their ground.

23 36 He smote all first-born in their land,
   Chief of their strength each one.
   37 With gold and silver brought them forth,
   Weak in their tribes were none.

24 38 Egypt was glad when forth they went,
   Their fear on them did light.
   39 He spread a cloud for covering,
   And fire to shine by night.

25 40 They asked, and He brought quails, with bread
   Of heaven supplied He them.
   41 He cleft the rock, floods gushed and ran
   In deserts like a stream.

26 42 For on His holy promise He,
   And servant Abr'ham thought.
   43 With joy His people, His elect
   With gladness, forth He brought.

27 44 And unto them the pleasant lands
   He of the nations gave;
   That of the peoples' labor they
   Inheritance might have;

28 45 That they His statutes might observe
  According to His word;
  And that they might His laws obey,
  Give praise unto the LORD.

Psalm CVI. C. M.

1 O PRAISE the LORD, thanks to the
  Give ye, for good is He;   [LORD
  Because His mercy doth endure
  To all eternity.

2 2 Who can Jehovah's mighty acts
  Express? tell all His praise?
  3 How blessed are they that judgment
  And justice do always.   [keep,

3 4 LORD, me remember with that love,
  Thou show'st Thy people dear;
  And with Thine own salvation now
  To visit me draw near.

4 5 That I Thy chosen's good may see,
  And in their joy rejoice;
  And may with Thine inheritance
  Triumph with cheerful voice.

5 6 We with our fathers all have sinned,
  And of iniquity
  Too long we have the workers been;
  We have done wickedly.

6 7 Our fathers did not understand
  Thy works in Egypt done;
  Remembered not the multitude
  Of mercies shown each one;

7   They at the sea did all rebel,
  At Red Sea Him disown;   [saved,
  8 Yet for His Name's sake He them
  To make His great might known.

8 9 The Red Sea also He rebuked,
And then dried up it was;
Through depths, as through the wilderness,
He safely made them pass.

9 10 From haters' hand He did them save,
From foe redemption give;
11 The waters overwhelmed their foes,
Not one was left alive.

10 12 Then they believed His word, and did
His praise in songs relate;
13 But soon forgat His mighty deeds,
Nor on His counsel wait.

11 14 They lusted in the wilderness,
In desert God did tempt.
15 He gave them what they sought, but to
Their soul He leanness sent.

12 16 At Moses in the camp, also,
They moved with envy were;
'Gainst Aaron, too, Jehovah's saint,
Their envy did appear.

13 17 The earth did therefore open wide,
And Dathan did devour,
And all Abiram's company
It covered in that hour.

14 18 And likewise 'mong their company
A fire was kindled then;
And so the hot consuming flame
Burnt up the wicked men.

15 19 At Horeb they did make a calf,
Cast image worshipped they;
20 They changed their Glory to the form
Of ox that eateth hay.

16 21 They did forget the mighty God,
   Who had their Saviour been,
 By whom such great things brought to pass
   They had in Egypt seen ;   [pass

17 22 The works within the land of Ham
   Which He wrought wondrously,
 And deeds most terrible that were
   Performed at the Red Sea.

18 23 Then said He, He would them destroy,
   Had not, His wrath to stay,
 His chosen Moses stood in breach,
   That them He should not slay.

19 24 Yea, they despised the pleasant land,
   Did not believe His word ;
 25 But they did murmur in their tents,
   Not heark'ning to the LORD.

20 26 In desert, therefore, them to slay
   He lifted up His hand ;
 27 'Mong nations to o'erthrow their seed
   And scatter in each land.

21 28 With Baal-peor they did join ;
   Ate off'rings of the dead.
 29 Their deeds to anger Him provoked ;
   The plague among them spread.

22 30 But Phin'has rose, and justice did,
   And so the plague did cease ;
 31 To ages all this counted was
   To him for righteousness.

23 32 And at the waters, where they strove,
   They did Him angry make,
 In manner such that it went ill
   With Moses for their sake.

24 33 Because against his spirit they
　　　Rebelled most grievously,
　　So that he uttered with his lips
　　　Words unadvisedly.

25 34 Nor, as Jehovah gave command,
　　　Did they the peoples slay,
　　35 But with the nations mingled were,
　　　And learned of them their way.

26 36 Their idols they did serve, and these
　　　Became to them a snare ;
　　37 They unto demons sacrificed
　　　Their sons and daughters there.

27 38 In their own children's guiltless blood'
　　　Their hands they did imbrue,
　　Whom unto Canaan's idols they
　　　For sacrifices slew ;

28　　So was the land defiled with blood.
　　39　Stained by their works were they ;
　　And with devices of their own
　　　They faithlessly did stray.

29 40 Against His people kindled was
　　　Jehovah's wrath the more,
　　So that His own inheritance
　　　He greatly did abhor.

30 41 He gave them to the nations' power;
　　　Their foes did them command ;
　　42 Their en'mies them oppressed, they
　　　Made subject to their hand.　　[were

31 43 He many times delivered them,
　　　But in their counsel so
　　They did rebel that for their sin
　　　They were brought very low.

32 44 Yet their affliction He beheld,
When He did hear their cry;
45 And He for them His covenant
Did call to memory.

33 And in His mercies' multitude
He did repent, and made
46 Them to be pitied of all those
Who did them captive lead.

34 47 Save, LORD our God, and gather us
The nations from among,
That we Thy holy Name may praise
In a triumphant song.

35 48 Blessed be Jehovah, Isr'el's God,
To all eternity;
Let all the people say, Amen.
Praise to the LORD give ye.

Psalm CVII. C. M.

1 JEHOVAH praise, for He is good,
His mercies lasting be;
2 The LORD'S redeemed say so, whom
From hand of foe did free. [He

2 3 And gathered them out of the lands,
From north, south, east and west.
4 They strayed in desert's pathless way,
No city found to rest.

3 5 For thirst and hunger faints in them
Their soul. When straits them
6 They to Jehovah cry, and He [press,
Them frees from their distress.

4 7 Them also in a way to walk
That right is, He did guide,
That they might to a city go,
Wherein they might abide.

5 8 O that men would Jehovah praise
For His great goodness then,
And for His works so wonderful
Done to the sons of men!

6 9 For He the soul that longing is
Doth fully satisfy ;
With goodness He the hungry soul
Doth fill abundantly.

7 10 Such as shut up in darkness deep,
And in death's shade abide,
Whom strongly hath affliction bound,
And irons fast have tied ;

8 11 Because against the words of God
They wrought rebelliously ;
And they the counsel did contemn
Of Him that is Most High ;

9 12 With labor He brought down their heart,
They fell, and help none gave ;
13 In grief they to Jehovah cried,
From straits He did them save.

10 14 He out of darkness did them bring,
And from death's shade them take ;
Their bands, wherewith they had been
He did asunder break.   [bound,

11 15 O that men would Jehovah praise
For His great goodness then,
And for His works so wonderful
Done to the sons of men!

12 16 Because the mighty gates of brass
In pieces He did tear,
By Him in sunder also cut
The bars of iron were.

13 17 Fools, for their trespass and their sins,
Do sore affliction bear ;
18 All kinds of meat their soul abhors ;
They to death's gates draw near.

14 19 In grief they to Jehovah cry,
He saves from miseries ;
20 He sends His word, them heals, and them
From their destructions frees.

15 21 O that men would Jehovah praise
For His great goodness then,
And for His works so wonderful
Done to the sons of men !

16 22 And let them sacrifice to Him
Off'rings of thankfulness ;
And let them show abroad His works
In songs of joyfulness.

17 23 Who go to sea in ships, and in
Great waters trading be,
24 Jehovah's works within the deep
And His great wonders see.

18 25 For He commands, and forth in haste
The stormy tempest flies,
Which makes the sea with rolling
Aloft to swell and rise.   [waves

19 26 They mount to heaven, then to the
They do go down again ;   [depths
Their soul doth faint and melt away
With trouble and with pain.

20 27 They reel and stagger like one drunk,
At their wits' end they be ;
28 In grief they to Jehovah cry,
From straits He sets them free.

21 29 He calms the angry storm, He stills
　　　The raging waves again.
　　30 He guides them to the haven sought ;
　　　They rest and joy obtain.

22 31 O that men would Jehovah praise
　　　For His great goodness then,
　　　And for His works so wonderful
　　　Done to the sons of men.

23 32 Among the people when they meet,
　　　　Let them exalt His name ;
　　　Among assembled elders spread
　　　　His most renownèd fame.

24 33 To dry land He turns water-springs
　　　　And floods to wilderness ;
　　34 For sins of those that dwell therein,
　　　　Fat land to barrenness.

25 35 The burned and parched up wilderness
　　　　To water pools He brings,
　　　The ground that was dried up before
　　　　He turns to water springs.

26 36 And there, for dwelling, He a place
　　　　Doth to the hungry give,
　　　That they a city may prepare,
　　　　Where they in peace may live.

27 37 There sow they fields, and vineyards
　　　　plant,
　　　Which yield fruits of increase ;
　　38 His blessing makes them multiply,
　　　　Lets not their herds decrease.

28 39 Again they much diminished are,
　　　　And brought to low estate,
　　　Through sorrow and adversity,
　　　　And through oppression great.

29 40 Contempt on princes poureth He,
And causeth them to stray,
And wander in a wilderness,
Wherein there is no way.

30 41 Yet setteth He the poor on high
From all their miseries,
And evèn like unto a flock
He makes them families.

31 42 They that are righteous shall rejoice,
When they the same shall see;
And, as confounded, stop her mouth
Shall all iniquity.

32 43 Whoso is wise, and will these things
Observe, and them record,
Even they shall understand the love
And kindness of the LORD.

Psalm CVIII. C. M.

1 MY heart is fixed, O God; I 'll sing,
And with my glory praise.
2 Awake up, psaltery and harp;
Myself I 'll early raise.

2 3 I 'll praise Thee 'mong the peoples,
'Mong nations sing will I; [LORD,
4 For 'bove the heavens Thy love is great,
Thy truth doth reach the sky.

3 5 Be Thou above the heavens, O God,
Exalted gloriously;
Thy glory all the earth above
Be lifted up on high.

4 6 That those who Thy belovèd are
May all delivered be,

O do Thou save with Thy right hand,
And answer give to me.

5 7 God in His holiness hath said,
In this exult I will ;
I Shechem will divide, and I
Will mete out Succoth's vale.

6 8 Gilead I claim as Mine by right ;
Manasseh Mine shall be ;
Ephraim is of My head the strength ;
Laws Judah gives for Me ;

7 9 Moab My washpot is ; My shoe
I 'll over Edom throw ;
And o'er Philistia My shout
Of triumph forth shall go.

8 10 O who is he will bring me to
The city fortified ?
O who is he that to the land
Of Edom will me guide ?

9 11 Is it not Thou, O God, who hast
Cast us from Thee afar ?
Yea, with our armies Thou dost not
Go forth, O God, to war.

10 12 Do Thou from trouble give us help,
For helpless is man's aid.
13 Through God we shall do valiantly ;
Our foes He shall down tread.

Psalm CVIII. L. M.

1 MY heart is firmly fixed, O God ;
I 'll sing and praise Thy Name to
laud:
2 My glory, harp, and lute awake,
The morning I will vocal make

2 3 I'll thank Thee 'mid the peoples, LORD,
  Among the nations praise accord;
  4 The heavens vast Thy grace transcends,
  And to the clouds Thy truth extends.

3 5 Be Thou above the heavens, O God,
  Thy glory o'er the earth abroad;
  6 That Thy belovèd free may stand,
  Hear us, and save with Thy right hand.

4 7 God spoken hath with holy voice,
  I will both triumph and rejoice;
  I'll Shechem's fields by lot assign,
  O'er Succoth's vale will draw the line.

5 8 Manasseh, Gilead too, are Mine,
  On Ephraim shall My head recline;
  My ruler I shall Judah greet,
  9 In Moab I shall wash My feet.

6   To Edom I will cast My shoe,
  In triumph o'er Philistia go.
  10 Who to the city fortified,
  To Edom, who will be my guide?

7 11 O God, do Thou our Leader be,
  Though we are now cast off from Thee;
  And when our hosts to battle go,
  O God, do Thou Thy presence show.

8 12 From trouble help, and us relieve,
  For vain the help that man can give.
  13 In God will we great valor show,
  And He our foes will overthrow.

Psalm CIX. C. M.

1 HOLD not Thy peace, God of my
praise ;
2 'Gainst me are opened wide
The mouths of vile, deceitful men ;
Whose false tongues 'gainst me lied.

2 3 They did beset me round about
With words of hateful spite ;
And, though to them no cause I gave,
Against me they did fight.

3 4 They for my love became my foes ;
I set myself to pray.
5 Yea, ill for good and hate for love
To me they did repay.

4 6 Set Thou the wicked over him ;
And there on his right hand
Against him in the judgment shall
The adversary stand.

5 7 And when by Thee he shall be judged,
He shall condemnèd be ;
And turned to sin shall be his prayer,
When he shall call on Thee.

6 8 His days shall be but few ; his charge
Another man shall take ;
9 Thou wilt his children fatherless,
His wife a widow, make.

7 10 His children shall be vagabonds,
And beg continually,
And from their places desolate
Seek bread for their supply.

8 11 The greedy creditors shall take
All that he hath away ;

Of all for which he labored hath
  Shall strangers make a prey.

9 12 To him none favor shall extend,
  Nor to his orphans show ;
  13 His seed shall fail, nor shall their names
  The age that follows know.

10 14 His father's guilt, Jehovah shall
  Still to rememb'rance call ;
  And never shall his mother's sin
  Be blotted out at all.

11 15 Before Jehovah's face they shall
  Appear continually,
  Until He wholly from the earth
  Cut off their memory.

12 16 Because he mercy minded not,
  But persecuted still
  The poor and needy, that he might
  The broken-hearted kill.

13 17 As he in cursing pleasure took,
  So doth it to him fall ;
  As he delighted not to bless,
  He is not blest at all.

14 18 As cursing he like clothes puts on,
  Into his bowels so,
  Like water, and into his bones,
  Like oil, it down doth go.

15 19 Like to the garment shall it be
  Which doth himself array,
  And for a girdle, wherewith he
  Is girt about alway.

16 20 This from Jehovah's their reward
That en'mies are to me,
And their reward that speak against
My soul maliciously.

17 21 But for Thine own name's sake do
Jehovah, Lord, for me ;   [Thou
Since good Thy loving kindness is,
From trouble set me free.

18 22 For I am poor and indigent,
Afflicted sore am I,
My heart within me also is
Wounded exceedingly.

19 23 I pass like a declining shade,
I 'm like the locust tossed ;
24 My knees, through fasting, weakened
My flesh hath fatness lost.   [are ;.

20 25 I also am a vile reproach
Made unto them to be ;
And when they do upon me look,
They shake their heads at me.

21 26 Help me, Jehovah, O my God ;
In Thy grace, save Thou me ;
27 That they may know this is Thy hand,
That, LORD, 'tis done by Thee.

22 28 When they shall curse with spite, then
Wilt bless with loving voice.   [Thou
When they arise they shall be shamed ;
Thy servant shall rejoice.

23 29 They that mine adversaries are,
Shall all be clothed with shame ;
And, as a mantle, shall their own
Confusion cover them

24 30 But as for me, I with my mouth
　　　Will greatly praise the LORD ;
　　And I among the multitude
　　　His praises will record.

25 31 For He shall stand at his right hand
　　　Who is in poverty,
　　To save him from all those that would
　　　Condemn his soul to die.

Psalm CX.　C. M.

1 　JEHOVAH said unto my Lord,
　　　Sit Thou at My right hand,
　　Until I make Thy foes a stool,
　　　Whereon Thy feet may stand.

2 　2 Jehovah shall from Zion send
　　　The rod of Thy great power ;
　　In midst of all Thine enemies
　　　Be Thou the Governor.

3 　3 A willing people in Thy day
　　　Of power shall come to Thee,
　　In holy beauties from morn's womb ;
　　　Thy youth like dew shall be.

4 　4 Jehovah made an oath, from it
　　　He never will depart,
　　Of th' order of Melchizedek
　　　A priest Thou ever art.

5 　5 The glorious and mighty Lord,
　　　That sits at Thy right hand,
　　Shall, in His day of wrath, strike
　　　through
　　Kings that do Him withstand.

6   6 He shall among the nations judge,
      He shall with bodies dead
    The places fill ; o'er many lands
      He wound shall every head.

7   7 The brook that runneth in the way
      With drink shall Him supply ;
    And, for this cause, in triumph He
      Shall lift His head on high.

Psalm CX. S. M.

1   THE LORD to My Lord said :
      At My right hand sit Thou,
    Until I make Thine enemies
      Beneath Thy feet to bow.

2   2 Thy rod of strength the LORD
      Shall send from Zion then ;
    Be Ruler o'er Thy foes ; and come
      In day of might to men.

3   3 Clothed then in holy robes,
      Thy people come to Thee,
    A free-will off'ring ; from morn's
      womb
    Thy youth like dew shall be.

4   4 Jehovah swore an oath,
      Which He will nowise break ;
    Forever like Melchizedek's,
      Thy priesthood I will make.

5   5 The sovereign Lord who sits
      At Thy right hand as King,
    Shall smite all kings who Him resist;
      His wrath's day woes shall bring.

6   6 He shall the nations judge,
      And fill the land with dead ;

O'er many countries great and wide
He'll wound the reigning head.

7 7 And in His way, the brook
His thirst shall satisfy;
And thus refreshed, the conq'ring One
Shall lift His head on high.

Psalm CXI. C. M.

1 1 O PRAISE the LORD; I'll with whole heart
Jehovah's praise declare,
Where the assemblies of the just
And congregations are.

2 2 The doings of Jehovah are
Exceeding great in might;
Sought out they are of every one
That doth therein delight.

3 3 His work most honorable is,
Most glorious and pure;
And His untainted righteousness
For ever doth endure.

4 4 His works most wondrous He hath
Remembered still to be;   [made
Jehovah is compassionate,
And merciful is He.

5 5 He giveth meat unto all those
That truly do Him fear;
And evermore His covenant
He in His mind will bear.

6 6 He did the power of His works
To His own people show,
When He the nations' heritage
Upon them did bestow.

7 7 His hands' works all are truth and
His precepts all are sure ; [right,
8 And, done in truth and uprightness,
They evermore endure.

8 9 He sent redemption to His folk,
His covenant for aye
He did command ; His holy Name
Is reverend alway.

9 10 Of wisdom the beginning is
Jehovah's fear ; all they
Who keep His laws true wisdom have.
His praise endures for aye.

Psalm CXII. C. M.

1 O PRAISE the LORD; the man is blessed
That fears Jehovah's might,
He who in His commandments doth
Exceedingly delight.

2 2 His offspring for their might shall be
Upon the earth renowned ;
The generation of the just
In blessings shall abound.

3 3 For wealth and riches shall remain
Within his house in store ;
And his unspotted righteousness
Endures for evermore.

4 4 Light to the upright doth arise,
Though he in darkness be ;
Compassionate, and merciful,
And ever just is he.

5 5 A good man doth his favor show,
And doth to others lend ;

  He in the judgment will his cause
   Maintain unto the end.

6 6 Surely there is not anything
   That ever shall him move;
  The righteous man's memorial
   Shall everlasting prove.

7 7 When he shall evil tidings hear,
   He shall not be afraid;
  His heart is fixed, his confidence
   Is on Jehovah stayed.

8 8 Established firmly is his heart,
   Afraid he shall not be,
  Until upon his enemies
   He his desire shall see.

9 9 He hath dispersed his wealth abroad,
   And givèn to the poor;
  His horn with honor shall be raised,
   His righteousness endure.

10 10 The wicked shall it see, and fret,
   His teeth gnash, melt away;
  What wicked men do most desire
   Shall utterly decay.

Psalm CXIII. C. M.

1 PRAISE ye the LORD; who serve the
   LORD,
  O praise, the LORD'S Name praise.
 2 Jehovah's Name, let it be blessed
   From this time forth always.

2 3 From rising sun to where it sets
   Jehovah's Name be praised.
 4 O'er nations all Jehovah 's high,
   'Bove heavens His glory raised.

3 5 And with the LORD our God, that
On high, who can compare, [dwells
6 Himself that humbleth things to see
In heaven and earth that are ?

4 7 He lifts the helpless from the dust,
The poor from low estate ;
8 That He may him with princes set,
His people's princes great.

5 9 The barren woman house to keep
He maketh, and to be
Of sons a mother full of joy.
Praise to the LORD give ye.

Psalm CXIV. C. M.

1 WHEN Isr'el out of Egypt went,
And did his dwelling change,
When Jacob's house went out from those
That were of language strange ;

2 2 Judah became his holy place,
Isr'el his own domain ;
3 The sea beheld and quickly fled,
Jordan turned back again.

3 4 Like rams the mountains, and like
The hills skipped to and fro. [lambs
5 O sea, why fledd'st thou ? Jordan,
Why wast thou driven so ?   [back

4 6 Why, mountains, do ye skip like rams,
Like lambs, ye little hills ?
7 Earth, tremble thou because the Lord
His presence here reveals,

5 For Jacob's God His presence shows;
8 Who from the rock did bring
A water-pool, and turned the flint
Into a water-spring.

Psalm CXV. C. M.

1 NOT unto us, LORD, not to us,
But do Thou glory take
To Thine own Name, even for Thy
And for Thy mercy's sake.   [truth,

2 2 O wherefore should the nations say,
Where is their God now gone?
3 But our God dwelleth in the heavens,
What pleased Him He hath done.

3 4 Their idols silver are, and gold,
Work of men's hands they be.
5 Mouths have they, but they do not
And eyes, but do not see;   [speak;

4 6 Ears have they, but they do not hear;
And noses, yet smell not;
7 Hands, feet, but handle not, nor walk;
Nor speak they through their throat.

5 8 Like them their makers are, and all
On them their trust that build.
9 O Isr'el, in Jehovah trust,
He is their help and shield.

6 10 O Aaron's house, Jehovah trust
Their help and shield is He.
11 Who fear Jehovah, trust the LORD,
Their help and shield He'll be.

7 12 Jehovah hath remembered us,
And He will bless us still:
He will the house of Isr'el bless,
Bless Aaron's house He will.

8 13 Who fear Jehovah, small and great,
　　He will them surely bless.
　14 Jehovah you, you and your seed,
　　Will more and more increase.

9 15 O blessed ye of Jehovah are,
　　Who made the earth and heaven.
　16 Jehovah's are the heavens, but earth
　　To men's sons He hath given.

10 17 Nor dead, nor who to silence go,
　　Jehovah's praise record.
　　But now and ever we the LORD
　　Will bless.　Praise ye the LORD.

Psalm CXVI.　C. M.

1　I LOVE the LORD, because my voice
　　And my prayers He did hear.
　2 I, while I live, will call on Him,
　　Who bowed to me His ear.

2　3 The cords of death on every side
　　Encompassed me around;
　　The sorrows of the grave me seized,
　　I grief and trouble found.

3　4 And then upon Jehovah's Name
　　I called, and thus did say,
　　O LORD, deliver Thou my soul,
　　I do Thee humbly pray.

4　5 Jehovah gracious is and just,
　　Our God doth mercy show;
　6 Jehovah keeps the meek, He saved
　　Me when I was brought low.

5　7 O thou my soul, do thou return
　　To thine own quiet rest;

    Because Jehovah unto thee
      His bounty hath expressed.

6   8 Thou rescued hast my soul from death,
      From tears and falls kept free;
   9 I 'll walk before the LORD in lands
      Of them that living be.

7   10 I did believe, I therefore spake;
      Afflicted sore was I,
   11 In fear I said, All men are false,
      On them I 'll not rely.

8   12 How shall I all His gifts repay,
      Which from Jehovah came?
   13 I 'll take salvation's cup, and call
      Upon Jehovah's Name.

9   14 I to Jehovah vows will pay
      Before His people's face.
   15 His saints' death in Jehovah's eyes
      Most precious is, and peace.

10 16 Jehovah, I Thy servant am,
      Thy servant true am I.
   I also am Thy handmaid's son;
      Thou didst my bands untie.

11 17 Thanks I will offer unto Thee,
      And on the LORD'S Name call;
   18 I 'll to Jehovah pay my vows,
      Before His people all;

12 19 Within Jehovah's temple-courts
      Within the midst of thee,
   O city of Jerusalem.
      Praise to the LORD give ye.

Psalm CXVII. C. M.

1 O DO ye give Jehovah praise,
  Ye nations all that be ;
  Likewise, ye peoples all, accord
  His Name to magnify.

2 2 For great to us-ward ever are
  His loving-kindnesses ;
  Jehovah's truth endures for aye.
  The LORD, O praise and bless.

Psalm CXVII. 6s and 4s.

1 ALL nations, praise the LORD ;
  All peoples in accord
    His glory raise.
  2 Because His mercy pure
  Is great to us ; and sure
    The LORD'S truth doth endure.
    The LORD, O praise.

Psalm CXVIII. C. M.

1 JEHOVAH praise, for He is good ;
  For His grace lasts for aye.
  2 That His grace ever doth endure,
  Let Israel now say.

2 3 Now let the house of Aaron say,
  His mercy lasts for aye.
  4 That His grace ever lasts, let them
  That fear Jehovah say.

3 5 I in distress called on the LORD,
  The LORD did answer me.
  He in a large place did me set,
  From trouble made me free.

4 6 The LORD is for me, I 'll not fear;
   What can man do to me?
  7 Jehovah with my helpers is,
   My haters' fall I 'll see.

5 8 To trust Jehovah better is
   Than trust in man's defence;
  9 Better Jehovah trust than place
   In princes confidence.

6 10 The nations, joining all in one,
   Did compass me about;
  But in Jehovah's holy Name
   I shall them all root out.

7 11 They compassed me about; I say,
   They compassed me about;
  But in Jehovah's holy Name
   I shall them all root out.

8 12 Like bees they compassed me about;
   They're quenched like thorns that
    flame;
  For I will surely them destroy,
   Even in Jehovah's Name.

9 13 Thou hast sore thrust that I might fall;
   Jehovah succored me.
  14 The LORD my Saviour is become,
   My strength and song is He.

10 15 In just men's tents the voice of joy
   And saving health shall be;
  The right hand of Jehovah doth
   Work ever valiantly.

11 16 The right hand of Jehovah is
   Exalted far on high;
  The right hand of Jehovah doth
   Work ever valiantly.

12 17 I shall not die, but live, and shall
    Jehovah's work make known.
  18 Jehovah me hath chastened sore,
    But not to death brought down.

13 19 O set ye open unto me
    The gates of righteousness ;
  Then will I enter in, and will
    Jehovah's praise express.

14 20 This is Jehovah's gate, by it
    The just shall enter in.
  21 Thee will I praise, for Thou me
    And hast my safety been. [heard'st,

15 22 That stone is made head corner-stone,
    Which builders did despise ;
  23 This is the doing of the LORD,
    And wondrous in our eyes.

16 24 This is the day Jehovah made,
    In it exult will we.
  25 Save, LORD, we pray Thee ; LORD,
    Send now prosperity.   [we pray

17 26 Blessed in Jehovah's Name is he
    That cometh us among ;
  We bless you from the house which to
    Jehovah doth belong.

18 27 God is Jehovah, who to us
    Hath made light to arise ;
  Bind ye unto the altar's horns
    With cords the sacrifice.

19 28 Thou art my God, I 'll Thee exalt ;
    My God, I will Thee praise.
  29 Jehovah bless, for He is good ;
    His mercy lasts always.

Psalm CXIX. C. M.

ALEPH. The 1st Part.

1 1 O BLESSED are they that undefiled
And straight are in the way;
Who in Jehovah's holy law
Do walk, and do not stray.

2 2 Those that His testimonies keep,
True blessedness do find;
Even those that after Him do seek,
With their whole heart and mind.

3 3 Such in His ways do walk, and they
Do no iniquity.
4 Thou hast commanded us to keep
Thy precepts carefully.

4 5 O that Thy statutes to observe
Thou wouldst my ways direct!
6 Then shall I not be shamed when I
All Thy commands respect.

5 7 Then with integrity of heart
Thee will I praise and bless,
When I the judgments all have learned
Of Thy pure righteousness.

6 8 That I Thy statutes will observe
Firmly resolved have I;
O do not Thou withdraw Thyself
And leave me utterly.

BETH. The 2nd Part.

7 9 By what means shall a young man
His way to purify?   [learn
If he according to Thy word
Thereto attentive be.

8 10 Unfeignedly Thee have I sought
With all my soul and heart;
O let me not from the right path
Of Thy commands depart.

9 11 Thy word I in my heart have hid,
That I offend not Thee,
12 Jehovah, ever blessed art Thou,
Thy statutes teach Thou me.

10 13 The judgments of Thy mouth, each
My lips declarèd have;   [one,
14 More joy Thy testimonies' way
Than riches all me gave.

11 15 Thy holy precepts I will make
My meditation still;
And unto Thy ways have respect
Most carefully I will.

12 16 Upon Thy statutes my delight
Shall constantly be set;
And, by Thy grace, I never will
Thy holy word forget.

GIMEL.   The 3rd Part.

13 17 With me, who am Thy servant, do
Thou bountifully deal,
That I may live; and so Thy word
Keep carefully I will.

14 18 Open mine eyes, that of Thy law
The wonders I may see.
19 I stranger am on earth; do not
Hide Thy commands from me.

15 20 My soul within me breaks, and doth
Much fainting still endure,
Through longing that it hath all times
To Thine own judgments pure.

16 21 Thou hast rebuked the proud accursed,
   From Thy commands who stray.
   22 Roll from me scorn and shame, I 've
   Thy testimonies' way.   [kept

17 23 Though princes in assembly sit,
   And counsel 'gainst me take,
   Thy statutes I, Thy servant, still
   My meditation make.

18 24 My comfort, and my heart's delight
   Thy testimonies be ;
   And they, in all my doubts and fears,
   Are counsellors to me.

DALETH.   The 4th Part.

19 25 My soul to dust cleaves ; quicken me
   As promised was by Thee.
   26 My ways I showed, and me Thou heardst ;
   Thy statutes teach Thou me.

20 27 Thy precepts' way O do Thou teach,
   And make me well to know ;
   So all Thy works that wondrous are
   I shall to others show.

21 28 My soul doth melt and drop away,
   For heaviness and grief ;
   To me, according to Thy word,
   Give strength and send relief.

22 29 O let the way of falsehood far
   From me removèd be ;
   And graciously Thy holy law
   Do Thou grant unto me.

23 30 I chosen have the perfect way
   Of truth and verity ;

Thy judgments, that most righteous
Before me laid have I.   [are,

24 31 I to Thy testimonies cleave ;
   No shame, LORD, on me lay.
32 When Thou 'lt enlarge my heart, I will
   Run Thy commandments' way.

HE.   The 5th Part.

25 33 O Thou, Jehovah, teach to me
   Thy statutes' way divine,
And to observe it to the end
   I shall my heart incline.

26 34 Give understanding unto me,
   So keep Thy law shall I ;
Yea, even with my whole heart I shall
   Observe it carefully.

27 35 Lead me in Thy commandments' path,
   For I delight therein.
36 To Thy pure testimonies turn
   My heart, and not to gain.

28 37 Turn Thou away my sight and eyes
   From viewing vanity ;
And in Thy good and holy way
   Be pleased to quicken me.

29 38 Confirm to me Thy gracious word,
   Which I did gladly hear ;
To me, who am Thy servant, and
   Devoted to Thy fear.

30 39 Turn Thou away my feared reproach :
   For good Thy judgments be.
40 Lo, for Thy precepts I have longed ;
   In Thy truth quicken me.

VAU. The 6th Part.

31 41 Let Thy sweet mercies also come
 And visit me, O LORD;
 Let Thy salvation come to me,
 According to Thy word.

32 42 So shall I have wherewith I may
 Give him an answer just,
 Who spitefully reproacheth me;
 For in Thy word I trust.

33 43 The word of truth out of my mouth
 Take Thou not utterly;
 For on Thy righteous judgments still
 Doth all my hope rely.

34 44 So shall I keep for evermore
 Thy law continually.
 45 Because I have Thy precepts sought,
 I'll walk at liberty.

35 46 Thy testimonies unto kings,
 I'll speak, with shame not moved;
 47 And will delight myself in Thy
 Commandments which I loved.

36 48 To Thy commandments, which I loved,
 My hands lift up I will;
 And I will also meditate
 Upon Thy statutes still.

ZAIN. The 7th Part.

37 49 The promise keep in mind, which
 Didst to Thy servant make, [Thou
 The word, which, as a ground of hope,
 Thou causedst me to take.

38 50 By this, in time of my distress,
   Great comfort I have known;
   For in my straits I am revived
   By this Thy word alone.

39 51 The men inflated with their pride
   Did greatly me deride;
   Yet from Thy good and holy law
   I have not turned aside.

40 52 The righteous judgments, which of old,
   Jehovah, Thou hast wrought,
   I have remembered, and to me
   Great comfort they have brought.

41 53 Horror took hold on me, because
   Ill men Thy law forsake.
   54 I in my house of pilgrimage
   My songs Thy statutes make.

42 55 Thy Name, Jehovah, I recalled
   By night, and kept Thy law.
   56 And this I had, for I observed
   Thy precepts all with awe.

CHETH.   The 8th Part.

43 57 Thou my sure portion art alone,
   Which I did choose, O LORD;
   I have resolved, and said, that I
   Would keep Thy holy word.

44 58 With my whole heart I did entreat
   Thy face and favor free;
   According to Thy gracious word
   Be merciful to me.

45 59 I thought upon my former ways
  And did my life well try;
And to Thy testimonies pure
  My feet then turn did I.

46 60 I did not stay, nor linger long,
  As those that slothful are;
But Thy commandments to observe
  Myself I did prepare.

47 61 Bands of the wicked me beset,
  Thy law I did not slight.
62 I'll rise at midnight Thee to praise,
  Even for Thy judgments right.

48 63 I am allied to all who keep
  Thy precepts and fear Thee.
64 Jehovah, earth Thy mercy fills;
  Thy statutes teach Thou me.

TETH. The 9th Part.

49 65 Good hast Thou done Thy servant,
      LORD,
  As Thou didst promise give.
66 Good judgment me, and knowledge,
  I Thy commands believe. [teach.

50 67 Ere I afflicted was I strayed·
  Thy word I now obey.
68 Good art Thou, and Thou doest good;
  Teach me Thy statutes' way.

51 69 The men inflated with their pride
  Against me forged a lie;
But as for me, Thy precepts keep
  With all my heart will I.

52 70 Their hearts, through worldly ease
and wealth,
As fat as grease they be ;
But in Thy holy law I take
Delight continually.

53 71 That I afflicted was, it hath
Been very good for me,
That I might learn Thy statutes all,
And well instructed be.

54 72 The law that cometh from Thy mouth
Is better unto me
Than many thousands and great sums
Of gold and silver be.

JOD. The 10th Part.

55 73 Thy hands me made and formed,
make wise
All Thy commands to know.
74 Who fear Thee see and joy, for I
Hope in Thy word do show.

56 75 Jehovah, just Thy judgments are,
I know, and do confess ;
And that Thou hast afflicted me
In truth and faithfulness.

57 76 O let Thy kindness merciful,
I pray Thee, comfort me,
As to Thy servant promised was
In faithfulness by Thee.

58 77 And let Thy tender mercies come
To me, that I may live ;
Because Thy holy law to me
Doth delectation give.

59 78 O let the proud be put to shame,
  For with injustice great
 They me o'erthrew ; but I will on
  Thy precepts meditate.

60 79 Who know Thy testimonies and
  Fear Thee, let turn to me.
 80 Sound in Thy statutes make my heart,
  That shamed I may not be.

  CAPH.   The 11th Part.

61 81 My soul for Thy salvation faints ;
  Yet I Thy word believe.
 82 Mine eyes fail for Thy word ; I say,
  When wilt Thou comfort give ?

62 83 For like a bottle I 'm become,
  That in the smoke is set ;
 But yet the statutes Thou hast given,
  I never do forget.

63 84 How many are Thy servant's days ?
  When wilt Thou execute
 Just judgment on those wicked men
  That do me persecute ?

64 85 The proud have digged their pits for
  Who Thy law will not have.   [me,
 86 All Thy commands are faithfulness ;
  From false pursuers save.

65 87 They so consumed me, that on earth
  My life they scarce did leave ;
 Thy precepts yet forsook I not,
  But close to them did cleave.

66 88 According to Thy gracious love
  Me quicken and preserve ;

The testimony of Thy mouth
So shall I still observe.

LAMED. The 12th Part.

67 89 Thy word for ever is, O LORD,
In heavèn settled fast ;
90 And unto generations all
Thy faithfulness doth last ;

68 The earth Thou hast established firm,
And it abides by Thee.
91 This day they stand as Thou or-
For all Thy servants be. [dain'dst ;

69 92 Unless in Thy most perfect law
My soul delights had found,
I should have perished at the time
My troubles did abound.

70 93 Thy precepts I will ne'er forget ;
They quick'ning to me brought.
94 I am Thine own ; O save Thou me ;
Thy precepts I have sought.

71 95 For me the wicked have laid wait,
Me seeking to destroy ;
But I Thy testimonies true
Consider will with joy.

72 96 To all perfection here I have
Beheld a boundary ;
But Thy command, how broad it is ,
How broad exceedingly.

MEM. The 13th Part.

73 97 O how I love Thy law ! it is
My study all the day ;

98 More wise than foes by Thy commands
    I 'm made ; they 're mine for aye.

74 99 Than all my teachers now I have
    More understanding far ;
    Because my meditation still
    Thy testimonies are.

75 100 In understanding I excel
    Those that the agèd are,
    For I endeavored have to keep
    Thy precepts with due care.

76 101 To keep Thy word, I have my feet
    From each ill way refrained.
    102 I from Thy judgments have not swerved,
    Because Thou hast me trained.

77 103 How sweet unto my sense of taste
    Are all Thy words of truth !
    Yea, I do find them sweeter far
    Than honey to my mouth.

78 104 I through Thy precepts, that are pure,
    Do understanding get ;
    I therefore every way that 's false
    With all my heart do hate.

NUN.   The 14th Part.

79 105 Thy word is to my feet a lamp,
    And to my path a light.
    106 As I have sworn, I will perform,
    To keep Thy judgments right.

80 107 I with affliction very sore
    Am overwhelmed ; O LORD,
    Do Thou give quick'ning unto me
    According to Thy word.

81 108 The free-will-off'rings of my mouth
Accept, I Thee beseech,
O LORD ; and unto me do Thou
Thy righteous judgments teach.

82 109 Though still my soul be in my hand,
Thy law I 'll not forget ;
110 Nor leave Thy precepts, though for
A snare the wicked set.   [me

83 111 I of Thy testimonies have
Above all things made choice,
To be my heritage for aye ;
For they my heart rejoice ;

84 112 Most carefully I have inclined
My heart still to attend,
That I Thy statutes may perform
Alway unto the end.

SAMECH.   The 15th Part.

85 113 I hate the men of double mind,
But love Thy law do I.
114 My shield and hiding-place Thou art;
I on Thy word rely.

86 115 All ye that evil-doers are
From me depart away ;
For the commandments of my God
I purpose to obey.

87 116 According to Thy faithful word
Uphold and stablish me,
That I may live, and of my hope
Ashamed may never be.

88 117 Hold Thou me up, so shall I be
　　　In peace and safety still ;
　　And to Thy statutes have respect
　　　Continually I will.

89 118 Thou scorn'st all who Thy statutes
　　　　leave ;
　　　False their deceit doth prove;
　119 Putt'st off, like dross, earth's wicked; I
　　　Thy testimonies love.

90 120 For fear of Thee my very flesh
　　　Doth tremble, all dismayed ;
　　And of the judgments wrought by
　　　I 'm very much afraid.　　[Thee

AIN.　The 16th Part.

91 121 To all men I have judgment done,
　　　Performing justice right ;
　　Then let me not delivered be
　　　To proud oppressors' might.

92 122 To Thine own servant, for his good,
　　　Do Thou a surety be ;
　　And from oppression of the proud
　　　Do Thou deliver me.

93 123 Mine eyes do fail with looking long
　　　For Thy salvation great,
　　While for Thy word of righteousness
　　　I earnestly do wait.

94 124 In mercy with Thy servant deal,
　　　Thy statutes to me show.
　125 I serve Thee, wisdom give ; I shall
　　　Thy testimonies know.

95 126 Jehovah, it is time to work ;
    They break Thy law divine.
  127 Hence Thy commandments more I love
    Than gold, yea, gold most fine.

96 128 Thy precepts all, I therefore judge
    In all things to be right ;
    And every false and wicked way
    Is hateful in my sight.

PE.   The 17th Part.

97 129 Thy testimonies wondrous are,
    My soul them keeps with care.
  130 The op'ning of Thy words gives
    Makes wise who simple are. [light,

98 131 My mouth I also opened wide
    And panted earnestly ;
    For after Thy commandments I
    Have longed exceedingly.

99 132 Turn Thou to me, and merciful
    Do Thou unto me prove,
    As Thou art wont to do to those
    Thy Name who truly love.

100 133 O let my footsteps in Thy word
    Aright still ordered be ;
    Let no iniquity obtain
    Dominion over me.

101 134 From man's oppression me redeem,
    Thy precepts keep I will.
  135 Thy face make on Thy servant shine,
    Teach me Thy statutes still.

102 136 The flowing waters from mine eyes
　　Ran down, because I saw
　That wicked men go on in sin,
　　And do not keep Thy law.

　　　TZADDI.　The 18th Part.

103 137 O Thou, Jehovah, righteous art;
　　Thy judgments upright be.
　138 Thy testimonies Thou command'st
　　In right and faithfully.

104 139 My burning zeal hath me consumed,
　　Because mine enemies
　Thy holy words have failed to keep
　　Within their memories.

105 140 Thy word is very pure, on it
　　Thy servant's love is set.
　141 Small and despised I am, yet I
　　Thy precepts not forget.

106 142 Thy righteousness is righteousness
　　Which ever doth endure;
　Thy holy law, moreover, is
　　The very truth most pure.

107 143 Distress and anguish have me found,
　　Fast hold on me they take;
　Yet in my trouble my delight
　　I Thy commandments make.

108 144 Eternal righteousness is in
　　Thy testimonies all;
　Give understanding unto me,
　　And ever live I shall.

KOPH. The 19th Part.

109 145 With my whole heart I cried,
  LORD, hear;
  Thy statutes I 'll obey.
  146 I cried to Thee; save me, I 'll keep
  Thy testimonies' way.

110 147 I did anticipate the dawn,
  That I for help might cry;
  For all my waiting confidence
  Did on Thy word rely.

111 148 Mine eyes anticipated, too,
  The watches of the night,
  That in Thy word, with careful
  Then meditate I might.   [mind,

112 149 According to Thy mercy hear
  My voice, that calls on Thee;
  According to Thy judgments just,
  Jehovah, quicken me.

113 150 The men who mischief seek draw
    nigh,
  They from Thy law are far;
  151 Jehovah, Thou art near; and truth
  All Thy commandments are.

114 152 From Thine own testimonies long
  Hath this been known to me,
  That Thou hast founded them to
  Through all eternity.   [last

RESH. The 20th Part.

115 153 On mine affliction do Thou look,
  And me in safety set
  . By Thy deliverance, for I
  Thy law do not forget

116 154 As Thou hast promised, me revive;
    Save me and plead my cause.
   155 Salvation is from sinners far;
    For They seek not Thy laws.

117 156 Jehovah, great and manifold
    Thy tender mercies be;
   According to Thy judgments just
    Revive and quicken me.

118 157 My persecutors many are,
    And foes that do combine,
   Yet from Thy testimonies pure
    My heart doth not decline.

119 158 I saw transgressors, and was
     grieved;
    For they keep not Thy word.
   159 Behold, Thy precepts I have loved,
    Do Thou me quicken, LORD.

120 160 The sum of Thy most holy word
    Is only truth most pure;
   Thy righteous judgments every one
    For evermore endure.

SCHIN.   The 21st Part.

121 161 The princes persecuted me,
    Although no cause they saw;
   But still of Thy most holy word
    My heart doth stand in awe.

122 162 I at Thy word rejoice as one
    Of spoil that finds great store.
   163 Thy law I love; but lying all
    I hate and do abhor.

123 164 Seven times a day it is my care
To give due praise to Thee ;
Because of all Thy judgments that
For ever righteous be.

124 165 Great peace have they who love
Thy law ;
Offence they shall have none.
166 I hope for Thy salvation, LORD,
And Thy commands have done.

125 167 My soul Thy testimonies pure
Observeth carefully ;
On them my heart is set, and them
I love exceedingly.

126 168 Thy testimonies I have kept,
Thy precepts, too, with care ;
For all my ways of life each one
Before Thee open are

TAU. The 22nd Part.

127 169 Jehovah, unto Thee my prayer
A near approach afford ;
Give understanding unto me,
According to Thy word.

128 170 Let my request before Thee come ;
After Thy word me free.
171 My lips shall utter praise, for Thou
Thy statutes teachest me.

129 172 My tongue of Thy most blessèd
word
Shall speak and it confess ;
Because all Thy commandments are
Most perfect righteousness.

130 173 O let Thy hand be for my help;
 Thy precepts are my choice.
 174 I longed for Thy salvation, LORD,
 And in Thy law rejoice.

131 175 O let my soul live, and it shall
 Give praises unto Thee;
 And let Thy judgments evermore
 Be helpful unto me.

132 176 I, like a lost sheep, went astray;
 Thy servant seek, and find;
 For Thy commands I suffered not
 To slip out of my mind.

Psalm CXIX. L. M.

PART I.

1 1 BLESSED are the upright in the way,
 Who in Jehovah's law progress.
 2 Blessed who His testimonies keep,
 And seek Him with whole-heartedness.

2 3 Yea, they do no iniquity;
 They in His ways progressing are.
 4 Thou hast commanded us to keep
 Thy precepts with our utmost care.

3 5 O that my ways established were,
 To keep Thy statutes void of blame!
 6 When I all Thy commands regard,
 I shall not then be put to shame.

4 7 When I Thy righteous judgments learn,
 I'll give Thee praise with upright heart.
 8 Thy statutes I will keep; from me
 O do not utterly depart.

PART II.

5 9 How can a young man cleanse his way?
  Let him with care Thy word observe.
 10 With all my heart I have Thee sought;
  From Thy commands let me not swerve.

6 11 I hid Thy word within my heart,
  Lest I should give offence to Thee.
 12 Jehovah, ever blessed art Thou;
  Thy statutes teach Thou unto me.

7 13 And all the judgments of Thy mouth
  I with my lips recounted have.
 14 Thy testimonies' way great joy,
  As much as riches all, me gave.

8 15 I 'll in Thy precepts meditate,
  And on Thy ways mine eyes will set.
 16 Thy statutes shall be my delight,
  And I Thy word will not forget.

PART III.

9 17 O to Thy servant give this grace,
  That I may live Thy word to keep.
 18 Open mine eyes, that of Thy law
  I may behold the wonders deep.

10 19 I am a stranger in the earth;
  O hide not Thy commands from me.
 20 My soul is breaking with desire
  Thy judgments at all times to see.

11 21. Thou hast rebuked the proud accursed
  Who have from Thy commandments swerved.
 22 Take scorn and shame from me, for I
  Thy testimonies have observed.

12 23 'Gainst me conspiring, princes sat;
  Thy servant of Thy statutes spake.
  24 Thy testimonies my delight,
  And for my counsellors, I take.

PART IV.

13 25 My soul to dust cleaves; quickening,
  In promised grace on me bestow.
  26 I told my ways, and Thou me heard'st;
  Thy statutes make me well to know.

14 27 Thy precepts' way do Thou me teach;
  Thy wonders shall my study be.
  28 My soul with grief dissolves away;
  In promised grace, O strengthen me.

15 29 Remove from me the way of lies;
  Grant me Thy law in gracious aid.
  30 I chosen have the way of truth;
  Thy judgments I before me laid.

16 31 I to Thy testimonies cleave;
  On me, O LORD, shame never cast.
  32 I'll run the way of Thy commands,
  When Thou my heart enlargèd hast.

PART V.

17 33 O LORD, teach me Thy statutes' way;
  I never will from it depart.
  34 Instruct me and I'll keep Thy law,
  Yea, keep it shall with all my heart.

18 35 Lead me in Thy commandments' path,
  For I therein delight obtain.
  36 To Thy pure testimonies turn
  My heart, and not to worldly gain.

19 37 O turn from vanity mine eyes,
    And in Thy ways revive Thou me.
  38 Sure to Thy servant make Thy word,
    Which tendeth to the fear of Thee.

20 39 Turn Thou away my feared reproach,
    Because Thy judgments all are good.
  40 Lo, for Thy precepts I have longed;
    Revive me in Thy rectitude.

PART VI.

21 41 Jehovah, let Thy mercies come,
    Salvation promised me afford.
  42 So I my sland'rer shall refute,
    Because I trust upon Thy word.

22 43 Take not Thy truth's word from my mouth,
    For on Thy judgments I depend.
  44 So shall I keep Thy holy law
    For evermore, unto the end.

23 45 And I shall walk at liberty,
    Because I do Thy precepts seek.
  46 And unashamed, before great kings,
    I'll of Thy testimonies speak.

24 47 In Thy commandments loved, I'll joy;
  48 To Thy commands, which I love still,
    I will lift up my hands, and on
    Thy statutes meditate I will.

PART VII.

25 49 Thy word unto Thy servant given
    Recall; Thou madst me hope in Thee.

50 This is my comfort in distress,
   Because Thy word has quickened me.

26 51 The proud did greatly me deride,
   Yet from Thy law I 've not declined.
52 Thy judgments, LORD, which are of
   I do recall, and comfort find.   [old,

27 53 Hot indignation hath me seized,
   Because ill men Thy law forsake.
54 But in my house of pilgrimage
   Thy statutes for my songs I take.

28 55 Thy name, Jehovah, in the night
   I 've borne in mind, and kept Thy
56 This I have had appointed me,   [law.
   For I Thy precepts kept with awe.

PART VIII.

29 57 Jehovah my sure portion is ;
   I said that I will keep Thy word.
58 I sought Thy face with my whole heart;
   Thy promised grace to me afford.

30 59 I viewed my ways and turned my feet
   Into Thy testimonies' way.
60 I hastened Thy commands to keep,
   And made not any more delay.

31 61 The wicked's cords environed me
   But I Thy law to mind recall.
62 I 'll rise at midnight Thee to praise,
   Because of Thy just judgments all.

32 63 To all who fear Thee I 'm a friend,
   To those Thy precepts who obey.
64 Jehovah, earth Thy mercy fills ;
   Instruct me in Thy statutes' way.

PART IX.

33 65 O LORD, according to Thy word
  Thou didst Thy servant favor give ;
  66 Good judgment me and knowledge teach,
  For Thy commandments I believe.

34 67 Before affliction came I strayed ;
  But now I do Thy word obey.
  68 Thou art good, and Thou doest good,
  Teach me Thy statutes' perfect way.

35 69 The proud against me forged a lie ;
  I 'll keep Thy precepts with whole heart.
  70 Their heart is fat and worldly grown ;
  Thy law to me doth joy impart.

36 71 I was afflicted for my good,
  That I might learn Thy statutes sure;
  72 Thy mouth's law I 'bove thousands prize
  Of silver and of gold most pure.

PART X.

37 73 Thy hands did make and fashion me ;
  To learn all Thy commands make wise.
  74 Thy fearers shall me see and joy,
  For on Thy word my hope relies.

38 75 Jehovah, right Thy judgments are
  I know ; Thou justly chast'nest me ;
  76 As Thy word to Thy servant came,
  O let Thy grace my comfort be.

39 77 Thy mercies send to me, I 'll live;
  Thy law to me gives pleasure great.
  78 The proud shame, who by lies me wrong;
  I 'll in Thy precepts meditate.

40 79 Let them that fear Thee turn to me,
  And know Thy testimonies all.
  80 Sound in Thy statutes make my heart,
  That shame may not upon me fall.

PART XI.

41 81 My soul for Thy salvation faints,
  But I upon Thy word believe;
  82 Mine eyes fail for Thy word, I say:
  O when wilt Thou me comfort give?

42 83 I 'm like a bottle in the smoke;
  Thy statutes I do not forget.
  84 How long Thy servant's days? O when
  Wilt Thou judge those who me beset?

43 85 For me the proud have opened pits,
  They after Thy law will not do.
  86 All Thy commandments faithful are;
  Help me, whom falsely they pursue.

44 87 They me almost consumed on earth,
  Yet I to all Thy precepts clave.
  88 In Thy grace quicken me, I 'll keep
  The testimony Thy mouth gave.

PART XII.

45 89 Thy word, Jehovah, settled is
  In heaven for ever to endure;
  90 Thy faithfulness is to each age;
  Earth fixed by Thee abideth sure.

46 91 By Thy decrees they stand this day,
    For all things serve Thee evermore.
 92 Had I not loved Thy law, I should
    Have perished in affliction sore.

47 93 Thy precepts I will ne'er forget,
    For Thou didst quicken me thereby.
 94 O save Thou me, for I am Thine,
    Because Thy precepts sought have I.

48 95 The wicked watched to ruin me ;
    Thy testimonies shall me lead.
 96 Of all perfection bounds I 've seen,
    But Thy commands all bounds exceed.

PART XIII.

49 97 O how I love Thy law ! it is
    My meditation all the day ;
 98 More wise than foes by Thy commands
    I 'm made ; they ever with me stay.

50 99 I know more than my teachers all ;
    My thought Thy testimonies are ;
 100 Than old men more I understand,
    For I Thy precepts kept with care.

51 101 From each ill way I kept my feet,
    That so I might Thy word obey ;
 102 I from Thy judgments did not swerve,
    Because Thou guidest all my way.

52 103 How sweet Thy sayings to my taste !
    Than honey to my mouth more sweet ;
 104 I from Thy precepts wisdom learn,
    And therefore every false way hate.

PART XIV.

53 105 Thy word is to my feet a lamp,
A shining light to show my way;
106 I' ve sworn, and will perform my oath,
Thy righteous judgments to obey.

54 107 I 'm sore distressed; Jehovah, me
According to Thy word restore.
108 Accept my mouth's free off'ring, LORD,
Thy judgments teach me to adore.

55 109 My soul is ever in my hand,
Yet I Thy law do not forget;
110 Nor from Thy precepts did I stray,
When snares for me the wicked set.

56 111 Thy testimonies, my heart's joy,
An endless heritage I find;
112 To do Thy statutes to the end
My heart I ever have inclined.

PART XV.

57 113 All those that are of double mind
I hate; but love Thy law do I.
114 Thou art my hiding place and shield;
I do upon Thy word rely.

58 115 Ye evil doers, hence from me,
My God's commands I will obey;
116 That I may live in hope not shamed,
According to Thy word me stay.

59 117 Uphold me, and I shall be safe,
And to Thy statutes look alway;
118 Who leave Thy statutes Thou dost scorn,
For their deceit is falsehood's stay.

60 119 Earth's wicked Thou putt'st off as
    dross;
    Thy testimonies I hold dear;
120 My flesh doth tremble, dreading Thee,
    And I Thy judgments greatly fear.

PART XVI.

61 121 To my oppressors leave me not;
    I justice do and righteousness;
122 For good Thy servant's surety be,
    And let not proud ones me oppress.

62 123 Mine eyes for Thy salvation fail,
    And for Thy word of equity.
124 In mercy with Thy servant deal;
    And all Thy statutes teach to me.

63 125 I am Thy servant; wisdom give
    Thy testimonies all to know;
126 Jehovah, it is time to work,
    For men Thy law abolish now.

64 127 I therefore Thy commandments love
    Above all gold, yea, finest gold;
128 And all Thy precepts right esteem,
    And each false way in hatred hold.

PART XVII.

65 129 Thy testimonies wondrous are;
    For this my soul to them gives
    heed.
130 The op'ning of Thy words gives light,
    And makes the simple wise indeed.

66 131 With open mouth I pant; I long
    For Thy commands all things
    above.

132 Turn unto me and gracious be,
   As due to all Thy Name that love.

67 133 My steps establish in Thy word,
   Let no iniquity me sway.
134 From man's oppression me redeem·
   And I Thy precepts will obey.

68 135 Thy face let on Thy servant shine,
   And me to know Thy statutes make.
136 In floods the tears run down mine eyes
   Because that men Thy law do break.

PART XVIII.

69 137 Thou, O Jehovah, righteous art,
   And in Thy judgments Thou art
138 Thy testimonies righteously   [just.
   Appointed are, and claim my trust.

70 139 My zeal consumeth me, because
   Mine enemies Thy words forget;
140 Thy word is very pure; on it
   Thy servant's love is therefore set.

71 141 Though I am little and despised,
   My soul Thy precepts yet retains;
142 Thy righteousness for ever lasts;
   Thy law eternal truth remains.

72 143 Distress and anguish on me seize;
   Yet Thy commands me solace give;
144 Thy testimonies righteous are;
   O make me wise, that I may live.

PART XIX.

73 145 To Thee with all my heart I call;
   LORD, hear; Thy statutes I'll obey;

PSALM CXIX. L. M. 285

146 To Thee I call; save me, and I
    Will keep Thy testimonies' way.

74 147 I rise before the dawn to pray,
    And for Thy word devoutly wait.
148 Mine eyes anticipate night's watch,
    Upon Thy word to meditate.

75 149 In grace my voice hear; quicken me,
    Jehovah, in Thy judgment's way.
150 Near me are those that crime pursue,
    That from Thy law go far astray.

76 151 But, O Jehovah, Thou art near;
    All Thy commands are truth alway.
152 Long from Thy testimonies known
    Have I, Thou didst them found for
    aye.

PART XX.

77 153 See mine affliction, and me save;
    Thy law is in my memory;
154 Plead Thou my cause and me re-
    deem;   [me.
    As Thou hast promised, quicken

78 155 Salvation is from sinners far,
    Who for Thy statutes do not strive.
156 Jehovah, great Thy mercies are,
    By Thine own judgments me re-
    vive.

79 157 Foes many me pursue; yet I
    Ne'er from Thy testimonies swerve.
158 The faithless I beheld, and grieved,
    For they Thy word do not observe.

80 159 Behold how I Thy precepts love ;
　　　In love, Jehovah, quicken me.
　　160 The substance of Thy word is truth,
　　　Thy judgments just eternally.

PART XXI.

81 161 Without cause princes me pursued ;
　　　Thy words with awe do fill my mind ;
　　162 And yet I in Thy word rejoice,
　　　As they who store of riches find.

82 163 I falsehood hate and do abhor,
　　　But dearly love Thy law always.
　　164 And for Thy righteous judgments I
　　　Do sevèn times a day Thee praise.

83 165 Great peace have they who love Thy law ;
　　　No stumbling-stone is in their way.
　　166 I hope for Thy salvation, LORD,
　　　And Thy commandments I obey.

84 167 My soul Thy testimonies keeps,
　　　And greatly love them all do I.
　　168 Thy precepts, testimonies, too,
　　　I keep ; my ways before Thee lie.

PART XXII.

85 169 Jehovah, let my cry reach Thee ;
　　　And by Thy word me wisdom give;
　　170 Let my request before Thee come ;
　　　As Thou hast promised, make me live.

86 171 My lips pour forth a song of praise,
　　　For Thou Thy statutes teachest me.

172 O let my tongue sing of Thy word,
   For Thy commands are verity.

87 173 O help me by Thy mighty hand ;
   For I Thy precepts made my choice.
174 I long for Thy salvation, LORD,
   And greatly in Thy law rejoice.

88 175 My soul shall live and Thee extol,
   Thy judgments surely aid me yet ;
176 A stray sheep, lost, Thy servant seek ;
   For Thy commands I'll not forget.

Psalm CXX. C. M.

1 1 IN grief I to Jehovah cried,
   And He gave ear to me.
2 From lying lips and guileful tongue,
   My soul, Jehovah, free.

2 3 What shall be givèn Thee? what more
   Be done to thee, false tongue ?
4 With burning coals of juniper,
   Sharp arrows of the strong.

3 5 Alas! that I in Meshech am
   A sojourner so long ;
   That I among the tents do dwell
   To Kedar that belong.

4 6 My soul with him that hateth peace
   Hath long a dweller been.
   I am for peace ; but when I speak,
   For battle they are keen.

Psalm CXXI. C. M.

1 1 I TO the hills will lift mine eyes,
   From whence doth come mine aid.
2 My safety cometh from the LORD,
   Who heaven and earth hath made.

2 3 Thy foot He'll not let slide, nor will
He slumber that thee keeps.
4 Behold, He that keeps Israel,
He slumbers not, nor sleeps.

3 5 The LORD thee keeps, the LORD
thy shade
On thy right hand doth stay;
6 The moon by night thee shall not
Nor yet the sun by day. [smite,

4 7 The LORD shall keep thy soul; He
Preserve thee from all ill. [shall
8 Henceforth thy going out and in
The LORD keep ever will.

Psalm CXXII. C. M.

1 1 JOYED, when unto me they said:
Let us together go
Into Jehovah's holy house,
His meeting place below.

2 2 Jerusalem, within thy gates
Our feet shall stand; thou art,
3 Jerusalem, a city fair,
Compact in every part.

3 4 Unto that place the tribes go up,
A testimony there
To Israel, before the LORD
His chosen tribes appear

4   To thank Jehovah's gracious Name
In loud and grateful tones :
5 For there are seats for judgment set,
The house of David's thrones.

5 6 Pray that Jerusalem may have
Peace and felicity;

Let them that love thee and thy peace
Have still prosperity.

6   7 Therefore I wish that peace may still
Within thy walls remain,
And ever may thy palaces
Prosperity retain.

7   8 Now, for my friends and brethren's
Peace be in thee, I 'll say.   [sake,
9 And for our God Jehovah's house,
I 'll seek thy good alway.

Psalm CXXII. 6s and 4s.

1   GLAD was I when to me,
Jehovah's house to see,
Let us go near,
They said, with Him to meet.
2 Jerus'lem, now our feet
Shall stand within thy street,
Thy gates so dear.

2   3 Jerusalem, by none
Surpassed, is built in one,
A city great.
4 The tribes assemble here,
Jehovah's tribes come near,
To testimony dear
To Isr'el's State.

3   Thanks ever they proclaim
Unto Jehovah's Name ;
5   For there are set
The thrones of judgment right,
The royal thrones of might,
Which David's house delight,
Exalted yet.

4 6 Pray for Jerus'lem's peace,
   Thy lovers ne'er shall cease
      To prosper well.
   7 Peace be within thy walls,
   And in thy palace halls,
   Whatever thee befalls,
      Let quiet dwell.

5 8 For brethren's sake I pray,
   And for my friends I 'll say,
      Peace with thee be.
   9 Thy good then seek will I;
   For our God's house is nigh,
   And there Jehovah high
      Doth dwell in thee.

Psalm CXXIII. C. M.

1 O THOU that dwellest in the heavens,
      I lift mine eyes to Thee.
   2 Behold, as servants' eyes do look
      Their master's hand to see,

2   As handmaid's eyes her mistress' hand,
      So do our eyes attend
   Upon the LORD our God, until
      To us He mercy send.

3 3 Jehovah, gracious be to us,
      To us now gracious be;
   Because replenished with contempt
      Exceedingly are we.

4 4 Our soul is filled with scorn of those
      That at their ease abide,
   And with the insolent contempt
      Of those that swell in pride.

Psalm CXXIV. C. M.

1 HAD not Jehovah been for us,
　　May Israel now say :
2 Had not Jehovah been for us
　　When men rose us to slay ;

2 3 Alive they had us swallowed, when
　　Their wrath 'gainst us did flame ;
4 Waters had whelmed us then ; our soul
　　Had sunk beneath the stream.

3 5 Then had the waters swelling high
　　Above our soul made way.
6 Blessed be the LORD, who to their
　　Us gave not for a prey.　　　[teeth

4 7 Our soul escaped is as a bird
　　Out of the fowler's snare ;
The snare asunder broken is,
　　And we escapèd are.

5 8 Our sure and all-sufficient help
　　Is in Jehovah's Name ;
His Name who did the heaven create,
　　And who the earth did frame.

Psalm CXXIV. 4s and 6s, or 10s.

1 NOW Israel
　　May say, and that truly,
If that the LORD
　　Had not our right maintained,
2 If that the LORD
　　Had not our cause sustained,
When cruel men
　　Who us desired to slay
Rose up in wrath
　　To make of us their prey ;

3 Then certainly
   They had devoured us all,
And swallowed quick,
   For aught that we could deem;
Such was their rage,
   As we might well esteem.
4 And as fierce floods
   Before them all things drown,
So had they brought
   Our soul to death quite down.

5 The raging streams,
   With their proud swelling waves,
Had then our soul
   O'erwhelmed within the deep.
6 Blessed be the LORD,
   Who doth us safely keep,
And gave us not
   A living prey to be
Unto their teeth
   And bloody cruelty.

7 Even as a bird
   Out of the fowler's snare
Escapes away,
   So is our soul set free;
Rent is their net,
   And thus escaped are we.
8 Therefore our help
   Is in Jehovah's Name,
Who heaven and earth
   By His great power did frame.

Psalm CXXV. C. M.

1 THEY who Jehovah firmly trust
   Shall be like Zion hill,
Which at no time can be removed,
   But stand for ever will.

2 2 As round about Jerusalem
     The mountains stand alway,
   Jehovah round His people is,
     From henceforth and for aye.

3 3 For ill men's rod upon the lot
     Of just men shall not lie;
   Lest righteous men stretch forth their
     To work iniquity.   [hands

4 4 Do Thou, Jehovah, to the good
     Thy goodness now impart;
   And also do Thou good to them
     Who upright are in heart.

5 5 But as for such as turn aside
     In their own crooked way,
   The LORD with ill men shall lead
     On Isr'el peace shall stay.   [forth;

Psalm CXXVI. C. M.

1 WHEN Zion's bonds the LORD removed,
     As men that dreamed were we.
   2 Then filled with laughter was our
     Our tongue with melody.   [mouth,

2   Jehovah, they 'mong nations said,
     Great things for them hath wrought.
   3 Jehovah did great things for us,
     Whence joy to us is brought.

3 4 As streams of water in the south,
     Our bondage, LORD, recall.
   5 Who sow in tears, a reaping time
     Of joy enjoy they shall.

4 6 The man who, bearing precious seed,
   In going forth doth mourn,
  He doubtless, bringing back his
   Rejoicing shall return.   [sheaves,

Psalm CXXVII. C. M.

1 EXCEPT Jehovah build the house,
   The builders lose their pain;
  Except the LORD the city keep,
   The watchmen watch in vain.

2 2 'Tis vain for you to rise betimes,
   Or late from rest to keep,
  To feed on sorrows' bread; so gives
   He His beloved ones sleep.

3 3 Lo, children, the LORD'S heritage,
   Our offspring, His reward.
  4 The sons of youth as arrows are,
   For strong men's hands prepared.

4 5 O happy is the man that hath
   His quiver filled with those;
  For unashamed they in the gate
   Shall speak unto their foes.

Psalm CXXVIII. C. M.

1 BLEST is each one that fears the LORD,
   And walketh in His ways;
  2 For of thy labor thou shalt eat,
   And prosper all thy days.

2 3 Thy wife shall as a fruitful vine
   By thy house' sides be found;
  Thy children like to olive-plants
   Thy table shall surround.

3 4 Lo, he that doth Jehovah fear
Thus blessed shall ever be.
5 Jehovah shall from Zion give
His blessing unto thee ;

4 Thou shalt Jerus'lem's good behold
Whilst thou on earth dost dwell.
6 Thou shalt thy children's children see,
And peace on Israel.

Psalm CXXVIII. 8s and 7s.

1 BLEST the man who fears Jehovah,
Walking ever in His ways ;
2 Thou shalt eat of thy hands' labor,
And be happy all thy days.

2 3 Like a vine in fruit abounding,
In thy house thy wife is found ;
And like olive-plants thy children
Compassing thy table round.

3 4 Lo, on him that fears Jehovah,
Shall this blessedness attend ;
5 Thus Jehovah, out of Zion,
Shall to thee His blessing send.

4 Thou shalt see Jerus'lem prosper,
Long as thou on earth shalt dwell ;
6 Thou shalt see thy children's children
And the peace of Israel.

Psalm CXXIX. C. M.

1 OFT did they vex me from my youth,
May Isr'el now declare ;
2 Oft did they vex me from my youth
Yet not victorious were.

2 3 The ploughers ploughed upon my
   back;
   They long their furrows drew;
 4 Jehovah righteous is, who did
   The wicked's cords cut through.

3 5 Let Zion's haters be turned back,
   And in confusion thrown;
 6 As grass on housetops let them be,
   Which fades ere it be grown;

4 7 Whereof enough to fill his hand
   The mower cannot find;
   Nor can the man his bosom fill
   Whose work is sheaves to bind.

5 8 Nor say the passers-by, On you
   Jehovah's blessing rest;
   We in Jehovah's holy name
   Do wish you to be blest.

Psalm CXXX. C. M.

1 LORD, from the depths to Thee I cried
 2 My voice, Lord, do Thou hear;
   And to my supplication's voice
   Give an attentive ear.

2 3 Lord, who shall stand, if Thou, O
   Shouldst mark iniquity?   [LORD,
 4 But yet with Thee forgiveness is,
   That feared Thou mayèst be.

3 5 I wait, my soul waits on the LORD,
   My hope is in His word.
 6 More than they that for morning watch,
   My soul waits for the Lord;

4   Yea, evèn more than they that watch
   The morning light to see.

7 Let Isr'el trust the LORD, for with
   The LORD sure mercies be ;

5 And plenteous redemption is
   For ever found with Him.
8 And from all his iniquities
   He Isr'el shall redeem.

Psalm CXXX. L. M.

1 FROM depths I on Jehovah call
   2 Jehovah, hearken to my prayer;
   Let me not unregarded sink
   In the deep waters of despair !

2 3 If Thou, LORD, shouldst transgression mark,
   Who shall, O Lord, from guilt be cleared ?
   4 Forgiveness is with Thee alone,
   To the intent Thou mayst be feared.

3 5 I wait, my soul waits for the LORD—
   By hope in His own word upborne—
   6 Waits for the coming of the Lord,
   As weary watchers for the morn.

4 7 Hope in the Lord, O Israel !
   For with the LORD is grace supreme,
   8 And plenteous redemption too.
   He Isr'el will from sins redeem.

Psalm CXXXI. C. M.

1 MY heart, Jehovah, is not proud,
   Mine eyes not lofty be ;
   Nor do I deal in matters great,
   Or things too high for me.

PSALM CXXXII.

2 2 I surely have myself behaved
With spirit calm and mild,
As child of mother weaned; **my soul**
Is like a weanèd child.

3 3 Upon Jehovah let the hope
Of Israel rely,
Even from the time that present **is**
To all eternity.

Psalm CXXXI. 6s and 4s.

1 MY heart 's not haughty, LORD,
Nor proud mine eyes;
Nor do I seek myself
To exercise
In matters great that be,
Or things too high for me.
2 At rest assuredly
My stilled soul lies,

2 Like weanèd child that rests
On mother's knee,
So rests, like weanèd child,
My soul in me.
3 O Israel, trust thou
Upon Jehovah now,
From this time forth unto
Eternity.

Psalm CXXXII. C. M.

1 DAVID, and his afflictions all,
Jehovah, think upon;
2 How to the LORD he sware, **and**
To Jacob's Mighty One.   [vowed

2 3 I will not come within my house,
Nor rest in bed at all;
4 Nor shall mine eyes take any sleep,
Nor eyelids slumber shall;

3 5 Till for Jehovah I do find
A place that He will own,
A place of habitation meet
For Jacob's Mighty One.

4 6 Lo, at the place of Ephratah,
Of it we understood;
And we did find it in the fields
And city of the wood.

5 7 We 'll to His tabernacles go,
And at His footstool bow.
8 Arise, Jehovah, to Thy rest,
Thine ark of strength and Thou.

6 9 O let Thy priests appareled be
With truth and righteousness;
And let all those that are Thy saints
Shout forth for joyfulness.

7 10 For Thine own servant David's sake,
Do not deny Thy grace;
Nor of Thine own anointed one
Turn Thou away the face.

8. 11 The LORD in truth to David sware,
He will not turn from it;
I of thy body's fruit will make
Upon thy throne to sit.

9 12 My cov'nant, if thy sons will keep,
And laws to them made known,
Their children then shall also sit
For ever on thy throne.

10 13 For Zion is Jehovah's choice;
There He desires to dwell.
14 This is my rest, here still I 'll stay;
For I do like it well.

11 15 Her food I 'll greatly bless ; her poor
With bread will satisfy.
16 Her priests I 'll clothe with health, her
Shall shout aloud for joy.   [saints

12 17 And there will I make David's horn
To bud forth pleasantly ;
For him that Mine anointed is
A lamp ordained have I.

13 18 As with a garment I will clothe
With shame his en'mies all ;
But yet the crown that he doth wear
Upon him flourish shall.

Psalm CXXXIII.   C. M.

1 1 BEHOLD how good a thing it is,
And how becoming well,
Together such as brethren are
In unity to dwell !

2 2 Like precious ointment on the head,
That down the beard did flow,
Even Aaron's beard, and to the skirts
Did of his garments go.

3 3 As Hermon's dew, the dew that doth
On Zion hills descend ;
Jehovah blessing there commands,
Life that shall never end.

Psalm CXXXIII.   7s and 6s.

1 1 BEHOLD how good and pleasant.
And how becoming well,
Where brethren all united,
In peace together dwell.

2   2 'T is like the precious ointment
      That on the head did flow,
      Which down the beard of Aaron,
      Did o'er his vesture go.

3   3 Like dews which on Mount Hermon
      And Zion hills descend;
      The LORD commands the blessing,
      Life that shall never end.

Psalm CXXXIV. C. M.

1   BEHOLD. Jehovah bless, all who
      Jehovah's servants are;
      Who in Jehovah's temple stand,
      And praise Him nightly there.

2   2 Your hands in holiness lift up
      And bless Jehovah's Name.
    3 From Zion thee Jehovah bless,
      Who heaven and earth did frame.

Psalm CXXXIV. 8, 7, 4.

1   LO, do ye ascribe due blessing
      To Jehovah in accord,
      All of you who faithful service
      To Jehovah do afford,
        Standing nightly
      In the dwelling of the LORD.

2   2 To His holy place of dwelling
        Let your hands be stretchèd forth.
      Bless the LORD. Jehovah blessing
        Give to thee, of priceless worth,
    3 Out of Zion;
        He that made the heaven and earth.

Psalm CXXXV. C. M.

1 O PRAISE the LORD. Do ye unto
   Jehovah's Name give praise ;
Jehovah's servants, unto Him
   Your alleluias raise.

2 2 Ye that within Jehovah's house
      Do stand and make abode
   Within the courts belonging to
      The temple of our God,

3 3 Praise ye the LORD ; the LORD is
      And do ye praises sing   [good;
   To His most holy Name, because
      It is a pleasant thing.

4 4 The LORD of Jacob for Himself
      A final choice did make,
   For His peculiar treasure He
      Did Isr'el also take.

5 5 Because I know assuredly
      Jehovah 's very great,
   And that our Lord above all gods
      In glory hath His seat.

6 6 What thing soe'er Jehovah pleased
      That in the heavens did He,
   And in the earth, the seas, and all
      The places deep that be.

7 7 He from the ends of earth doth make
      The vapors to ascend ;
   For rain He lightnings makes, and
      Doth from His treasures send. [wind

8 8 Egypt's first born, from man to beast
   9   Who smote. Strange tokens He
   On Phar'oh and his servants sent,
      Egypt, in midst of thee.

9 10 He smote great nations, slew great
11 Sihon, the Am'rite king, [kings;
And Og of Bashan, and to nought
Did Canaan's kingdoms bring :

10 12 And for a wealthy heritage
Their pleasant land He gave,
A heritage which Israel,
His chosen folk, should have.

11 13 Thy Name, Jehovah, ever is;
And Thy memorial,
Jehovah, shall continued be
To generations all.

12 14 Because Jehovah govern will
His people righteously ;
Concerning those that do Him serve
Himself repent will He.

13 15 The nations' gods are made by men,
They silver are and gold ;
16 Mouths have they, but they do not speak ;
Their eyes can nought behold..

14 17 Ears have they, but they do not hear;
Their mouths no breath receive.
18 Their makers like them are ; and all
Who do in them believe.

15 19 Bless ye Jehovah, Isr'el's house ;
The LORD bless, Aaron's race ;
20 The LORD bless, Levi's tribe; who fear
The LORD, the LORD'S Name bless.

16 21 From Zion, His own holy hill,
Blessed let Jehovah be,
Who dwelleth at Jerusalem,
Praise to the LORD give ye.

Psalm CXXXVI. 8s and 7s.

1
1 JEHOVAH praise, for good is He;
   For mercy hath He ever.
2 Thanks to the God of gods give ye;
   For His grace faileth never.

2
3 Thanks give the Lord of lords unto;
   For mercy hath He ever;
4 Who only wonders great can do;
   For His grace faileth never.

3
5 Who by His wisdom made heavens high;
   For mercy hath He ever;
6 Who stretched the earth above the sea;
   For His grace faileth never.

4
7 To Him that made great lights to shine;
   For mercy hath He ever;
8 The sun to rule till day decline;
   For His grace faileth never.

5
9 The moon and stars to rule by night;
   For mercy hath He ever;
10 Who Egypt's first-born all did smite;
   For His grace faileth never.

6
11 And Isr'el brought out from their land;
   For mercy hath He ever;
12 With outstretched arm, and with
      strong hand;
   For His grace faileth never.

7
13 By whom the Red Sea parted was;
   For mercy hath He ever;
14 Who through its midst made Isr'el pass;
   For His grace faileth never.

8
15 Pharaoh and host in Red Sea cast;
   For mercy hath He ever;

16 His people led through desert vast ;
  For His grace faileth never.

9 17 To Him great kings who overthrew ;
  For mercy hath He ever ;
18 Yea, famous kings in battle slew ;
  For His grace faileth never.

10 19 Even Sihon, king of Amorites ;
  For mercy hath He ever ;
20 And Og, the king of Bashanites ;
  For His grace faileth never.

11 21 Their land as heritage to have ;
  For mercy hath He ever ;
22 His servant Isr'el right He gave ;
  For His grace faileth never.

12 23 In our low state who on us thought ;
  For mercy hath He ever ;
24 And from our foes our freedom
    wrought ;
  For His grace faileth never.

13 25 Who doth all flesh with food relieve ;
  For mercy hath He ever ;
26 Thanks to the God of heaven give ;
  For His grace faileth never.

Psalm CXXXVI. H. M.

1 JEHOVAH praise, He 's kind ;
    His mercy lasts for aye.
  2 Give thanks with heart and mind
      To God of gods alway ;
    For certainly
      His mercies dure
      Most firm and sure
    Eternally.

2 3 The Lord of lords praise ye,
       Whose mercies ever stand.
    4 Great wonders only He
       Doth work with mighty hand;
    For certainly, &c.

3 5 Praise Him the heavens who made,
       Whose wisdom doth abide.
    6 Praise Him who earth did spread
       Above the waters wide.
    For certainly, &c.

4 7 Great lights who made of old;
       For His grace lasteth aye;
    8 The sun, which we behold,
       To rule the lightsome day;
    For certainly, &c.

5 9 Who made the stars so clear,
       The moon to rule the night.
    10 Who Egypt's first-born dear
       Did in just anger smite.
    For certainly, &c.

6 11 Thence Isr'el out He brought;
       His mercies ever stand;
    12 With outstretched arm He wrought,
       And with a mighty hand;
    For certainly, &c.

7 13 The sea He clave in two;
       For His grace lasteth still;
    14 And through its midst to go,
       Made His own Israel;
    For certainly, &c.

8 15 His host and Pharoah He
       Did in the Red Sea cast;
    16 His people thus set free,
       He led through desert vast.
    For certainly, &c.

9 17 To Him great kings who smote:
    For His grace hath no bound ;
  18 Who did to death devote
    Kings famous and renowned ;
    For certainly, &c.

10 19 Sihon, the Am'rites' prince ;
    For His grace lasteth aye ;
  20 And mighty Og, who once
    In Bashan's land had sway ;
    For certainly, &c.

11 21 Their land by lot He gave,
    For His grace lasts alway ;
  22 That Isr'el might it have
    In heritage for aye.
    For certainly, &c.

12 23 Who thought on us when low,
    For His grace still endures ;
  24 And from our evil foe
    Deliverance secures.
    For certainly, &c.

13 25 Who to all flesh gives food ;
    For His grace lasteth on ;
  26 Give thanks, for this is good,
    To God of heaven alone.
    For certainly, &c.

Psalm CXXXVII. C. M.

1 BY Babel's streams we sat and wept,
    When Zion we thought on.
  2 In midst thereof we hung our harps
    The willow trees upon.

2 3 For there a song did they require,
    Who did us captive bring ;

    Our spoilers called for mirth, and said,
      A song of Zion sing.

3 4 How shall we sing Jehovah's song
      Within a foreign land?
    5 If thee, Jerus'lem, I forget,
      Skill part from my right hand.

4 6 My tongue to my mouth's roof let
      If I do thee forget,   [cleave
    Jerusalem, and thee above
      My chief joy do not set.

5 7 Jehovah, Edom's sons recall,
      Who in Jerus'lem's day,
    Even unto its foundation, Raze,
      Yea, raze it quite, did say.

6 8 O thou unto destruction doomed,
      Daughter of Babylon;
    Happy the man that do'th to thee
      As thou to us hast done.

7 9 Yea, happy, surely shall he be,
      Thy tender little ones
    Who shall lay hold upon, and them
      Shall dash against the stones.

Psalm CXXXVII. L. M.

1 BY Babel's streams we sat and wept,
      For mem'ry still to Zion clung;
    2 The winds alone our harp-strings swept,
      Which we upon the willows hung.

2 3 There cruel captors, flushed with pride,
      A song required to mock our wrongs:
    Our spoilers called for mirth, and cried;
      Come, sing us one of Zion's songs.

3 4 O how can we, sad exiles yet,
  The LORD'S song sing in foreign land ?
  5 If thee, Jerus'lem, I forget,
  Let skill depart from my right hand.

4 6 My mouth and tongue be parched and dumb
  If I hold not Thy mem'ry dear,
  If loved Jerusalem shall come
  Below chief joys I cherish here.

5 7 Remember, LORD, 'gainst Edom's crowd
  Jerus'lem's day of bitter woe ;
  For they with anger shouted loud :
  Remove her walls, o'erthrow, o'erthrow.

6 8 O Babel's daughter, stern decree
  Dooms thee to cruel foes a prey ;
  Yea, glad shall that avenger be,
  Who shall to thee our wrongs repay.

7 9 Yea, truly shall that man be pleased,
  And with triumphal honor crowned,
  By whom thy children shall be seized,
  And dashed to death upon the ground.

Psalm CXXXVIII. C. M.

1 THEE will I praise with all my heart,
  I will sing praise to Thee
  2 Before the gods ; and worship will
  Toward Thy sanctuary.

2 I 'll praise Thy Name, even for Thy
  And kindness of Thy love ; [truth,

For Thou Thy word hast magnified
All Thy great Name above.

3 3 Thou didst me answer in the day
When I did cry to Thee;
And Thou my fainting soul with
Didst strengthen inwardly. [strength

4 4 Jehovah, all the kings of earth
To Thee shall thanks accord,
What time they from Thy mouth shall
Thy true and faithful word. [hear

5 5 Yea, in Jehovah's righteous ways
With gladness they shall sing;
For great Jehovah's glory is,
Who evermore is King.

6 6 Jehovah's high, yet He regards
All those that lowly be;
Whereas the proud and lofty ones
Afar off knoweth He.

7 7 Though I in midst of trouble walk,
I life from Thee shall have;
'Gainst my foes' wrath Thou 'lt stretch
Thy hand;
Thy right hand shall me save.

8 8 All that concerns me surely will
Jehovah perfect make;
Jehovah, Thy grace lasts; do not
Thine own hands' works forsake.

Psalm CXXXIX. C. M.

1 O LORD, Thou hast me searched and known,
2 Thou know'st my sitting down,
And rising up; yea, all my thoughts
Afar to Thee are known.

2 3 My footsteps, and my lying down,
   Thou compassest always;
   Thou also most entirely art
   Acquaint with all my ways.

3 4 Because before a single word
   Upon my tongue can be,
   Behold, Jehovah, it is known,
   Yea, all are known to Thee.

4 5 Behind, before, Thou hast beset,
   And laid on me Thy hand.
  6 Such knowledge is too strange for me,
   Too high to understand.

5 7 Where from Thy Spirit shall I go?
   Or from Thy presence fly?
  8 Ascend I heaven, lo, Thou art there;
   There, if in grave I lie.

6 9 Take I the wings of morn, and dwell
   In utmost parts of sea,
  10 Thy hand shall evèn there me lead,
   Thy right hand hold shall me.

7 11 If I do say that darkness shall
   Me cover from Thy sight,
   Then surely shall the very night
   About me be as light.

8 12 Yea, darkness hideth not from Thee,
   But night doth shine as day;
   To Thee the darkness and the light
   Are both alike alway.

9 13 For Thou my inmost being hast
   Possessed, and covered me
   Thou hast, within my mother's womb,
   I will give praise to Thee.

10 14 Yea, Thee I'll praise, for fearfully
    And strangely made I am;
  Thy works are wondrous, and right
  My soul doth know the same. [well

11 15 My substance was not hid from Thee,
    When as in secret I
  Was made; and in earth's lowest parts
    Was wrought most curiously.

12 16 My unformed substance Thine eyes
    My days were every one   [saw;
  In Thy book written, all ordained
    When of them there was none.

13 17 How precious also are Thy thoughts,
    O gracious God, to me!
  And in their sum how passing great
    And numberless they be!

14 18 If I should count them, than the sand
    They more in number be!
  What time soever I awake,
    I ever am with Thee.

15 19 Thou 'lt sure the wicked slay, O God;
    Hence from me, bloody men.
  20 Thy foes against Thee loudly speak,
    And take Thy name in vain.

16 21 Jehovah, do not I hate those
    That hatred bear to Thee?
  With those that up against Thee rise
    Can I but grievèd be?

17 22 With perfect hatred them I hate,
    My foes I them do hold.
  23 Search me, O God, and know my heart,
    Try me, my thoughts unfold;

18 24 And see if any wicked way
   There be at all in me;
   And in Thine everlasting way
   To me a leader be.

Psalm CXL. C. M.

1 JEHOVAH, from the wicked man
   Give me deliverance,
   And do Thou safe preserve me from
   The man of violence;

2 2 Who in their heart things mischievous
   Do meditate alway;
   And they for war together are
   Assembled every day.

3 3 For even like a serpent's tongue
   Their tongues they sharp do make;
   And underneath their lips there lies
   The poison of a snake.

4 4 LORD, keep me from the wicked's
   From vi'lent man me save; [hands,
   Who utterly to overthrow
   My goings purposed have.

5 5 The proud have hid a snare for me
   And cords; for me a net
   Close by the wayside they have spread,
   And traps for me have set.

6 6 Then to Jehovah thus I said:
   My God alone art Thou;
   Jehovah, hear my voice, when I
   In supplication bow.

7 7 Jehovah, Lord, Thou who the strength
   Of my salvation art,

Thou to my head in day of war
   Protection dost impart.

8   8 Jehovah, to the wicked man
      His wishes do not grant;
   Nor further Thou his ill device,
      Lest they themselves should vaunt.

9   9 As for the head of those that do
      About encompass me,
   Even by the mischief of their lips
      Let Thou them covered be.

10 10 Let burning coals upon them fall,
      Them throw in fiery flame,
   And in deep pits, that they no more
      May rise out of the same.

11 11 A man of evil tongue shall not
      On earth established be;
   Mischief shall hunt the violent
      And waste him utterly.

12 12 The LORD, I know, will judge the poor,
      Maintain the suff'rer's right.
   13 The righteous shall extol Thy Name;
      The just dwell in Thy sight.

Psalm CXLI. C. M.

1   JEHOVAH, I to Thee do cry,
      Do Thou make haste to me,
   And to my voice give Thou an ear,
      When I cry unto Thee.

2   2 O let my prayer before Thy face
      As fragrant incense rise;
   And the uplifting of my hands
      As evening sacrifice.

3 3 Set watch, Jehovah, on my mouth;
      Guard of my lips the door.
  4 My heart incline Thou not unto
      The ills I should abhor,

4   To practise wicked works with men
      That work iniquity;
     And of their dainties let me not
      With them partaker be.

5 5 Let him that righteous is me smite,
      It shall a kindness be;
    Let him reprove, I shall it count
      A precious oil to me;

6   Such oil my head shall not refuse;
      For yet the time shall fall
    When I, in their calamities,
      Prayer offer for them shall.

7 6 When as their judges down shall be
      In stony places cast,
    Then shall they hear my words; for
      Shall sweet be to their taste.   [they

8 7 About the grave's devouring mouth
      Our bones are scattered round,
    As wood, which men do cut and cleave,
      Lies scattered on the ground.

9 8 But unto Thee, Jehovah, Lord,
      Mine eyes uplifted be;
    My soul do not leave destitute;
      My trust is set on Thee.

10 9 O keep me safely from the snares
      Which they for me prepare;
    And from the subtle gins of those
      That wicked workers are.

11 10 Let workers of iniquity
    Down in their own nets fall,
Whilst I do, by Thy help, escape
    The danger of them all.

Psalm CXLII. C. M.

1 1 WITH voice I to Jehovah cry;
    With voice the LORD I pray;
2 Pour out to Him my plaint, and all
    My grief before Him lay.

2 3 When faints my spirit me within,
    Then knowest Thou my way;
Where I did walk a snare for me
    They privily did lay.

3 4 Look on the right hand, and behold
    There's none to know me there;
All refuge hath me failed, and none
    Doth for my soul take care.

4 5 I cried to Thee, Jehovah; Thou,
    I said, my refuge art;
And in the land of those that live
    The portion of my heart.

5 6 Because I am brought very low,
    Do Thou attend my cry;
Me from my persecutors save,
    Who stronger are than I.

6 7 From prison bring my soul, that I
    Thy Name may glorify;
The just shall compass me, when Thou
    With me deal'st bounteously.

Psalm CXLIII. C. M.

1 LORD, hear my prayer, regard my
   And in Thy faithfulness [cries;
Give Thou an answer unto me,
And in Thy righteousness.

2 Thy servant also bring Thou not
In judgment to be tried;
Because no living man can be
In Thy sight justified.

3 Because the foe pursues my soul,
My life to earth doth tread;
In darkness he hath made me dwell,
As those that are long dead.

4 My spirit, then, is overwhelmed
With sore perplexity;
Within me also is my heart
Amazèd wondrously.

5 I call to mind the days of old,
I think upon Thy deeds;
On all the work I meditate
Which from Thy hand proceeds.

6 My hands to Thee I stretch; my soul
Thirsts as dry land for Thee.
7 Haste, LORD, to hear, my spirit fails;
Hide not Thy face from me;

Lest like to them I do become
That go down to the dust.
8 At morn let me Thy kindness hear;
For in Thee do I trust.

Teach me the way that I should walk;
I lift my soul to Thee.
9 LORD, free me from my foes; I flee
To Thee to cover me.

9 10 Because Thou art my God, to do
  Thy will do me instruct;
 Good is Thy Spirit; in a land
  That plain is me conduct.

10 11 Jehovah, do Thou quicken me,
  Even for Thine own Name's sake;
 And do Thou, in Thy righteousness,
  My soul from trouble take.

11 12 And of Thy mercy slay my foes;
  Let all destroyed now be
 That do afflict my soul; for I
  A servant am to Thee.

Psalm CXLIII. 6s.

1 JEHOVAH hear my prayer,
  And to my suppliant cry
 In faithfulness give ear,
  In righteousness reply.
 2 In judgment call not me,
  Thy servant, to be tried;
 No living man can be
  In Thy sight justified.

2 3 The foe my soul hath sought,
  My life to earth doth tread;
 To darkness me hath brought,
  As those that long are dead.
 4 My spirit therefore vexed
  O'erwhelmed is me within;
 My heart in me perplexed
  And desolate hath been.

3 5 The days of old I call
  Again unto my thought,
 Thy works I ponder all,
  Works which Thy hands have wrought.

6 And I spread forth my hands
  To Thee beseechingly;
My soul, like thirsty lands,
  Is longing after Thee.

4   7 LORD, let my prayer prevail,
      To answer it make speed;
    My spirit quite doth fail;
      Hide not Thy face in need;
    Lest I be like to those
      That do in darkness sit,
    Or him that downward goes
      Into the dreadful pit.

5   8 Because I trust in Thee,
      Do Thou cause me to hear
    Thy loving-kindness free,
      When morning doth appear;
    Make me to know the way
      Wherein my path should be;
    Because my soul each day
      I do lift up to Thee.

6   9 Jehovah, rescue me
      From all who me oppose;
    I unto Thee do flee,
      To hide me from my foes.
   10 No God have I but Thee,
      Teach me to do Thy will;
    Thy Spirit 's good; lead me
      On evèn pathway still.

7 11 Jehovah, for the sake
      Of Thy Name quicken me;
    In righteousness O take
      My soul from misery.
   12 In mercy cut off those
      That en'mies are to me;
    Slay of my soul the foes;
      I servant am to Thee.

Psalm CXLIV. C. M.

1 O LET Jehovah blessèd be,
    Who is my rock of might.
  Who doth instruct my hands to war,
    My fingers teach to fight;

2 2 My goodness, fortress, my high tower,
    Deliverer, and shield.
  In whom I trust; who under me
    My people makes to yield.

3 3 Jehovah, what is man, that Thou
    Of him dost knowledge take?
  Or son of man, that Thou of him
    So great account dost make?

4 4 Man is like vanity; his days,
    As shadows, pass away.
  5 Jehovah, bow Thy heavens; come down,
    Touch hills, and smoke shall they.

5 6 Cast forth Thy lightning, scatter them;
    Thine arrows shoot, them rout.
  7 Thy hand send from above; me save;
    From great depths draw me out;

6   And from the hand of children strange,
  8   Whose mouth speaks vanity;
  And their right hand a right hand is
    That works deceitfully.

7 9 O God, a new song I will sing
    Assuredly to Thee;
  And on a ten stringed instrument
    To Thee make melody.

8 10 Even He it is that unto kings
    Doth His salvation send;

Who His own servant, David, doth
From hurtful sword defend.

9 11 O free me from strange children's
Whose mouth speaks vanity; [hand,
And their right hand a right hand is
That works deceitfully.

10 12 That, as the plants, our sons may be
In youth grown up that are;
Our daughters like to corner-stones,
Carved like a palace fair;

11 13 That to afford all kind of store
Our garners may be filled;
That our sheep thousands, in our fields,
Ten thousands they may yield;

12 14 That strong our oxen be for work,
That no inbreaking be,
Nor going forth; and that our streets
From outcry may be free:

13 15 Blessed is the people that is found
In such a case as this;
Yea, greatly is the people blessed,
Whose God Jehovah is.

Psalm CXLV. C. M.

1 I 'LL Thee extol, my God, O King;
I 'll bless Thy Name always.
2 Thee will I bless each day, and will
Thy Name for ever praise.

2 3 Jehovah's great, much to be praised;
His greatness search exceeds.
4 Race unto race shall praise Thy works,
And show Thy mighty deeds.

3 5 Upon the splendor glorious,
    O let me meditate,
  Which to Thy majesty belongs,
    And works of wonder great.

4 6 Men of Thine acts the might shall
    Thine acts that dreadful are; [show,
  And I, Thy glory to advance,
    Thy greatness will declare.

5 7 The mem'ry of Thy goodness great
    They largely shall express;
  With songs of praise they shall extol
    Thy perfect righteousness.

6 8 Jehovah very gracious is,
    In Him compassions flow;
  In mercy He is plentiful,
    And unto anger slow.

7 9 The LORD is good to all, His works
    All mercy still express;
  10 Jehovah, Thee all creatures praise,
    Thy saints Thee thank and bless.

8 11 Thy kingdom's glory they proclaim,
    And tell Thy wondrous might;
  12 To show men's sons His deeds, who
    In majesty most bright.   [reigns

9 13 Thy kingdom everlasting is,
    Thy reign through ages all.
  14 Jehovah all the prostrate lifts,
    Upholdeth all that fall.

10 15 The eyes of all look unto Thee,
    Thou giv'st them timely food;
  16 Thine open hand all things that live
    Doth satisfy with good.

11 17 Jehovah 's just in all His ways,
  And kind in His works all.
  18 Jehovah 's near to all that call,
  In truth that on Him call.

12 19 His fearers' wish He will perform,
  Their cry hear and them free ;
  20 Jehovah guards His friends, but all
  The wicked slay will He.

13 21 My mouth Jehovah's praises shall
  Assuredly express ;
  And let all flesh His holy Name
  Ever and ever bless.

Psalm CXLV. L. M.

1 I 'LL Thee exalt, my God and King,
  I will Thy Name bless o'er and o'er;
  2 Each day I will Thee bless, and sing
  The praise of Thy Name ever more.

2 3 Jehovah 's great, He praise exceeds,
  His greatness duly search can none ;
  4 Race shall to race extol Thy deeds,
  And tell Thy mighty acts each one.

3 5 Upon Thy majesty most bright,
  Thy grace and miracles I 'll muse ;
  6 Of Thy dread acts men tell the might,
  Thy storied greatness I 'll diffuse.

4 7 They utter shall abundantly
  The mem'ry of Thy goodness great ;
  And shall sing praises cheerfully,
  Whilst they Thy righteousness relate.

5 8 Jehovah very gracious is,
   And He doth great compassion show;
 Abundant mercy, too, is His,
   And unto anger He is slow.

6 9 Jehovah's good to all that live;
   O'er all His works His mercy is.
 10 Thy works all praise to Thee shall give,
   Jehovah; Thee Thy saints shall bless.

7 11 The glory of Thy kingdom show
   Shall they, and of Thy power tell,
 12 That so men's sons His deeds may know,
   His kingdom's glories that excel.

8 13 Thy kingdom hath no end at all,
   It doth through ages all remain.
 14 Jehovah bears up all that fall,
   The prostrate lifteth up again.

9 15 The eyes of all upon Thee wait;
   In season Thou their food dost give.
 16 Thine open hand, with bounty great,
   Fills the desire of all that live.

10 17 Jehovah's just in His ways all,
   And gracious in His works each one.
 18 Jehovah's near to all that call,
   Who call in truth on Him alone.

11 19 His fearers' wishes He will grant,
   Will hear and save them when they call;
 20 Jehovah keeps His friends from want,
   But will destroy the wicked all.

12 21 O let me therefore my mouth frame
Jehovah's praises to express,
And let all flesh His holy Name
For ever and for ever bless.

Psalm CXLVI. C. M.

1 1 THE LORD praise. Praise the LORD,
my soul.
2 Through life I'll praise the LORD,
While I have being, to my God
In songs I'll praise accord.

2 3 Trust not in princes, nor man's son,
In whom there is no stay;
4 His breath departs, to 's earth he turns;
That day his thoughts decay.

3 5 O happy is that man, and blessed,
Whom Jacob's God doth aid;
Whose hope upon Jehovah rests,
And on his God is stayed;

4 6 Who made the earth and heavens high,
Who made the swelling deep,
And all that is within the same;
Who truth doth ever keep;

5 7 Who righteous judgment executes
For those oppressed that be,
Who feeds the hungry, 'tis the LORD
Who sets the pris'ners free.

6 8 Jehovah gives the blind their sight;
Jehovah them doth raise
That are bowed down; Jehovah loves
The man of upright ways.

7 9 Jehovah strangers doth preserve;
Orphan and widow He
Sustains; by Him the wicked's way
Turned upside down shall be.

8 10 Jehovah reigns for evermore;
Thy God, O Zion, He
Reigns unto generations all.
Praise to the LORD give ye.

Psalm CXLVII. C. M.

1 O PRAISE the LORD; for it is good
Praise to our God to sing;
For it is pleasant, and to praise
Is a becoming thing.

2 2 Jehovah builds Jerusalem,
And He it is alone
That the dispersed of Israel
Doth gather into one.

3 3 Those that are broken in their heart
And grievèd in their minds
He healeth, and their painful wounds
He tenderly up binds.

4 4 He counts the number of the stars;
He names them every one.
5 Great is our Lord, and of great power;
His wisdom search can none.

5 6 Jehovah lifts the meek, and casts
The wicked to the ground.
7 With thanks Jehovah praise; on harp
Let our God's praise resound.

6 8 Who covereth the heaven with clouds,
Who for the earth below
Prepareth rain, who maketh grass
Upon the mountains grow.

PSALM CXLVII.

7 9 He gives the beast its food, He feeds
The ravens young that cry.
10 His pleasure not in horse's strength,
Nor in man's legs doth lie.

8 11 But in all those that do fear Him
The LORD doth pleasure take;
In those that to His mercy do
In hope themselves betake.

9 12 Jehovah praise, Jerusalem;
Zion, Thy God confess;
13 For Thy gates' bars He maketh strong;
Thy sons in thee doth bless.

10 14 He in thy borders maketh peace;
With fine wheat filleth thee.
15 He sends forth His command on earth,
His word runs speedily.

11 16 Hoar-frost, like ashes, scatters He;
Like wool He snow doth give;
17 Like morsels casteth forth His ice;
Who in His cold can live?

12 18 He sendeth forth His mighty word,
And melteth them again;
His wind He makes to blow, and then
The waters flow amain.

13 19 The doctrine of His holy word
To Jacob He doth show;
His statutes and His judgments He
Gives Israel to know.

14 20 With none of all the nations round
So kindly dealt hath He;
For they His judgments have not
Praise to the LORD give ye. [known.

Psalm CXLVIII. C. M.

1
1 O PRAISE the LORD; Jehovah praise
From heavens; Him glorify
2 In heights; praise Him, His angels all;
His hosts all, praise Him ye.

2
3 O praise ye Him, both sun and moon,
Praise Him, all stars of light.
4 Ye heavens of heavens Him praise,
and floods
Above the heavens' height.

3
5 O let them all due praise unto
Jehovah's name accord;
For He commanded, and they were
Created by His word.

4
6 He also, for all times to come,
Hath them established sure;
He hath appointed them a law,
Which ever shall endure.

5
7 Praise ye Jehovah from the earth,
Dragons, and every deep;
8 Fire, hail, snow, vapor, stormy wind,
His word that fully keep.

6
9 All hills and mountains, fruitful trees,
And all ye cedars high;
10 Beasts, and all cattle, creeping things,
And all ye birds that fly;

7
11 Kings of the earth, all nations, too,
Earth's princes, judges all;
12 Young men, and maidens everywhere,
Old men and children small.

8 13 O let them praise Jehovah's Name;
    His Name alone on high
    Exalted is; His glory shines
    Above the earth and sky.

9 14 His people's horn, the praise of all
    His saints He high doth raise;
    Of Isr'el's sons, a people near
    To Him. Jehovah praise.

Psalm CXLVIII. H. M.

1 1 THE LORD of heaven confess,
        On high His glory raise.
    2 Him let all angels bless,
        Him all His armies praise.
    3   Him glorify
            Both moon and sun,
            And stars each one
        That lights the sky.

2 4 Ye heavens His power proclaim,
        And floods that heaven o'erspread.
    5 They praise Jehovah's Name,
        Who spake and they were made.
    6   And in their place
            Firm fixed they be
            By His decree,
        Which cannot pass.

3 7 From earth extol the LORD,
        Ye dragons, depths below;
    8 Storm-wind that keeps His word,
        Fire, hail, the clouds, and snow.
    9   Hills, mountains high,
            The cedars tall,
            Trees great and small
        That fruit supply.

4 10 Wild beasts, and cattle tame,
    Things creeping, fowls that fly,
  11 All peoples, kings of fame,
    Earth's judges, princes high,
      Young men and maids,
      Both old and young,
  12   Let now be sung
    One Name's great deeds.

5 13 The LORD'S great Name be praised,
    Extolled 'bove earth and sky;
  14 His people's horn He raised,
    His saints did magnify.
      Even those that be
      Of Isr'el's race
      Near to His grace,
    The LORD praise ye.

Psalm CXLVIII. 7s.

1 HALLELUJAH! Praise the LORD!
    From the heavens, with one accord,
  Praise be to Jehovah given;
  Praise Him in the heights of heaven.

2 2 Praise Him, all His angel choir,
  Praise Him, ye, His hosts of fire;
  3 Praise Him, sun and moon so bright,
  Praise Him, all ye stars of light.

3 4 Praise Him, heaven of heavens so high,
  Praise Him, floods above the sky;
  5 In the LORD'S Name all be glad,
  For He spake, and they were made.

4 6 Them for ever 'stablished He
    By unchangeable decree;
  7 From the earth, praise, praise the LORD,
  Dragons, deeps, with one accord.

5 8 Hail and lightning, snow and mists,
Storm-winds doing His behests,
9 Hills and mighty mountains all,
Fruitful trees and cedars tall.

6 10 Praise Him, all ye birds of wing,
Beast and herd and creeping thing,
11 Peoples on this earthly ball,
Kings and princes, judges all.

7 12 Youths and maidens, old and young,
13 Praise Jehovah's Name in song;
For His Name alone is high,
Glory His fills earth and sky.

8 14 He His people's horn doth raise,
Of His holy ones the praise;
Sons of Isr'el, people nigh,
Praise the LORD eternally.

Psalm CXLIX. C. M.

1 PRAISE ye the LORD; Sing to the LORD
A new song; and His praise
In the assembly of His saints
In sweet psalms do ye raise.

2 2 Let Isr'el in his Maker joy,
And to Him praises sing;
Let all that Zion's children are
Be joyful in their King.

3 3 O let them unto His great Name
Give praises in the dance;
Let them with timbrel and with harp
In songs His praise advance.

4 4 For in His people, whom He chose,
Jehovah pleasure takes;

And with salvation all the meek
Most beautiful He makes.

5 5 In glory let the saints exult,
On beds sing loud for joy;
6 God's praises in their mouth, their
A two-edged sword employ. [hands

6 7 'Mong nations vengeance to inflict,
'Mong peoples punish wrong;
8 To bind their kings with chains, their
With iron fetters strong. [chiefs

7 9 On them the judgment to perform
Found written in His word;
This honor is to all His saints.
O do ye praise the LORD.

Psalm CL. C. M.

1 O PRAISE the LORD. God's praise
His sanctuary raise; [within
And to Him in the firmament
Of His power give ye praise.

2 2 Because of all His mighty acts,
With praise Him magnify;
O praise Him, as He doth excel
In glorious majesty.

3 3 Praise Him with trumpet's sound; His
With harp and lyre advance; [praise
4 With timbrel, pipe, stringed instru-
Him praise ye in the dance. [ments,

4 5 Praise Him on cymbals loud; Him
On cymbals sounding high. [praise
6 Let each thing breathing praise the
LORD.
Praise to the LORD give ye,

www.ingramcontent.com/pod-product-compliance
Lightning Source LLC
Chambersburg PA
CBHW030004240426
43672CB00007B/814